Living with the East Florida shore

Living with the shore

Series editors

Orrin H. Pilkey, Jr.
William J. Neal

The beaches are moving: the drowning of America's shoreline,
new edition

Wallace Kaufman and Orrin H. Pilkey, Jr.

Living with the West Florida shore

Larry J. Doyle, Dinesh C. Sharma, Albert C. Hine, Orrin H. Pilkey, Jr.,
William J. Neal, Orrin H. Pilkey, Sr., and Daniel F. Belknap

Living with the Alabama-Mississippi shore

Wayne F. Canis, William J. Neal, Orrin H. Pilkey, Sr., and Orrin H. Pilkey, Jr.

Living with the Louisiana shore

Joseph T. Kelley, Alice R. Kelley, Orrin H. Pilkey, Sr., and Albert A. Clark

Living with the Texas shore

Robert A. Morton, Orrin H. Pilkey, Jr., Orrin H. Pilkey, Sr., and William J. Neal

Living with the East Florida shore

Orrin H. Pilkey, Jr.
Dinesh C. Sharma
Harold R. Wanless
Larry J. Doyle
Orrin H. Pilkey, Sr.
William J. Neal
Barbara L. Gruver

Duke University Press   Durham, North Carolina   1984

The publication of this book was supported by a grant from the Florida Coastal Management Office.

Publication of the various volumes in the Living with the Shore series has been greatly assisted by the following individuals and organizations: the American Conservation Association, an anonymous Texas foundation, the Charleston Natural History Society, the Coastal Zone Management Agency (NOAA), the Geraldine R. Dodge Foundation, the Federal Emergency Management Agency, the George Gund Foundation, the Mobil Oil Corporation, Elizabeth O'Connor, the Sapelo Island Research Foundation, the Sea Grant programs of North Carolina, Florida, Mississippi/Alabama, and New York, The Fund for New Jersey, M. Harvey Weil, and Patrick H. Welder, Jr. The Living with the Shore series is part of the Duke University Program for the Study of Developed Shorelines.

Library of Congress Cataloging in Publication Data
Main entry under title:

Living with the East Florida shore.

  Bibliography: p.
  1. Shore protection—Florida 2. Coastal zone
management—Florida. 3. Beach erosion—Florida.
4. Shore-lines—Florida. 5. House Construction. I. Pilkey, Orrin H., 1934–
TC224.F6L58 1984   333.91'716'09759   84-10297
ISBN 0-8223-0514-3
ISBN 0-8223-0515-1 (pbk.)

ARCH

Contents

Figures and tables

Tables

Foreword

During the 1920s, that anomalous period of American history when consumption of alcohol was forbidden by law, a great deal of illicit booze entered the country across the beaches of Florida. Prosperous Palm Beach was a community with a great thirst for illegal liquids, and as a consequence there were frequent flurries of late-night clandestine activity on local beaches. Young John Rybovich, later to become famous as the builder of the country's premier yachts, made the magnificent sum of $15 per night by giving a helping hand. Rybovich and other young men of the island carried burlap bag after burlap bag of whiskey and beer from small boats bobbing in the surf, across the beach, through a tunnel under the road, and up to the beautiful mansion whose owner was conveniently absent. There cars and limousines waited to speed through the night and deliver their precious loads to thirsty customers.

The task of hauling booze across the beach was hard work. The beach was a lot wider in those days than it is now. Today, in many stretches of Palm Beach, the crates of booze could probably be transferred almost directly from a boat to a car parked on a road atop a seawall or revetment. Like many stretches of South Florida shoreline, the beaches of Palm Beach are a mere shadow of what they once were. They have disappeared for two reasons: buildings were built too close to the beach, and the eroding shoreline caught up with the houses. Beach erosion, which is caused by a variety of natural processes including a rise in sea level, is affecting all of Florida. Twenty-story condominiums, unheard of in John Rybovich's youth, are hugging the shoreline from Jacksonville Beach to Miami Beach, and more and more beaches are getting narrower and narrower.

Still, there are many miles of East Florida shoreline where beaches are broad and beautiful and the vista of the sea is unencumbered by seawalls and groins. The beautiful beaches are a primary reason for Florida's unprecedented growth and prosperity. Today, beach-front property is at a premium in the state.

But the rush to the Florida shore has created problems, the most important of which is a real danger to the inhabitants. Most of Florida's beach-front property lies on thin, narrow strips of sand called barrier islands. These islands are low in elevation and are subject to flooding during storms and hurricanes. Some of the construction of buildings is poor, adding to the hazards facing homeowners, most of whom come from other parts of the country with little awareness of the hazards of beaches.

Those who live on Florida barrier islands and those who live next to beaches should understand how these dynamic systems work. This is important for both their physical and economic well-being. More than one transplanted Floridian has plunked down $150,000 for a beautiful condominium with a sea view only to find that in order to keep the building from becoming part of the view, a lot more money must be spent to build and repair seawalls or to pump up new beaches by dredging sand from offshore.

Lots of other surprises may await the unwary property owner along Florida's shoreline, and one important purpose of this book is to provide a good basis for where and what to buy and not buy.

As with all things in life, there is a right way and a wrong way. The right way of living near the beach is to live with the forces of nature rather than to confront them. The right way is to learn respect for the big storms that will inevitably strike the shoreline and to build homes and condominiums that will minimize the hazards if one must ride out the storm. The right way is to clearly understand the escape routes from an island. Most important of all, the right way is citizen support for a strong local and state coastal zone management program that will ensure that the beautiful beaches of Florida will still be around for our children and grandchildren to enjoy.

In this book we sometimes may seem to be critical of the efforts of engineers, developers, and state officials in their role in the development of the East Florida shoreline. But we fully recognize that usually they are simply carrying out the dictates of a public that is ever-anxious to get a better view of the sea. During the last couple of decades, however, coastal scientists and engineers have made great advances in understanding the nearshore oceanographic environment. The time has come when developers can no longer say, "How were we to know?"

This book is one of a multivolume series called the "Living with the Shore" series. Eventually there will be a book for each coastal state as well as for Lake Erie and Lake Michigan. All will be published by Duke University Press. We also have published an "umbrella" volume entitled *Coastal Design* through Van Nostrand Reinhold (1983, $25.50). The Living with the Shore series emphasizes, state by state, very detailed site-safety analyses of the American shoreline. *Coastal Design* is a generalized volume intended to be applicable for all coastal areas, with emphasis on principles of safe construction for near-the-shore areas. The prudent coastal dweller will own both *Coastal Design* and the individual state volume.

A word about the authors: Orrin Pilkey, Jr., is a James B. Duke Professor of geology at Duke University. Larry J. Doyle is a professor of marine science at the University of South Florida. Dinesh C. Sharma is an environmental resources consultant in Fort Myers, Florida. Harold R. Wanless (author of the field trip guide) is a professor of geology at the University of Miami's Rosentiel School of Marine and Atmospheric Sciences. William J. Neal is a professor of geology at Grand Valley State Colleges, Michigan. Orrin H. Pilkey, Sr., is a retired civil engineer residing in Charlottesville, Virginia. And Barbara Gruver is a geologist/technician/draftsperson from Durham, North Carolina.

A lot of people have helped us produce this book. Larry Doyle was supported by the Florida Sea Grant College Program. This is Sea Grant Report #64. The Florida Department of Community Affairs, through a grant to coauthor Dinesh Sharma, provided funds to cover some research and printing costs. We also would like to extend special thanks to Dr. Asish Mehta and Dr. T. Y.

Chia of the Coastal Engineering and Oceanographical Engineering Department at the University of Florida for providing a great deal of information for the compilation of the hazard profiles of individual counties. Lucille Lehman at the coastal engineering archives secured several hundred reports and documents during our research, and the Jacksonville District Headquarters of the Corps of Engineers was very helpful in providing a number of hard-to-get reports. Various county and regional planners provided copies of technical reports and ordinances for our review and research.

The overall coastal book project is an outgrowth of initial support from the National Oceanic and Atmospheric Administration through the Office of Coastal Zone Management. The project was administered through the North Carolina Sea Grant Program. Most recently we have been generously supported by the Federal Emergency Management Agency (FEMA). The FEMA support has enabled us to expand the book into a nationwide series including Lake Erie and Lake Michigan. Without the FEMA support, the series would have long since ground to a halt. The technical conclusions presented herein are those of the authors and do not necessarily represent those of the supporting agencies.

We owe a debt of gratitude to many individuals for support, ideas, encouragement, and information. Doris Schroeder has helped us in many ways as Jill-of-all-trades over a span of more than a decade and a dozen books. Doris, along with Ed Harrison, compiled the index for this volume. The original idea for our first coastal book (*How to Live with an Island*, 1972) was that of Pete Chenery, then director of the North Carolina Science and Technology Research Center. Richard Foster of the Federal Coastal Zone Management Agency supported the book project at a critical juncture. Richard Pough of the Natural Area Council has been a mainstay in our fund-raising efforts. Myrna Jackson of the Duke Development Office has been most helpful in our search for support.

Mike Robinson, Jane Bullock, and Doug Lash of the Federal Emergency Management Agency have worked hard to help us chart a course through the shifting channels of the federal government. Richard Krimm, Peter Gibson, Dennis Carroll, Jim Collins, Jet Battley, Melita Rodeck, Chris Makris, and many others opened doors, furnished maps and charts, and in many other ways helped us through the Washington maze.

We also received a lot of help from Tallahassee officialdom. We would like to particularly note Jorge Southworth of the Department of Commerce and James Stoutamire of the Department of Environmental Regulation. Along the way we received help and encouragement from many of our fellow geologists. We particularly wish to mention our gratitude to Charles Finkle.

Orrin H. Pilkey, Jr.
William J. Neal
series editors

Living with the East Florida shore

1. Highway A1A—the road to riches

Highway A1A, the "boulevard" of Jimmy Buffett's song, connects some of America's most fabled real estate. From south to north the A1A traveler whizzes and bumps through the faded glory of Miami Beach, the fabulous wealth of Palm Beach, the youthful exuberance of Fort Lauderdale beaches, the engineering marvels of Cape Canaveral, the race-crazy community of Daytona Beach, and ancient, colorful St. Augustine, the oldest town in America. There are a lot of other things for the alert A1A driver to see: endless rows of condominiums hugging the beach, signs tacked to trees offering a few acres of land for millions of dollars, brand-new, sparkling white beaches pumped up from offshore at a cost of millions of dollars per mile, and, if the driver chooses to step out of the car and walk to the beach, seawall after seawall after seawall.

Florida's shorelines, including the sections traversed by Highway A1A, are her greatest natural assets. What Florida tourism brochure has failed to feature a scene with some variation of the beautiful couple strolling down the sparkling white, palm tree-lined beach next to the beautiful blue sea? The advertisement is a reality. Florida does have a beautiful shoreline, and the shore is to a large degree responsible for much of the tourist trade and even for much of the state's phenomenal growth of permanent residents (fig. 1.1). Thousands upon thousands of Americans from colder and harsher climes continue to pour south to the promised land of Florida. Thousands upon thousands also pour northward from the mercurial political regimes of the Caribbean. The common meeting ground is the infinite vista of the sea, the rumble of the surf, and the bracing smell of the shoreline.

If Floridians could be satisfied with just seeing, hearing, and smelling the sea, the problems and potential dangers of shoreline development could have been avoided. The beaches and islands could have been left as places to visit or stroll on, as places to swim, surf, or fish from, and simply as places to enjoy.

Because Floridians are subject to the laws of human nature, too, it has not worked out that way. Florida's open ocean shoreline is the site of ever-larger, ever-closer-to-the-beach, and ever-more-exclusive development. The waterfront is so precious that hundreds of miles of canals have been dug on East Florida's islands allowing more thousands of people to live right next to the water. The participants in this rush to the shore often hail from Indiana or Pennsylvania or someplace where one's life experiences do not lead to an understanding of the forces of the sea. Some of those who rush to the Florida shore are simply taking advantage of tax benefits for those who buy vacation property. Orchestrating this rush are entrepreneurs, developers, and realtors who understandably intend to make a profit from the shore. In the normal scheme

Fig. 1.1. Happy swimmers frolicking in the beautiful sea off Palm Beach in 1900. Photo courtesy of the Palm Beach Historical Society.

of things in our democratic, free enterprise system, the views of those who come to make money should be balanced by the guardians of the quality of our life and environment, that is, the local governments. As in most rapidly developing parts of America, this balance in Florida has not worked very well; some are making money at the expense of undue destruction of the environment and the safety of people.

How else can the development on Florida's coast be described other than unsafe? Consider the high density of development on hurricane-prone islands with only a drawbridge or two for escape routes; development that is increasingly in the form of high-rise buildings built very close to an eroding shoreline and protected by seawalls and other structures that in themselves increase the rate of erosion and beach degradation. Neil Frank, director of the National Hurricane Center, sometimes sounds like a broken record when he warns again and again that beachfront development in Florida is setting the stage for a great natural disaster. The unprecedented gap in big hurricanes since Hurricane Donna (1960) leveled the Keys has fostered a complacent attitude that is not justified by the facts.

Things are looking up, however. In the early 1980s a number of events came together that will have a positive impact on the future of Florida's shore. In 1982 the federal government instituted barrier island legislation that effectively takes the federal government out of the development picture on heretofore undeveloped stretches of barrier islands. That is, the federal government will no longer help pay for bridges, roads, sewage and water facilities, and flood insurance for certain designated islands. Beginning in 1981 the Federal Emergency Management Agency (FEMA) began to raise the price of federal flood insurance to its real cost, so the taxpayer is not in the position of subsidizing unsafe development (figs. 1.2 and 1.3). Last, but not least, the state of Florida began to buy up undeveloped lands under the Save Our Coast (SOC) program.

But the news of the eighties is not all good. In 1983 the Environmental Protection Agency (EPA) dropped its "greenhouse effect"

Fig. 1.2. New home construction in New Smyrna Beach. This building is well forward of the state's construction setback line. It also is built on an actively eroding shoreline as evidenced by the erosion scarp (bluff) in the first dune. Photo by Dinesh C. Sharma.

Fig. 1.3. New construction (1983) in Wilbur-by-the-Sea. The building sits in front of the first dune instead of safely behind it. Furthermore, the dune was removed in order to make a conveniently flat spot to build the foundation. Photo by Barb Gruver.

bombshell with a report that warned of warming atmospheres, melting glaciers, and rising sea levels. The prestigious National Academy of Sciences said the same thing. What their warnings boil down to, as far as Florida's coastal areas are concerned, is continued and accelerated shoreline erosion. As discussed in chapter 3, a very small rise in sea level can cause a very large horizontal shoreline retreat.

Those who arrive on the east coast of Florida in coming years have an opportunity to benefit from the experience of the past and to build a better Florida. That is the purpose of this book: to let those who wish to know where the path of sound development lies, and to give those who wish to share in the Florida dream the wisdom to do so safely.

The stormy past

Juan Ponce de León, famous for his unsuccessful search for a fountain of youth, completed the first recorded cruise along Florida's east coast in the spring of 1513, a mere 21 years after the discovery of the New World. Some years later, in 1565, Pedro Mencadez de Aviles established a Spanish settlement at St. Augustine, and Florida's east coastal development began in earnest, albeit slowly. By 1599 the population of St. Augustine had survived Indians on the warpath and attacks by the British, plus a hurricane, and to those early residents Florida was not an impressively habitable place.

A shoreline milestone for East Florida was achieved with the completion of the St. Augustine seawalls, Florida's first, in 1690. By 1761 the English had pushed the Spanish out of Florida. During the next few years settlers dribbled in from several directions, but political instability continued as the British gave Florida back to Spain when they lost the American Revolution. Florida became U.S. territory in 1821 under the terms of the Adams-Onis Treaty. Shortly before the Revolutionary War, 100 plantations had been established along the east coast, but in the early 1800s development was hampered because the land was in the hands of people without much money; in addition, nobody wanted to buy land anyhow after the Seminoles went on the warpath in 1836.

Soon events along the east coast began to occur more rapidly. The site of Miami was picked in 1843. By 1854 Volusia County had a population (in the language of the day) of 300 plus 318 slaves. In 1865 the first land rush by northerners began. In 1868 Ormond (later called Ormond Beach) was founded, and in 1871 M. Day began to develop a tract of land that would someday be called Daytona. By 1875 Daytona's population had shot up to 70, but only 2 houses were on the adjacent island. In 1882 Henry M. Flagler, the first of a string of colorful Florida developers, appeared on the development scene with the purchase of a large portion of Miami Beach. In 1885 Flagler began buying marsh land near St. Augustine, which he filled in for development. He built the 450-room Ponce de Leon Hotel, among others, at a cost of $250,000. Flagler also was responsible for building the East Coast Railway to Miami, with the first train arriving in April 1896. In 1895 construction began on the Breakers Hotel in Palm Beach. It burned down in 1903 and was rebuilt in 1906 (fig. 1.4), burned down again in 1925 and was once more replaced—this time with the present-day structure.

In 1902 James Hathaway, trying out his Stanley Steamer on the beach, "discovered" the great Ormond-Daytona race course (fig. 1.5). In 1903 Ransom E. Olds and his "Pirate" hit speeds in excess of 57 mph on the beach, but beach racing received a black eye when F. Marriott totaled his car "Rocket" on an uneven stretch of sand. Car racing recommenced in 1927 at Ormond Beach; speeds now reached 200 mph. The big annual races continued until World War II. By 1913 Miami Beach was connected to the mainland by the Collins Bridge, and three developers (Messrs. Lummus,

Fig. 1.4. The 1917 version of the Breakers Hotel in Palm Beach. Note the wide beach where today no beach at all exists. Photo courtesy of the Palm Beach Historical Society.

Fig. 1.5. Horses, carriages, and beach strollers on the 1904 Daytona Beach. Library of Congress.

Fisher, and Collins) began to build what would soon be regarded as the world's most famous beach resort. By 1920 Miami Beach had a population of 644, and Miami contained more than 110,000 souls. A brand-new smuggling industry sprang up overnight with the onslaught of Prohibition, and Florida soon proved to be one of the "leakiest" states with regard to illicit booze.

The boom bubble burst for much of East Florida after the 1926 hurricane, to be followed shortly by the Depression. During the 1930s Floridians began to realize that they had to attract people 12 months a year, not just in winter, so at the end of World War II, with the advent of bulldozers and unprecedented individual wealth in America, the year-round boom was on. The results are there to see, for all who drive Highway A1A.

Throughout the history of Florida's east coast, hurricanes have played an important role in the success and failure of various development schemes. In fact, Florida and hurricanes became almost synonymous—a view that was helped along by Hollywood's penchant for emphasis of the violent and exciting. Who can forget the hurricane scenes in *Key Largo*, a Humphrey Bogart–Edward G. Robinson thriller still playing on late night TV screens?

One vivid memory of the senior author of this book was a visit to the Florida Keys a few days after Hurricane Donna struck in 1960. The sight of the destruction was awe-inspiring, but even more striking was the widespread pessimism of the survivors. Everyone seemed to feel that so many storms had hit the Keys in this century that Hurricane Donna had dealt a fatal blow to future development. However, the developers who came after Donna's

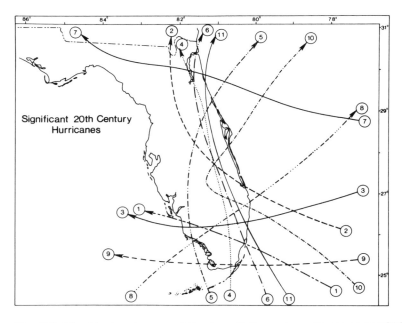

Fig. 1.6. The big hurricanes of the twentieth century: September 1926, September 1928, September 1947, October 1950 ("King"), September 1960 (Donna), August 1964 (Cleo), September 1964 (Dora), October 1964 (Isabell), August–September 1965 (Betsy), October 1969 (Gerda), August–September 1979 (David).

destruction ignored Mother Nature's danger signals. Now many thousands of new inhabitants live on sites cleared of debris from Hurricane Donna, and there is no way to evacuate the present population living on the Florida Keys in a hurricane emergency situation.

Figure 1.6 shows the paths of most East Coast hurricanes of this century and some of the big ones from times further past. Given Florida's past hurricane history, more lines will have to be drawn on this map in coming years.

Where would you want your parents to live?

During the final stages of writing this book, some of the authors (Pilkey, Jr., Neal, and Gruver) took a trip up Highway A1A, traveling the entire length of the east coast of Florida (fig. 1.7). It was a revealing experience and one that we would recommend to all potential beach-front homeowners *before* their purchase of property. The trip showed us far better than the reading of technical reports and the scanning of maps and aerial photographs what is happening to the Florida shoreline. The A1A traveler can see the wide variation in the quality of development practices along the shoreline. A surprising (to us) number of communities are doing the right thing by holding development back from the beach (for example, the beaches south of St. Augustine). But those communities are the exception rather than the rule. More often, newly developing areas are allowing buildings to crowd the shore (for example, the beaches south of Daytona Beach) where seawalls are often built simultaneously with high-rise construction.

As we drove along A1A, we decided the stiffest standard we could apply to judging the safety of a beach community was this one: would we recommend to our parents or our children that they live there? Recognizing fully that this is probably an unduly stringent standard by which to judge coastal development, we found few areas that would satisfy this criterion. Stepping back and looking at the big picture of all of Florida's shoreline, we have concluded (partly as a result of writing the West Florida companion volume to this book) that we would prefer that our parents live on the east coast of Florida rather than the west coast. This is because so many of West Florida's barrier islands are low in elevation and because in some areas (the Tampa–St. Petersburg coast) the evacuation problem borders on hopeless. Exceptions to these generalities may be found on the Panhandle coast.

Having settled on the east coast as the safest side of Florida for our parents, we found a number of communities here that we classified as low risk (see chapter 4 for our risk analysis). Even in some of the low-risk zones we would worry about the evacuation problem, especially for aging parents. Only two areas stand out as having few or minor evacuation problems, especially if one chooses a good site according to the criteria outlined in chapter 4. These are the Juno Beach area in Palm Beach County and Amelia Island in Nassau County next to the Georgia border.

The best way to satisfy your own instincts regarding the relative safety of your proposed living site is to make your own A1A odyssey. Take along this book and see for yourself.

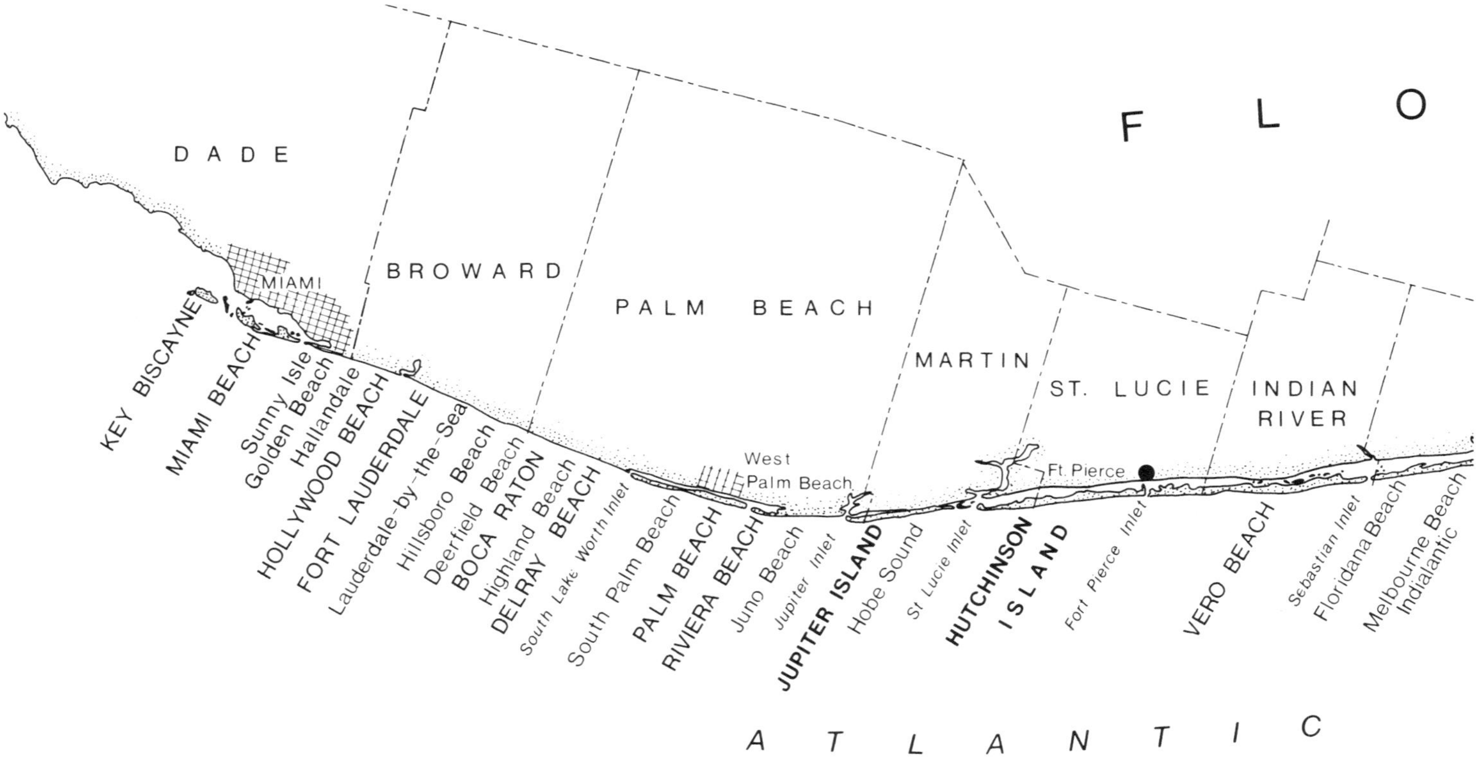

Fig. 1.7. Index map of the east coast of Florida showing the main islands and communities.

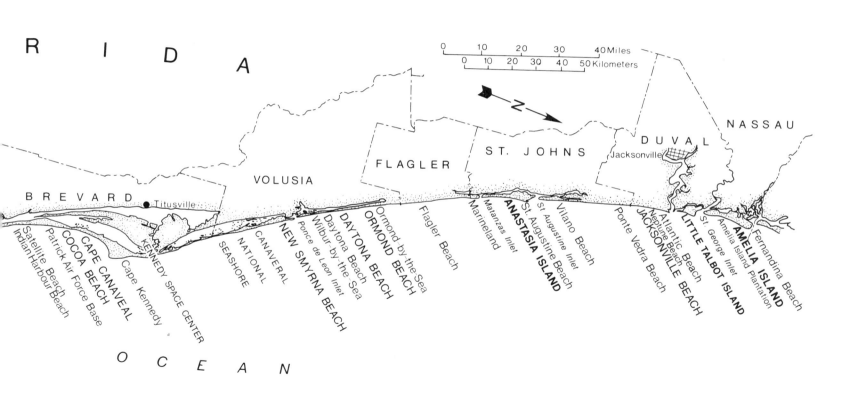

2. How the shoreline works

Most of Florida's east coast consists of a chain of *barrier islands*. These barriers, including capes and peninsulas, are narrow strips of sand that in comparison with any other portion of the continents are extremely dynamic. These islands act as a buffer for storm waves—hence the term by which they are known. Barrier islands are found off every coastal plain coast in the world, and along U.S. shores the barrier chain extends from the south shore of Long Island to the Mexican border. The Florida Keys represent one of the few breaks in the chain. The Keys are a string of upraised coral reefs that flourished more than 100,000 years ago when the sea level was higher. They are hard, immobile rock, not unconsolidated, movable sand like barrier islands.

There is a considerable variation in the size and shape of barrier islands. For example, Fernandina Island near the Georgia border is 3 miles wide compared to Hutchinson Island, a mere 200 yards in width in places. This difference in shape and size is due to many factors, but the most important is the volume of sand that comes ashore from the beach. The difference between East and West Florida's barrier islands can be explained by sand supply. West Florida's islands are almost all narrow and much lower in elevation than East Florida's. Less sand has been blown ashore on the west side to form the all-important sand dunes, and as a consequence West Florida islands are generally less safe for development.

In this chapter we will discuss how the East Florida shoreline works. Ironically, considering how important it is to Floridians, the chain of Florida islands making up the east coast are the least studied of any such islands along the Atlantic coast. In contrast, the islands of North Carolina, South Carolina, Delaware, and Texas have been drilled, trenched, mapped, and photographed by a whole generation of coastal geologists. Nonetheless, the basic principles of island and beach evolution are well established, and we can apply them with confidence to East Florida.

If you plan to live in an East Florida beach community, you must understand the natural processes at work there. Your safety and well-being depend on it. The safety and well-being of your community depend on it. A good place to start in your understanding of the shore is with the origin of barrier islands.

Barrier islands: where they come from

Florida has barrier islands because of the interaction of a rising sea level with a coastal plain indented by river valleys (fig. 2.1). Approximately 15,000 years ago, when sea level was as much as 300 feet lower than today, the Florida shoreline was many miles offshore, on what is now the continental shelf. Vast glaciers covered the high latitudes of the world, tying up a great volume of water.

But then the ice started melting and the sea began to rise. The rising water flooded the valleys, forming bodies of water called

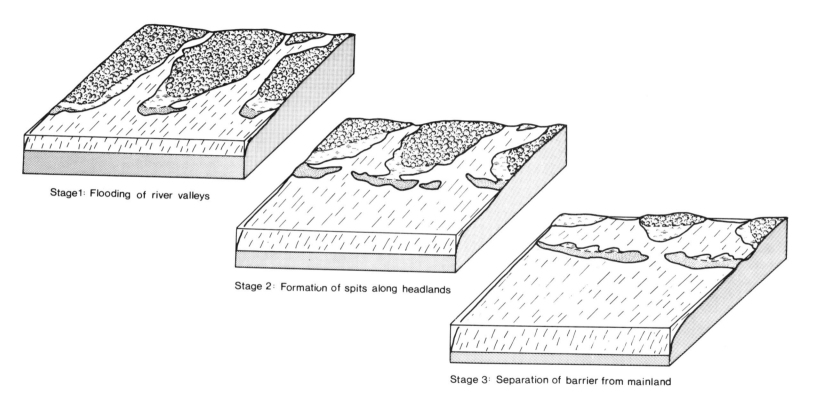

Stage 1: Flooding of river valleys

Stage 2: Formation of spits along headlands

Stage 3: Separation of barrier from mainland

Fig. 2.1. The origin of barrier islands in a rising sea level.

estuaries. If you look at a map of today's continental shoreline, you can see many such inundated valleys, especially along the Atlantic coast of the United States. Chesapeake Bay and Delaware Bay are two prominent examples. Along Florida's east coast the best examples of estuaries are the St. Johns and St. Marys rivers to the north.

If this were all that occurred, the shoreline today would be jagged. Nature, however, tends to straighten jagged shorelines. Wave action cut back the headlands—the areas of land that extended seaward between flooded valleys—and built spits extending from the headlands across the bay mouths. As sea level continued to rise, the low-lying land behind such spits, plus the sand dunes of the old headland shorelines, then became flooded. The flooding behind the old dune beach complexes resulted in their becoming detached from the mainland, and the barrier islands were born.

This concept of barrier island origin and growth was developed by a number of geologists, including the late John Hoyt of the University of Georgia and Donald Swift who is now with Arco Oil and Gas Company.

The operation of barrier islands

Islands on the move

You might ask why, if sea level continued to rise, the newly formed islands were not themselves covered by the sea. The answer, which only recently has been agreed upon by geologists, is that islands do not simply stay in one place when the sea level threatens to rise over them. The islands move or migrate toward the mainland. The more rapid the sea-level rise, the more rapid the island migration.

Needless to say, for the islands to have remained islands, the mainland shore must have moved, too. This is indeed what happened: the shoreline on the mainland retreated as the island advanced. Otherwise the islands would have run aground. Miami Beach probably migrated 5 or so miles to its present position. Fernandina Beach probably formed 50 miles or so offshore. Some barrier islands along the Texas and Mississippi Gulf coasts may have migrated more than 100 miles.

The sea-level rise was quite rapid until about 5,000 years ago, at which time it slowed down considerably (fig. 2.2). Hence, up until 5,000 years ago Florida's barrier islands were moving landward at an impressive clip. The most rapidly moving islands tend to be low, very narrow strips of sand. Cape Island, South Carolina, and Sand Key in Florida Bay (fig. 2.3) are small-scale examples of this kind of island. Fernandina Beach is an example of a wide, very slow-moving island.

When the slowdown in sea-level rise came, many islands stopped migrating altogether. And because they then remained in one position long enough for sand from various sources to accumulate, they also began to widen. This relative stability, however, has recently come to an end (fig. 2.4).

The accelerating rise in sea level

Recent studies suggest that in the 1930s the rise in sea level suddenly accelerated. Sea level is now rising at a rate of perhaps

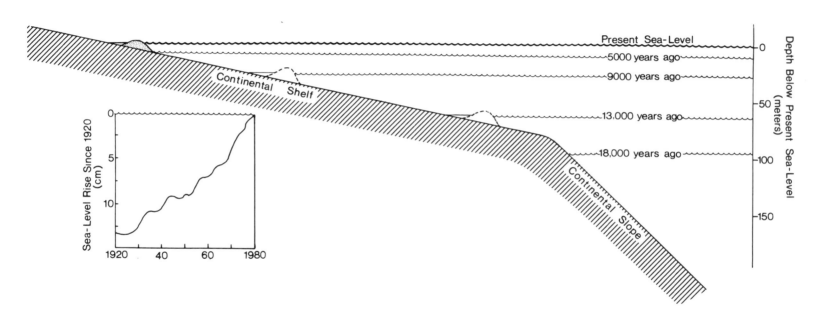

Fig. 2.2. The history of the sea-level rise off the east coast of Florida. The insert shows the rise in sea level since 1920.

slightly more than 1 foot per century. Keep in mind that this refers to a vertical rise. The horizontal change—the distance islands migrate as a consequence—is much greater (fig. 2.5) than the vertical rise. In theory, a 1-foot rise in sea level should produce a horizontal shoreline retreat of more than 1,000 feet. How much a specific island moves depends on the slope of its migration surface:

the gentler the slope, the more the island will migrate.

The safest assumption you can make about the future of sea-level rise is that it will continue and accelerate. The National Academy of Sciences has warned that all evidence points to a warming of the earth's climate. The burning of fossil fuels has resulted in excessive production of carbon dioxide, which causes

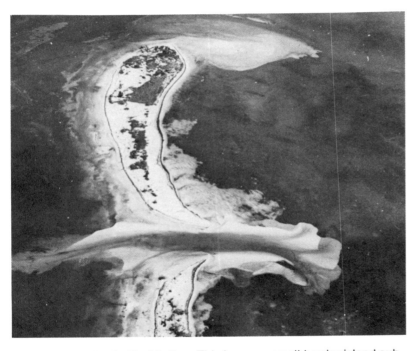

Fig. 2.3. Sand Key in Florida Bay. This is a very small barrier island subject to overwash by storm waves. The inlet splitting the island into 2 parts has developed an excellent example of a tidal delta. The body of sand extending to the right of the inlet is the flood-tidal delta produced by flood or incoming tides. To the left is the smaller ebb-tidal delta. Photo by Harold R. Wanless.

the atmosphere to retain heat. This warming is expected to increase the melting of the polar ice caps, which, in turn, will raise sea level.

The Environmental Protection Agency, in a report released during October 1983, suggests that sea level should rise between 2 feet and 10 feet by the year 2100. Four feet is the most plausible figure, but there is a lot of educated guesswork in these numbers. In any event, almost certainly the sea-level rise will accelerate and shoreline erosion will increase accordingly.

Barrier island migration

Do you want to prove to yourself that barrier islands migrate? If you are standing on one now, walk to the oceanside beach and look at the seashells. Chances are that on most natural Florida beaches you will find the shells of oysters, clams, or snails that once lived in the lagoon or river on the back side of the barrier island between the island and the mainland. How did shells from the back side get to the front side? The answer is that the island migrated over the lagoon, and waves attacking and breaking up the old lagoon sands and muds threw the shells up onto the present-day beach. (This assumes you are looking at a natural beach where sand has not been pumped in from behind the island or from the shelf in front of the island; see chapter 3.) It follows that if some of the shells on Florida's beaches are from preexisting environments, the average age of the shell material must be quite old. In fact, many of the shells one picks up on a Florida beach are several

1949   **1981**

Fig. 2.4. The sea-level rise illustrated by the level of barnacles on Miami Beach Pier. Photo by Harold R. Wanless.

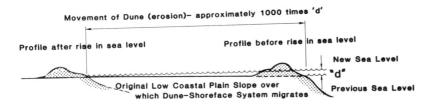

Fig. 2.5. A diagram illustrating the theoretical relationship between sea-level rise and shoreline retreat. A very small rise produces a very large retreat.

thousand years old and are actually fossils. The U.S. Army Corps of Engineers, a few years back, obtained some radiocarbon dates of the shell material on three South Florida beaches. The samples dated contained a number of shells, and all 3 revealed ages of around 13,000 years. In addition, salt-marsh peats that formed in back of the islands at some earlier time are exposed occasionally on oceanside beaches after storms. On Whale Beach, New Jersey, a patch of mud that appeared on the beach after a storm contained (much to the surprise of some beach strollers) cow hooves and fragments of colonial pottery. The mud was formerly salt marsh on the back side of the island where a colonist had dumped a wagonload of garbage. Since colonial times this particular section of the island had migrated its entire width! On some Florida islands, evidence of beach erosion (or of the front side of the island moving back) can be seen by stumps on the beach. For example, stumps protrude from the beach at the north end of Jupiter Island and on portions of Hutchinson Island (fig. 2.6).

Fig. 2.6. A ghost forest on the beach of Hutchinson Island. Very rapid shoreline retreat is indicated by the presence of such stumps in an environment where they obviously did not grow.

For an island to migrate (fig. 2.7), the side on the ocean (the front side) must move landward by erosion, and the side toward the mainland (the back side) must do likewise by growth. Also, as it moves, the island must somehow maintain its elevation and bulk. If you have not guessed already, *island migration* is the term that geologists use for what beach cottage or condo owners call *beach erosion* (fig. 2.8).

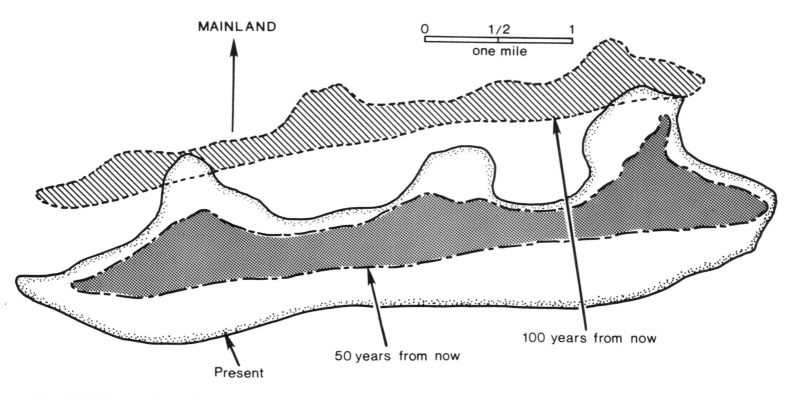

MAINLAND

0   1/2   1
one mile

100 years from now

50 years from now

Present

Fig. 2.7. A diagram showing how a barrier island similar to Anastasia Island might behave during the next 100 years. The island should be expected to initially thin by erosion on both the back and front sides, following which migration will begin in earnest (assuming an accelerating rise in sea level).

Fig. 2.8. A striking example of island migration. The jetties built at the south end of Ocean City, Maryland (top of photo), caused sand starvation of adjacent Assateague Island. In the early 1930s the 2 islands formed a more or less straight line.

Front side moves back by erosion

The beach on the front side moves back because the sea level is rising. The rise in sea level is a major cause of beach erosion worldwide, although man can make erosion worse, sometimes much worse, by interfering with the sand supply. For example, the groins and seawalls on many of Florida's beaches have increased rates of erosion on nearby beaches. The seawall effect is amply illustrated by beachless Palm Beach. The impact of groins could once be seen during the sixties and seventies on beachless Miami Beach before the new beach was pumped up in 1981. Even greater erosion of beaches is usually caused by jetties and artificially cut inlets, examples of which abound on Florida's east coast. Jetties that have caused serious problems for nearby beaches include those for Miami Harbor, Lake Worth Inlet, and St. Lucie Inlet.

Back side moves back by growth

There are several ways for an island to widen. On the narrow, low Florida islands that are separated from the mainland by an open body of water (called a *lagoon* or a *sound*) rather than by a marsh, a common widening process is that of incorporation of old flood-tidal deltas from closed inlets.

An *inlet* is the channel of water between adjacent barrier islands. The inlet may be a permanent feature in front of the mouth of a river or stream, or it may be a short-lived feature that forms when water breaches the island during a hurricane. Eyewitness accounts and other evidence confirm that water sometimes breaks through the island from the sound side, or back side, as the storm subsides and high tides retreat. Over the years following the formation of an inlet, sand carried by incoming tides pours through the gap and into the sound. This mass of sand is called a *flood-tidal delta* (see fig. 2.3) and forms the shallows on which boats go aground and through which the Corps of Engineers must dredge to maintain channels. (There also is a delta, called an *ebb-tidal delta*, on the ocean side of an inlet. This is formed by currents flowing out of the sound during falling tide.)

After a few decades many inlets either close or they migrate away from the flood-tidal delta. Salt marsh establishes itself on the shallow delta, and then the salt marsh grasses trap sediment and cause the land to be built up almost to high-tide level. Thus, new land is added to the back of the island. The inlet's former position is marked only by a marsh bulging into the lagoon.

When an inlet migrates laterally to a new position, the flood-tidal delta moves with it. In other words, as the inlet migrates, sand continues to pour into the lagoon, and a series of new flood-tidal deltas are formed along the entire area of inlet migration. In this way the island is widened over the full distance that the inlet shifts.

Another way that islands—especially narrow ones—can be widened is by direct frontal *overwash* of storm waves from the ocean side. All barrier islands receive overwash during storms. On large islands the overwash may barely penetrate the first line of dunes. On low, narrow islands overwash may be carried across the island to reach the lagoon. Overwash waves carry sand that is deposited in tongue-shaped or fan-shaped masses called *overwash fans*. When such fans reach into the lagoon, the island may be widened. If islands are backed by salt marshes or mangrove swamps, overwash sediment may bury them. Interestingly enough, the vegetation on many islands actually flourishes when buried by an overwash fan. In a few months some plants grow right up through the sand layer.

Overwash is the method of back-side growth used by islands in a hurry—that is, those that are migrating rapidly landward. Cape Island, South Carolina, and some of Louisiana's islands are examples of islands migrating perhaps tens of feet per year. Between 15,000 and 5,000 years ago when the sea level was rising rapidly, most American barrier islands were probably of the overwash type. If the EPA is correct in its predictions concerning the upcoming accelerated rise in sea level, we can expect many of our islands to begin thinning down to use the overwash migration mechanism.

The island maintains its elevation during migration

The remaining problem of a migrating island is how to retain its bulk or elevation as it moves toward the mainland. This problem is solved by two processes: dune formation and overwash-fan deposits.

Dunes are formed by the wind, and if a sufficiently large supply of sand comes to the beach from the continental shelf via the waves, a high-elevation island can be formed. Winds blowing on shore across the beach carry sand that dune plants trap, causing the sand to accumulate and build up. The wider the beach the more sand can be picked up by winds. Examples of well-developed ridges of dune sand on Florida's east coast include Daytona Beach, where several parallel ridges afford high elevation and a relatively safe location for construction. More commonly on East Florida's islands a single beach ridge or dune line is found next to the beach. Frequently Highway A1A, the coastal highway, occupies the top of this ridge. A particularly good example of a high dune ridge fronting a beach can be seen along the open ocean shore off Delray Beach and Boynton Beach. Such a ridge makes development safer, but not if condos and homes are built in front of the ridge, as often happens.

Sometimes the reason for the lack of dune formation on islands of low elevation (for example, many of Florida's west coast islands) is the lack of sand supply from the adjacent continental shelf. Sometimes dunes do not form on an island because the dominant winds do not blow across the beach and into the island. Finally, if the natural sand is too fine, it will not build up into dunes.

Size and shape of barrier islands

The most untrained eye can readily see that Florida's islands come in a wide variety of shapes and sizes. Ponte Vedra Beach and vicinity consists of a single ridge of sand a few yards wide, backed up by salt marsh. Fernandina Beach on Amelia Island occupies a wide, high island that is heavily forested. Amelia Island is actually the southernmost of the Sea Islands that make up the coast of Georgia. Miami Beach occupies a seemingly wide island

with broad Biscayne Bay between it and the mainland. However, the natural island before clearing in 1882 was a fairly narrow strip of dune sand backed by a broad band of low-elevation mangrove swamps. At Fort Lauderdale the island is only an island because the intracoastal waterway separates a strip of land from the mainland. Before the development of Fort Lauderdale, a narrow mangrove swamp separated mainland and island, but all signs of this swamp have disappeared.

Cape Canaveral occupies a piece of land that geologists call a cuspate foreland. Cape San Blas on the other side of the Florida peninsula and Cape Hatteras, North Carolina, are similar features. There is no unanimity of opinion as to how such capes form, and their origin remains a major unresolved question for shoreline geologists. Offshore from each of the capes is a large bar of sand called a shoal that extends seaward and upon which many unwary mariners have come to grief.

The factors responsible for all of these differences in island shape are numerous. The most important of them is sand supply. If a lot of sand can come ashore from beaches either by wind or overwash, the island will be high and wide. Low sand supply produces narrow, low islands.

The dominant mineral in most of East Florida's beach sands is quartz, a very stable form of silicon dioxide. The nearest sources of quartz are the rivers of Georgia and South Carolina. The quartz sand has been slowly pushed south by the waves over a period of several millions of years, and some grains must have traveled as much as 400 miles. Looking at the sand supply problem from a

A particularly intriguing example of man's effect was discovered by Dr. Paul Godfrey of the University of Massachusetts. He observed that the long, continuous, artificial dune built on the open ocean side by the National Park Service on the Outer Banks of North Carolina near Cape Hatteras is causing erosion on the *lagoon side* of the island. The problem is that the artificial dune prevents overwash fans from crossing the island during storms. Before the dune was built, overwash frequently reached the back side of the island, and new salt marsh was formed on the edge of the new overwash fan. Newly formed *Spartina* marsh is an excellent erosion buffer against lagoon-side waves. By preventing overwash, the frontal dune on the ocean side of the island precludes new marsh growth. Old salt marsh (20 to 30 years old) is a poor erosion buffer, so the lagoon-side erosion rate increases.

If overwash on a low-elevation island (such as portions of Jupiter and Hutchinson islands) is not obstructed, the marsh in time (10 years or more) builds up its elevation and essentially chokes itself. The grass thins out and becomes shorter and less healthy. The most casual observers walking along the back side of any marsh-fringed island in its natural state note that they are walking through alternately tall and short grass. The tall grass is new or fresh grass on recent overwash; the short grass is old grass on an old overwash fan. Old marsh is a poor buffer against shoreline erosion and soon begins to give way.

The maritime forests found in Florida's larger islands also illustrate the integration of island environments. The large trees are salt-tolerant and form a canopy over the less tolerant undergrowth. The undergrowth, in turn, stabilizes the larger trees by holding down the soil. If trees are thinned or removed, salt spray can attack and eliminate the undergrowth. Loss of vegetation allows sediment to be eroded by wind or other processes, thereby destroying the larger trees.

Much has been said about the damage to islands by dune buggies and other off-road vehicles. This problem further attests to the integration of island environments. Dune buggies can prevent dunes from stabilizing (becoming stationary), and destabilization (moving sand) may result in destroyed dunes and vegetation, followed by sand dune migration into maritime forests or developments.

The most common cause of excessive sand movement on barrier islands is construction. The problem is particularly acute during the early stages of construction, and in many instances sand movement has halted a building project altogether. Also, a common mistake made on barrier islands is the type of road construction leading to developments. On many American barrier islands you can drive along roads that parallel the beach and observe that at the end of each feeder road there is a giant notch cut through the last row or two of dunes. Such notches are certain someday to provide a path for storm-wave overwash. Beach access roads should go over not through dunes, and they should be curved rather than straight.

Beaches: the dynamic equilibrium

The beach is one of the earth's most dynamic environments. The beach—or zone of active sand movement—is always changing and always moving, and we now know that it does so in accordance with the earth's natural laws. The natural laws of the beach control a beautiful, logical environment that builds up when the weather is good, and strategically (but only temporarily) retreats when confronted by big storm waves. This system depends on four factors: waves, sea-level rise, beach sand, and shape of the beach (fig. 2.10). The relationship among these factors is a natural balance referred to as a *dynamic equilibrium:* when one factor changes, the others adjust accordingly to maintain a balance. When we enter the system incorrectly—as man often does—the dynamic equilibrium is destroyed.

The beach quiz

Answers to the following often-asked questions about beaches may clarify the nature of this dynamic equilibrium. It is important to keep in mind that the beach extends from the toe of the dune to a depth of 30 to 40 feet, which may be miles offshore. It is the zone of sand movement during storms. The part on which we walk or sunbathe is only the upper beach.

How does the beach respond to a storm?

Old-timers and storm survivors from barrier islands frequently have commented on how flat and broad the beach is after a storm. The flat beach can be explained in terms of the dynamic equilibrium. As wave height increases, the dunes at the back of the

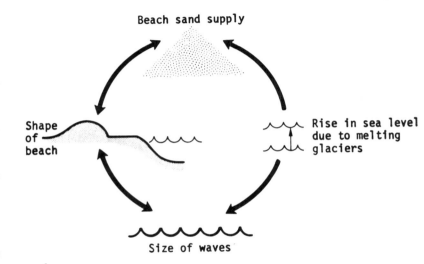

Fig. 2.10. The dynamic equilibrium of the beach.

beach are eroded and sand is moved seaward across the beach, changing its shape. The reason for this storm response is quite logical. The beach flattens itself so that storm waves expend their energy over a broader, more nearly level surface. On a steeper surface—take a vertical seawall, for example—storm-wave energy would be expended on a smaller area, causing greater damage.

Figure 2.11 illustrates the way in which the beach flattens. In summary, the waves take sand from the upper beach or the first

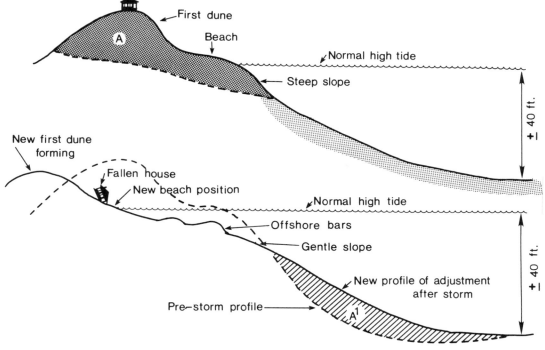

(Shaded area A¹ is approximately equal to shaded area A.)

Fig. 2.11. Storm response by the healthy natural beach.

dune and transport it to the lower beach. If a hot dog stand or beach cottage happens to be located on the first dune, it may disappear along with the dune sands. This also is the reason why condos must be built on deeply embedded stilts in case storm waves begin to eat away at the base of the building.

An island can lose a great deal of sand during a storm. Much of it will come back, however, gradually pushed shoreward by fair-weather waves. As the sand returns to the beach, the wind takes over and slowly rebuilds the dunes, storing sand to respond to nature's next storm call. In order for the sand to come back, of course, there should be no man-made obstructions—such as a seawall—between the first dune and the beach. Return of the beach may take months or even years.

Sometimes besides simply flattening, a storm beach also will develop one or more offshore bars. The bars serve the function of tripping the large waves long before they reach the beach. The sand bar produced by storms pulling sand offshore from the beach is easily visible during calm weather as a line of surf a few tens of yards off the beach. Geologists refer to the bar as a ridge and the intervening trough as a runnel.

How does the beach widen or build seaward?

Beaches grow seaward in several ways, principally by (1) bringing in new sand on the so-called *longshore* (surf-zone) currents, or (2) bringing in new sand from offshore by forming a *ridge-and-runnel* system. Actually, these two ways of beach widening are not mutually exclusive.

Longshore currents are familiar to anyone who has swum in the ocean; they are the reason you sometimes end up somewhere down the beach, away from your towel. Such currents result from waves approaching the shore at an angle; this causes a portion of the energy of the breaking wave to be directed along the beach. When combined with breaking waves, the weak current is capable of carrying large amounts of very coarse material for miles along the beach. The sand transported along the shore may be deposited at the end of the island, or it may cross to the next island.

In general, sand along the beaches of Florida travels from north to south. As mentioned earlier, over a period of many thousands of years the quartz sand that made up the old Miami Beach traveled from source rivers in faraway Georgia.

Ridges and runnels formed during small summer storms virtually march onto the shore and are welded to the beach. The next time you are at the beach, observe the offshore ridge for a period of a few days and verify this for yourself. You may find that each day you have to swim out a slightly shorter distance in order to stand on the sand bar.

At low tide during the summer, the beach frequently has a trough filled or partly filled with water. This trough is formed by the ridge that is in the final stages of welding onto the beach. Several ridges combine to make the berm, or beach terrace, on which sunbathers loll.

Where does the beach sand come from?

Along the east coast of Florida and along most of the Atlantic portion of the American barrier coast—which runs approximately 10,000 miles from the south shore of Long Island down and around to where the Texas coast meets Mexico—the sand comes from the adjacent continental shelf. It is pushed up to the beach by fair-weather waves. Additional sand, sometimes very large quantities of it, is carried laterally by longshore currents that move in the surf zone parallel to the beach. Rivers contribute sand directly to barrier beaches only along the Gulf coast, starting with Florida's Apalachicola River. Along the rest of America's barrier chain, sand carried by rivers does not make it to the coast. Rather it is deposited far inland at the heads of estuaries or behind man-made dams.

It is important for beach dwellers to know about or at least have some sense of the source of sand for their beach. If, for example, there is a lot of longshore sand transport in front of your favorite beach, the beach may well disappear if someone builds a groin or even a seawall upstream. Community actions taken on adjacent islands or inlets potentially could affect your beach, just as your actions may affect your coastal neighbors.

Where do seashells come from?

The main source of shells on a beach is from animal communities that line the nearshore zone adjacent to the beach. As we already have discussed, some of the shells on Florida's beaches were originally deposited behind the island and came to the beach after the island migrated right over them. If you use a shell book to identify all of the specimens from a beach, you will find a number of species that do not belong near an open ocean beach. Instead, they came from the lagoon or estuary.

Another source of shells on a number of beaches south of Cape Canaveral (for example, Boynton Beach, Vero Beach, and Jupiter Island) are outcropping rocks containing abundant fossil shells. As waves break the rock up, the fossil shells (which are often stained brown) become part of the beach sand and usually are transported south by longshore currents.

Why do beaches erode?

As we have already pointed out, beach erosion (figs. 2.12 and 2.13) is the cottage owner's term for the larger process called island or shoreline migration. Its principal cause is the sea-level rise —presently judged to average about 1 foot per century along American shores. We in Florida can be thankful that we do not have the more rapid 3-feet per century rise of portions of the New England coast. (The reason sea-level rise can be different in different coastal areas is that the land also may be sinking or rising slowly relative to sea level.)

On a year-to-year basis this sea-level rise is imperceptible. The actual erosion is still achieved by waves, so our short-term observation is to associate extensive erosion with a particularly intense storm. Our responses tend to be directed at such storm events when we design "protective" structures such as groins and revetments. The prime cause for erosion, however, is the sea-level rise. The impact of this rise is within one's lifetime and should not be regarded as such a long-term event as to be of no consequence.

Fig. 2.12. Beach erosion is about to catch up with this condo and has already caught up with the house down the beach. This is a low-tide scene from Vero Beach, looking north. Photo by Dinesh Sharma.

Increasingly, along the East Florida shore, man is becoming the major cause of shoreline erosion. Take jetties, for example. Almost every Florida inlet is jettied, and almost everywhere erosion is rampant south of the jetty. This is discussed in more detail in chapter 3.

Fig. 2.13. The roots on this palm tree on Key Biscayne are exposed due to beach lowering or loss of sand, that is, beach erosion. Photo by Bill Neal.

Are the shorelines on the back sides of our islands eroding?

The back side (lagoon side) of most American barrier islands is eroding just like the open ocean side. The reason for this, in large part, is the rise in sea level. However, most of Florida's heavily developed islands now have seawalls on the back side that halt the erosion. Where development is less heavy, particularly north of Cape Canaveral, many examples of eroding marshes and beaches can be seen on the back sides of islands.

What can I do about my eroding beach?

This question has no simple answer, but it is briefly addressed in chapter 3. If you are talking about an open ocean shoreline, there is nothing you can do unless (1) you are wealthy or (2) the U.S. Army Corps of Engineers steps in. Your best response, especially from an environmental standpoint, is to move your threatened building back. The bottom line in trying to stop erosion of an open ocean shoreline is that the methods employed will ultimately increase the erosion rate. For example, the simple act of hiring a friendly bulldozer operator to push sand up from the lower beach will steepen its profile and cause the beach to erode more rapidly during the next storm. Pumping in new sand (replenishment) costs a great deal of money, and in most cases the artificial beach will disappear much more rapidly than its natural predecessor. For example, artificial beaches at Pompano Beach and Hobe Sound disappeared much faster than originally predicted.

There are many ways to stop erosion in the short run if lots of money is available. But, in the long run, erosion cannot be halted except at the cost of losing the natural beach.

If most ocean shorelines are eroding, what is the long-range future of beach development?

The long-range future of beach development will depend on how individual communities respond to their migrating shoreline. Those communities that choose to protect their front-side houses at all costs need only look to portions of the New Jersey shore to see the end result. The life span of houses can unquestionably be extended by stabilizing a beach (i.e., slowing the erosion). The ultimate cost of slowing erosion, however, is loss of the beach. The time required for destruction of a beach is highly variable and depends on the shoreline or island dynamics. Usually an extensive seawall on a barrier island will do the trick in 10 to 30 years. Often a single storm will permanently remove a beach in front of a seawall.

If, when the time comes, a community grits its teeth and moves the front row of buildings or lets it fall in, the beaches can be saved in the long run. Unfortunately, so far in America, the primary factor involved in shoreline decisions, which every beach community must sooner or later make, has been money. Poor communities (Folly Beach in South Carolina or Sargent Beach in Texas) let the island roll on. Rich ones try to stop it.

Therein lies a problem of high-density development right next to the surf zone. As the shoreline recedes naturally and predictably, it is one thing for a community to allow individual cottages to fall in, but 20-story condominiums would be a "bit" more painful to allow to disappear.

The future of shoreline development in East Florida appears to be one of increasing expenditure of money leading to increasing loss of beach.

A word about storms and hurricanes

Sea-level rise may be the ultimate villain in the shoreline saga, but *hurricanes* are the most memorable actors. Coastal processes or wind, wave, storm surge (the increase in water level during a storm), and overwash are greatest during hurricanes, but the majority of today's coastal residents and property owners have not experienced such storms. The relatively hurricane-free period from the 1960s to the present has contributed to an apathetic disregard of the hurricane menace and has increased development in high-hazard zones. Time is not on the side of such development.

Although hurricanes get the lion's share of the publicity and public awareness campaigns, the shorelines of the east coast of Florida are probably more endangered by "common, old, every-day" winter storms, particularly *northeasters*. In the county-by-county descriptions of East Florida shoreline safety classifications (chapter 4) quite a bit is said about northeaster storms in recent years. Northeasters differ from hurricanes in that they hang around longer and pound the shoreline for days rather than hours. The two biggest storms in recent years were the Ash Wednesday storm of 1962 and the Lincoln's Birthday storm of 1973. The 1962 storm

was the biggest Atlantic storm of this century. It struck during the full moon, the time of spring tides, and it hovered offshore for 3 long days. A great deal of shoreline retreat and severe damage to buildings built too close to the shore were reported from South Florida to Massachusetts. The greatest damage was done along the New York–New Jersey shoreline. Flooding of low areas on barrier islands also can be severe during big northeasters. Floodwaters from the ocean are pushed up into lagoons and estuaries by these storms just as in the case of hurricanes. The wise Florida coastal dweller will watch out for northeasters as well as hurricanes!

Each year on June 1 the official hurricane season begins. For the next 6 to 7 months conditions are favorable for hurricane formation over the tropical to subtropical waters of the Western Hemisphere. Hurricanes that ultimately strike the eastern United States tend to originate in the Gulf of Mexico or Caribbean Sea early in the season, and later in the season (August, September, and October) in the eastern North Atlantic Ocean.

Although meteorologists are still seeking answers to the causes and mechanics of hurricanes, the basic model of what happens is known. During the summer the surface waters off West Africa heat up to at least 79° F. Evaporation produces a layer of warm, moist air over the ocean. This moist air is trapped by warm air coming off the African continent, but some is drawn upward. As the moist air rises, it cools and condenses, releasing heat, which in turn warms the surrounding air, causing it to rise. As a result of the increasing mass of rising air, a low-pressure area forms (tropical depression), and warm, easterly winds rush in to replace the rising air. The effect of the earth's rotation deflects the air flow, and the counterclockwise-rotating air mass begins to take on the familiar shape of a hurricane. Air forced to the middle of the spiral can only move upward, producing a chimneylike column of rising air—the "eye" of the storm.

So a heat engine effect evolves, with rising, moist air cooling and condensing, releasing heat to cause more air to rise, allowing more air to rush in over the sea, an endless source of moisture. Heavy rainfall characterizes the edges of the cloud mass, and when sustained wind velocities reach 74 mph the storm is classed as a hurricane. The strongest winds of a hurricane may exceed 200 mph, and the maximum winds of the largest storms to hit coastal areas are generally unknown because the wind-measuring instruments are blown away!

Once formed, the hurricane mass begins to move and may continue to grow in size and strength. The velocity of this tracking movement can vary from nearly stationary to greater than 60 mph. If you consider that the diameter of a hurricane ranges from 60 to 1,000 miles, and that gale-force or higher winds may extend over most of this area, the total energy released over the thousands of square miles covered by the storm is almost beyond comprehension. No ship or seawall, cottage, condominium, or other static structure will be immune from the impact of such forces. For a hurricane making landfall on the east coast of Florida, these forces will be at their maximum in the area to the right (north or east) of the eye (fig. 2.14), but the entire landfall area will experience the severity of the storm. If the hurricane comes on a high tide, espe-

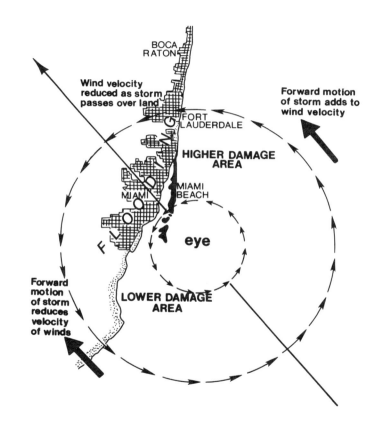

Fig. 2.14. A hypothetical hurricane striking the east coast of Florida.

cially a spring tide during a full moon, the effects of storm-surge flooding, waves, and overwash will be magnified.

Today the hurricane watchers of the National Oceanic and Atmospheric Administration track hurricanes and provide advance warning for the evacuation of threatened coastal areas. Yet as little as 9 to 12 hours advance warning may be all that is possible, given the unpredictable turns a hurricane may take. That is not much lead time.

Hurricane probability and rank

In modern times, storms have been compared in terms of dollar loss, but this comparison reflects the nature of the development damaged rather than the strength of the hurricane. Likewise, smaller storms of less than a century ago were more deadly than the largest of today's storms. Today, advance warning, efficient evacuation, and safer construction *should* result in low casualty rates even in a major hurricane. But unsafe development, allowing population growth to exceed the capacity for safe evacuation, and complacency on the part of coastal residents could reverse this trend with shocking results.

Many of the areas of dense population on Florida's islands are virtually impossible to evacuate completely before the onslaught of a storm. In southern Florida care must be taken in choosing a place to evacuate because many inland areas also will be flooded by the same storm that will inundate the island. Juno Beach and environs is an example of a beach area where high elevations are available for evacuation immediately adjacent to the beach. But the Miami Beach–Fort Lauderdale shoreline stretch is backed by

Table 2.1. The Saffir/Simpson Scale with pressure ranges, winds, surge, and damage classification.

Scale number	Central pressures		Winds (mph)	Surge	Damage
	Millibars	Inches			
1	980	28.94	74–95	4–5	Minimal
2	965–979	28.5–28.91	96–110	6–8	Moderate
3	945–964	27.91–28.47	111–130	9–12	Extensive
4	920–944	27.17–27.88	131–155	13–18	Extreme
5	920	27.17	155+	18+	Catastrophic

large areas of low-elevation mainland, and care must be taken to choose your storm haven.

The National Weather Service has adopted the Saffir-Simpson scale (table 2.1) for communicating the strength of a hurricane to public safety officials of communities in the storm's potential path. The scale ranks a storm on three variables: wind velocity, storm surge, and barometric pressure. Although hurricane paths are still unpredictable, the scale communicates quickly the nature of the storm—what to expect in terms of wind, waves, and flooding.

Do not be misled by such scales, however. A hurricane is a hurricane. The scale simply defines how bad is bad. When the word comes to evacuate, *do it*. Wind velocity may change, or the configuration of the coast may amplify storm-surge level, so the category rank can change. Do not gamble with your life or the lives of others.

See appendix A for a checklist of things to do when a hurricane threatens.

3. Shoreline engineering: the impossible dream?

Rising sea level, diminishing sand supplies, and barrier island migration have caused shoreline retreat along much of the American coast. The common response to this natural process has been to try and stop it—stabilize the beach so it no longer moves landward.

Shoreline engineering is a term that refers to methods of changing or altering the natural shoreline system in order to stabilize it, that is, to hold it in place. *Shoreline stabilization* is a synonym for shoreline engineering. Stabilization methods range from the simple planting of dune grass to the complex construction of large seawalls using draglines, cranes, and bulldozers. Stabilization is usually carried out in response to a recognized danger to buildings located next to a beach. Examples of such stabilization abound on Florida's east coast: Fernandina Beach, Jacksonville Beach, St. Augustine Beach, Daytona Beach, Cocoa Beach, Vero Beach, Jupiter Island, Palm Beach, Hillsboro Beach, Fort Lauderdale, and Key Biscayne, to name just a few. Sometimes stabilization, especially beach replenishment, is carried out both to prevent buildings from falling into the sea and to increase the recreation value of a beach. This is the case in Jacksonville Beach, Pompano Beach, Jupiter Island Beach, and Miami Beach.

Local rhetoric to the contrary, most shoreline engineering is carried out to save buildings and not beaches. Beaches never need saving. When left alone in their natural state, beaches change their position in space but always remain "healthy" strips of sand.

Another way of saying this: if we allow all of the cottages and condos to fall in as the shoreline erodes, the beaches will remain perfectly healthy and usable by all who wish to fish, swim, picnic, surf, camp, hike, stare at the surf, or whatever. It may not be realistic on the Florida political scene to allow 20-story condos presently located at the surf's edge to topple into the ocean as the beach retreats, but it should be made clear to all concerned that the natural beach itself never needs man's help and that shoreline stabilization becomes necessary only when man builds his structures too close to the sea. Man is the only enemy the beach knows (figs. 3.1 and 3.2).

The economic and environmental price of stabilizing a beach can be stiff indeed. Replenishment of beaches costs on the order of $1 million to $6 million per mile. Seawalls cost $300, $800, and even $1,000 per foot of shoreline.

There are, of course, a few situations in which stabilization is an economic necessity. Channels leading to our major state ports such as Miami and Jacksonville, for instance, must be maintained, and damage to local beaches may be an acceptable price. In other cases recreational value may be used as justification for groins and replenishment. For example, Jones Beach, New York, may have hundreds of thousands of swimmers on a single summer weekend day. Such beaches can be considered to be national treasures and if their maintenance requires a great deal of tax money and even

Fig. 3.1. This beach scene of 1909 clearly shows that Palm Beach has lost a great deal of beach in the interim and that the formality of beach attire has changed during the same time period. Photo courtesy of the Palm Beach Historical Society.

some damage to nearby beaches and structures, so be it. Perhaps Fort Lauderdale's jammed beaches fall in the national treasure category.

There are three major types of shoreline stabilization: (1) beach replenishment, (2) groins and jetties, and (3) seawalls. These are discussed below in order of increasing environmental damage.

Stabilizing the unstable

Beach replenishment (nourishment)

If you must "repair" a beach, *beach replenishment* is the most gentle approach. Replenishment, sometimes called nourishment, consists of pumping or trucking sand onto the beach and building up the dunes and upper beach that have been lost to erosion (fig. 3.3). Sufficient money is almost never available to replenish the entire beach that extends out into the water to a depth of about 30 to 40 feet. Thus, only the upper beach is covered with new sand. In effect, a steeper beach is created (fig. 3.4).

The steepened beach quickly becomes less steep, because a replenished beach erodes very rapidly as the beach system attempts to come to a more natural profile. Experience suggests that (depending on a number of factors such as the grain size of the sand) erosion of a replenished beach will occur at a rate that is at least 10 times that of the natural beach. Even more fundamental than steepening as a cause of erosion is the problem of sea-level rise (discussed in chapter 2 and later in this chapter).

For beach replenishment, sand is either pumped from the back

Fig. 3.2. Palm Beach today. Note the reflected wave. Photo by Orrin Pilkey, Jr.

side of the island, from a nearby inlet during periodic dredging, from a pit on the island, or from the continental shelf; most often it is taken from the shelf. Sand from the landward side of the island tends to be too fine; it quickly washes off the beach. Furthermore, dredging in back of the island disturbs the ecosystem, and the resulting hole affects waves and currents there, and this can cause harm.

The best source of sand environmentally, but also the most costly, is the continental shelf. Extreme care must be taken not to destroy coral colonies and other organisms away from the imme-

Fig. 3.3. Molding sand recently pumped up on a beach with a bulldozer, Lauderdale-by-the-Sea. Photo by Bill Neal.

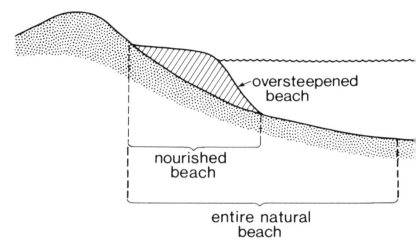

Fig. 3.4. Why replenished beaches disappear faster than natural beaches.

diate shelf-dredging area. Also coral head fragments greatly reduce the recreational value of the beach (figs. 3.5 and 3.6), for example, both Miami and Pompano beaches. Another problem, warns Dr. Victor Goldsmith, formerly of the Virginia Institute of Marine Science, is that when a hole is dug on the shelf, wave patterns on

the adjacent shoreline will likely be affected. Off the Connecticut coast wave patterns were altered by a hole dredged on the shelf, and the replenished beach quickly disappeared as a result. This may be part of the reason why the Pompano Beach and Jupiter Island Beach nourishment projects disappeared so quickly.

Beach replenishment also can create a false sense of security about storms because past damage is concealed. In addition, the value of property behind a nourished beach is maintained or increased, and this spurs an increase in development, including

Fig. 3.5. Removing coral fragments from a replenished beach to increase the "swimmability." North of Hollywood Beach. Photo by Bill Neal.

condominiums. This has happened at Jacksonville Beach. The growth in development density will increase the demand and political pressure from the community for continuing rounds of beach replenishment. The presence of beach-front condominiums makes the building relocation alternative response to the eroding shoreline an impossible dream.

Fig. 3.6. A pocket of coral head fragments on Miami Beach. Photo by Orrin Pilkey, Jr.

Beaches cannot be replenished ad infinitum. Sand supplies become exhausted, more distant, and always more costly. Naturally sand supply diminishes as the stabilized island, held in place where we think it "should be," becomes more and more out of equilibrium with the rising sea level. Past experience tells us that, inevitably, the island community will resort to more drastic stabilization measures such as a seawall.

The most celebrated replenishment project of recent years took place in Miami Beach where 15 miles of beach were replaced at a cost of $68 million. Completed in 1981, the project unquestionably has revitalized the tourist industry of Miami Beach (figs. 3.7 and 3.8), and at the same time the new beach is a very important element in hurricane protection. Before the storm waves can begin to smash into buildings, they first must smash into and remove the new beach.

The new Miami Beach is the envy of many coastal communities with narrowed or nonexistent beaches, but the $68 million price tag to benefit 10 miles of shoreline makes it a very costly solution. The costs do not end here. The new Miami Beach will gradually disappear in response to normal erosion processes and the rising sea level. It will need frequent re-replenishment or what the Corps of Engineers calls beach maintenance. In a big storm it could all disappear almost overnight, but that is one of the purposes of the beach; to sacrifice itself to save the community from direct wave attack.

There is a possibility that the new Miami Beach berm will

Fig. 3.7. The "old" Miami Beach, 1972. The principal reason that the beach disappeared in Miami Beach may simply be that buildings were built virtually out on the beach. Photo by Orrin Pilkey, Jr.

up largely of hard quartz sand. The new beach is made up of the much more delicate shells of marine organisms, some of which are microscopic in size. At the other end of the size spectrum are cobbles of limestone and reef fragments that are hazards to the bare feet of swimmers. The fine size and delicate nature of much of the new Miami Beach is responsible for the murky water in a surf zone once renowned worldwide for its clarity.

Beach replenishment seems to be the wave of the future for all the Florida shore. It is certainly an approach preferable to the old New Jersey method of building bigger and bigger seawalls. In the summer of 1983 Pompano Beach was pumping up its second major beach in just a few years. Almost certainly in 2 to 5 more years the new beach will have largely disappeared and will need re-replenishment at an additional cost of millions. In the case of Pompano Beach there is a good likelihood that the sand is being pumped from too close to shore, and the new beach may simply be "falling back" into the hole whence it came. Expert geological or oceanographic advice is needed to choose an offshore dredging site, but so far Florida beach replenishment projects seem to be the exclusive realm of the engineering profession.

Hobe Sound (Jupiter Island Beach) is now replacing its beach for the third time since 1974. In all, this very exclusive and wealthy community will have spent more than $7 million in a decade to maintain about 5 miles of beach. The money is entirely raised from the 400 or so families on the island, and, as a consequence, the community's beach front remains private property except for a public park. When state or federal tax money is used, as on

Fig. 3.8. The north end of the new Miami Beach, 1983. Photo by Bill Neal.

actually increase flooding on the lagoon side of the island in the next storm. This along with other aspects of the new beach are discussed in the field trip guide at the end of this book.

Material for the beach was derived by dredging on the continental shelf in front of the beach. The old Miami Beach was made

Pompano Beach and Miami Beach, convenient public access must be maintained.

There is an additional problem that must be addressed (fig. 3.9) when beach replenishment is contemplated: we observed a high density of turtle tracks and turtle egg nests on Hobe Sound beach at the location of the ongoing 1983 summer replenishment project. Burial of turtle nests will, of course, prevent their hatching.

In general, the minimum cost of beach replenishment is approaching $2 million per mile in the United States. Consider that virtually thousands of miles of American shoreline have buildings crowded close to the beaches, and that all of these communities will soon be in danger from shoreline erosion because the sea level is rising. If the majority of these communities seek to stabilize their shorelines, the potential cost to taxpayers, local and federal, is tremendous. So much so in fact that a taxpayers' rebellion is brewing, as reflected by the passage of the barrier island bill in the 1982 session of Congress (see chapter 5). This legislation removes all future expenditures (federal subsidies) on presently undeveloped barrier islands. Future federal support for beach replenishment most likely will become more and more difficult to obtain.

In summary, beach replenishment is unquestionably superior to other forms of stabilization. However, it upsets the natural system, and it is costly and temporary, requiring subsequent replenishment projects to remain effective. The Corps of Engineers refers to its beach nourishment projects as "ongoing," but "eternal" might be a better word. Also, serious economic questions can be raised when the facts associated with beach nourishment are considered—

especially since it is not the general public (which pays for these projects through taxes) that typically receives the greatest benefit from them. Cries for beach nourishment projects invariably come from those with direct economic interest associated with beach use—that is, from owners of cottages, motels, beachwear and gift shops, and other commercial ventures in the community, especially owners whose buildings are in danger of falling into the sea. Beach nourishment paid for with tax money is a form of government subsidy for the "well-off."

Thus, there are many problems associated with beach nourishment, but you can say this for it—it is a lot better than the following types of stabilization.

Groins and jetties

Groins and *jetties* are walls extending into the ocean from the shore, perpendicular to the shoreline. A jetty, often very long (sometimes miles), is intended to keep sand from flowing into a ship channel; jetties frequently come in pairs, one on each side of the channel. Groins are much smaller walls built on straight stretches of beach away from channels and inlets. They are intended to trap sand flowing in the longshore (surf-zone) current. There are groins present today on many Florida beaches; in fact, it is hard to find a developed community without at least a few groins. Groins can be made of wood, stone, concrete, steel, nylon bags filled with sand, and even wrecked cars.

Both groins and jetties are very successful sand traps. If a groin is working correctly, more sand should be piled up on one side of

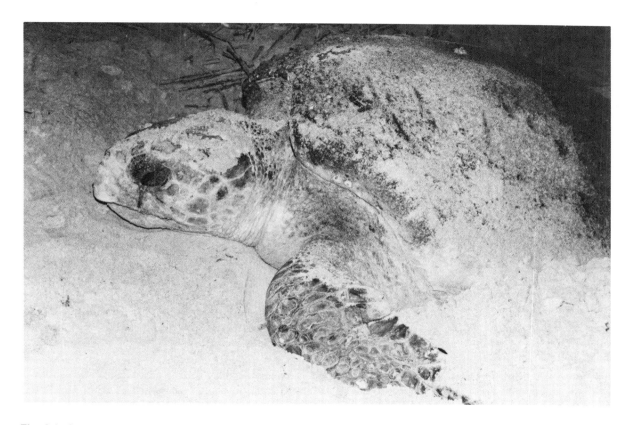

Fig. 3.9. A nesting loggerhead turtle.

Fig. 3.10. A small groin incorrectly labeled as a jetty. North is to the right. Photo by Bill Neal.

Fig. 3.11. Jetties at Lake Worth Inlet, Palm Beach. Sand has piled up on the north side of the channel, and the shoreline to the south is eroding. Photo by Bill Neal.

it than on the other. The problem with the groin is that it traps sand that is flowing to a neighboring beach. Thus, if a groin on one beach is functioning well, it must be causing erosion elsewhere by starving another beach (fig. 3.10). The same is true, of course, for jetties. Sand trapped on the north side of Florida's east coast jetties is usually destined for the next island to the south (fig. 3.11).

Miami Beach illustrates the results of groin use. After one was built in the 1920s, countless others had to be constructed—in self-defense. Prior to the 1980 beach renourishment project, Miami Beach looked like a military obstacle course, with groins obstructing both pedestrian and vehicular traffic. Groins and other forms of shoreline engineering, combined with too-close-to-the-beach construction, destroyed what remained of Miami Beach after the 1926 hurricane.

Most inlets between Florida's barrier islands are jettied, and severe beach erosion problems have resulted. As mentioned above, usually sand is trapped on the north side of the jetty while to the south the beaches are eroding. Adding to the problem is hopper dredging. Most of Florida's inlets are "cleaned out" periodically by hopper dredges that dump their loads at sea. The sand thus lost entirely from the beach system would be better pumped up on the southerly side of inlets. However, this is much more costly than dumping at sea. Floridians would improve their beaches considerably if they would outlaw hopper dredging and then come up with extra funds to pump inlet channel sand onto the adjacent beaches on a routine basis.

One way to reduce the bad effects of jetties is by pumping sand across inlets (sand bypassing). A well-known example of this can be found in the permanent pumping station at Lake Worth Inlet at the north end of Palm Beach (fig. 3.12). This station pumps sand from the north side of the jetty to the south side. The pumping station must help to some degree, but the offset of North Palm Beach Island and the general lack of beaches in Palm Beach attest to the fact that there is still a sand shortage.

The beach buildup on the north side of Florida's jettied inlets may cause erosion elsewhere, but at least it provides a wide beach for the upstream community. Unfortunately, more often than not,

Fig. 3.12. The sand bypass system on the north side of Lake Worth Inlet. Photo by Bill Neal.

buildings creep out onto the new beach, thus losing the safety and aesthetic advantage afforded by the broad beach. In one east coast case a 26-story condominium has been built next to the beach just north of a jetty. This massive building is in danger from both the beach and the inlet, 2 very dynamic environments during a storm.

Better to have built away from the inlet and back from the beach.

Examples of construction creeping out on the new beach next to a jetty include buildings in Fort Lauderdale, Jupiter Inlet Colony, and Singers Island.

Seawalls

Seawalls, built parallel to the shoreline, are designed to receive the full impact of the sea at least once during a tidal cycle. Present in almost every highly developed coastal area, seawalls (fig. 3.13) are very common along the East Florida shore. Also common along the Florida shore are *bulkheads* and *revetments*. Bulkheads are a type of seawall placed farther from the shoreline in front of the first dune—or what *was* the first dune. They are meant more to hold back the land than to hold back the sea. Revetments are usually stone facings placed on eroding dune scarps or bluffs (fig. 3.14) or at the base of seawalls (fig. 3.15) to slow storm-wave erosion. These are frequently made of loose stacks of large stones. A wave breaking on a stone revetment will lose part of its water volume in the spaces between the rocks, and this reduces the erosive effect of the backwash of the wave. The Corps of Engineers' shore protection manual, the "bible" of engineering at the shore, notes that seawalls, bulkheads, and revetments have the same deleterious effect on the beach.

Building a seawall, bulkhead, or revetment is a very drastic measure. Such structures harm the environment in the following ways:

1. Walls reflect wave energy, ultimately removing the beach and

Fig. 3.13. The seawall in front of the Marco Polo Hotel, Sunny Isle. Photo by Bill Neal.

steepening the offshore profile. The length of time required for this damage to occur is from 1 to 30 years. The steepened offshore profile increases the storm-wave energy striking the shoreline; this in turn increases erosion.

2. Walls increase the intensity of longshore currents, which hastens removal of the beach.

Fig. 3.14. Revetment at the north end of Jupiter Island. Columns in the water are probably remnants of destroyed groins. Photo by Barb Gruver.

Fig. 3.15. Neptune Beach seawall and revetment. Photo by Dinesh C. Sharma.

3. Walls prevent the exchange of sand between dunes and beach. Thus, the beach cannot supply new sand to the dunes on the island, and the beach cannot flatten as it tends to do during storms.

4. Walls concentrate wave and current energy at the ends of the wall, which increases erosion at these points.

The emplacement of a seawall or other hard structure is an irreversible act. By gradually removing the beach in front of it, every seawall must eventually be replaced with a bigger ("better"), more expensive one (fig. 3.16). Although a seawall may extend the lives of beach-front buildings in normal weather, it cannot protect those on a low-lying barrier island from the damage (fig. 3.17) caused by hurricanes; it cannot prevent overwash or storm-surge

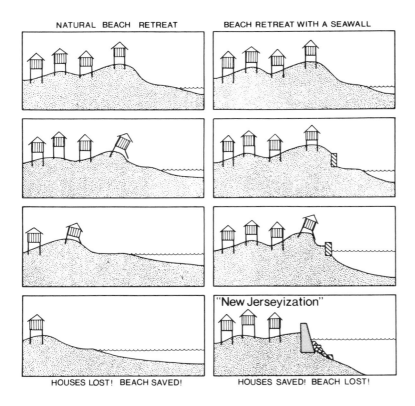

NATURAL BEACH RETREAT

BEACH RETREAT WITH A SEAWALL

"New Jerseyization"

HOUSES LOST! BEACH SAVED!

HOUSES SAVED! BEACH LOST!

Fig. 3.16. The Seawall Saga. Beaches or buildings, take your choice!

Fig. 3.17. The revetment at Ocean Ridge, South Palm Beach. Photo by Dinesh C. Sharma.

flooding. In fact, floodwaters may be trapped and held behind such a wall during a storm.

If a wall is truly massive like the one in Galveston, Texas, it can save lives and protect property even during hurricanes. Hurricane Alicia (1983) passed just west of Galveston, and 50,000 people rode out the storm in town. The massive Galveston-type wall is far too costly for most communities. It was built in response to the 1900 storm that killed 6,000 people. If a storm with the intensity of Hurricane Camille (1969, Mississippi) were to strike Galveston with 50,000 inhabitants still on the island, the death toll would be similar to the 1900 catastrophe.

The long-range effect of seawalls can be seen in New Jersey. In Monmouth Beach, New Jersey, a few years ago the town building inspector told of the town's seawall history. Pointing to a seawall he said, "There were once houses and even farms in front of that wall. First we built small seawalls and they were destroyed by the storms that seemed to get bigger and bigger. Now we have come to this huge wall which we hope will hold." The wall he spoke of, adjacent to the highway, was high enough to prevent even a glimpse of the sea beyond. There was no beach at all in front of it; instead there were remnants of old seawalls, groins, and bulkheads for hundreds of feet out to sea.

Hardly a beach community in Florida exists without revetments and seawalls (fig. 3.18), and the situation is deteriorating. Some communities and counties are doing better than others in preventing their construction. For example, the new construction in beach areas south of St. Augustine includes few seawalls, but south of Daytona there are condos being constructed *simultaneously* with seawalls jutting out on the beach.

If the techniques of shoreline stabilization have such a poor long-range survival record and cause so much destruction, why are they used? The answer is (1) seawalls have been very successful in protecting buildings, and jetties have been very successful in maintaining channels; (2) only recently have we begun to understand the great environmental damage done by these structures. When the earliest of these structures were built, they were thought to be "solutions." Most shoreline engineering projects have a design life of less than 20 years, and long-term geologic effects beyond, say,

Fig. 3.18. Most of the heavily developed Florida islands are completely bulkheaded on the back side. This example is in Hallandale Beach. Photo by Orrin Pilkey, Jr.

50 years are simply not considered. Our experiences with the erosive effects of the Charleston jetties, the Cape May, New Jersey, jetties and seawall, the Miami Beach groin field, and numerous other projects should send a clear message to Floridians that the long-term consequences must be considered, figured into cost-

benefit ratios, and entered into the final decision of whether to pursue a stabilization project or not.

Some states such as North Carolina and Maine are in the process of legislating against seawalls. These states are recognizing that the recreational beach is the property of all citizens and must not be harmed, even if buildings must fall into the sea. However, compared to the heavily developed areas of the Florida shoreline, the North Carolina and Maine shores look like a pristine wilderness.

Sea-level rise: built-in obsolescence

There are several reasons why shoreline stabilization is growing by leaps and bounds in East Florida, but the most important and fundamental reason is that the sea level is rising. (See chapter 2 for a discussion of sea-level rise and its effects on barrier islands.) In Florida this rise may amount to more than 1 foot per century. All along the American shore, what we now call beach erosion may largely be a response to the rising sea.

Figure 2.7 shows a hypothetical island responding to a hypothetical rise in sea level. The island becomes thinner and moves back. If the island is prevented from doing this and is held in the original position, it will become increasingly precarious as the years go by. As an extreme example, imagine what would happen if engineers had tried to hold an island in place when it first formed at the edge of the continental shelf 12,000 years ago. Now it would be 150 feet or so below sea level, and the seawalls indeed would

have to be spectacular in size! Stabilization is an attempt to hold back a sea that is rising, but shoreline structural designs do not take this phenomenon into account. Obsolescence is built into the structures.

Questions you should ask, or how to talk to your consultant

When a community is considering some form of shoreline engineering, it is almost invariably done in an atmosphere of crisis. Buildings and commercial interests are threatened, time is short, an expert is brought in, and a solution is proposed. Under such circumstances the right questions are sometimes not asked. The following is a list of questions you might ask if you find yourself a member of such a community.

1. Will the proposed solution for our shoreline erosion problem damage the recreational beach? in 10 years? in 20 years? in 30 years? in 50 years?
2. How much will maintenance of the solution cost in 10 years? in 20 years? in 30 years? in 50 years?
3. If the proposed solution is carried out, what is likely to happen in the next big northeaster? southwester? mild hurricane? severe hurricane?
4. What is the natural erosion rate of the shoreline here during the last 10 years? 20 years? since the late 1930s when the first coastal aerial photography took place? since the mid-1800s (the time when the first accurate Florida shoreline maps were surveyed by the old U.S. Geodetic Survey)?
5. What will the proposed solution do to the beach front along

the entire island? Will the solution for one portion of an island create problems for another portion?

6. What will happen if an adjacent inlet migrates? closes up? What will happen if the tidal delta offshore from the adjacent inlet changes its size and shape? Or what if the channel moves?

7. If the proposed beach erosion solution is carried out, how will it affect the type and density of future beach-front development? Will additional building density and location controls on beach-front development be needed at the same time as the solution?

8. What will happen 20 years from now if the inlet nearby is dredged for navigation? if jetties are constructed two inlets to the north? if seawalls and groins are built in front of nearby communities, especially to the north?

9. What is the 30- to 50-year environmental and economic prognosis for the proposed erosion solution if predictions of an accelerating sea-level rise are accurate?

10. If stabilization—for instance a seawall or revetment—is permitted here, will this open the door to seawalls elsewhere on the island? (The answer to this question has always been "yes" in Florida, as well as in most other coastal states.)

11. What are the alternatives to the proposed solution to shoreline erosion? Should the threatened buildings be allowed to fall in? Should they be moved? Should tax money be used to move them? Why not? If we can spend tax money for seawalls and nourishment, why not for relocation?

12. What are the long-range environmental and economic costs of the various alternatives from the standpoint of the local property owners? the beach community? the entire island? the citizens of Florida and the rest of the country?

13. Does the proposed solution meet with the approval of objective (noninvolved) consulting geologists and engineers?

A philosophy of shoreline conservation: "We have met the enemy and he is us"

In 1801 Postmaster Ellis Hughes of Cape May, New Jersey, placed the following advertisement in the Philadelphia *Aurora*:

The subscriber has prepared himself for entertaining company who uses sea bathing and he is accommodated with extensive house room with fish, oysters, crabs, and good liquors. Care will be taken of gentlemen's horses. Carriages may be driven along the margin of the ocean for miles and the wheels will scarcely make an impression upon the sand. The slope of the shore is so regular that persons may wade a great distance. It is the most delightful spot that citizens can go in the hot season.

This was the first beach advertisement in America and sparked the beginning of the American rush to the shore.

In the next 75 years six presidents of the United States vacationed at Cape May. At the time of the War Between the States it was certainly the country's most prestigious beach resort. The resort's prestige continued into the twentieth century. In 1908

Henry Ford raced his newest model cars on Cape May beaches.

Today, Cape May is no longer found on anyone's list of great beach resorts. The problem is not that the resort is too old-fashioned but that no beach remains on the cape.

The following excerpts are quoted from a grant application to the federal government from Cape May City. It was written by city officials in an attempt to get funds to build groins to "save the beaches." Though it is possible that its pessimistic tone was exaggerated to enhance the chances of receiving funds, its point was clear:

> Our community is nearly financially insolvent. The economic consequences for beach erosion are depriving all our people of much needed municipal services. . . . The residents of one area of town, Frog Hollow, live in constant fear. The Frog Hollow area is a 12 block segment of the town which becomes submerged when the tide is merely 1 to 2 feet above normal. The principal reason is that there is no beach fronting on this area. . . . Maps show blocks that have been lost, a boardwalk that has been lost. . . . The stone wall, one mile long, which we erected along the ocean front only five years ago has already begun to crumble from the pounding of the waves since there is little or no beach. . . . We have finally reached a point where we no longer have beaches to erode.

Truths of the shoreline

From examples of Cape May and other shoreline areas, certain generalizations or "universal truths" about the shoreline emerge quite clearly. These truths are equally apparent to scientists and engineers who have studied the shoreline and to old-timers who have lived there all their lives. As aids to safe and aesthetically pleasing shoreline development, these general truths should be the fundamental basis of planning on any barrier island.

There is no erosion problem until a structure is built on a shoreline. Beach erosion is a common, expected event, not a natural disaster. Beach erosion in its natural state is not a threat to a barrier island (fig. 3.19). It is, in fact, an integral part of island evolution (see chapter 2) and the dynamic system of the entire barrier island. When a beach retreats it does not mean that the island is disappearing. The beach retreat is part of the larger process of island migration. Whether the beach is growing or shrinking does not concern the visiting swimmer, surfer, hiker, or fisherman. It is when man builds a "permanent" structure in this zone of change that a problem develops.

Construction by man on the shoreline itself causes erosion. The sandy beach exists in a delicate balance with sand supply, beach shape, wave energy, and sea-level rise. This is the dynamic equilibrium discussed in chapter 2. Most construction on or near the shoreline changes this balance and reduces the natural flexibility of the beach. The result is change that often threatens man-made structures. Dune removal, which often precedes construction, reduces the sand supply used by the beach to adjust its profile during storms. Beach cottages—even those on stilts—may obstruct the normal sand exchange between the beach and the shelf during

Fig. 3.19. An eroding beach on an undeveloped portion of Hutchinson Island. Since trees do not grow on the beach, the stumps are proof of erosion. Photo by Bill Neal.

storms, while at the same time engineering devices interrupt or modify the natural cycle.

Shoreline engineering protects the interests of a very few, often at a very high cost in federal and state tax dollars. Shoreline engineering is carried out to save beach property, not the beach itself.

Shore stabilization projects are in the interest of the minority of beach property owners rather than the general public. If the shoreline were allowed to migrate naturally over and past the cottages and hot dog stands, the fisherman and swimmer would not suffer. Yet beach property owners apply pressure for the spending of tax money—public funds—to protect the beach. Because these property owners do not constitute the general public, their personal interests do not warrant the large expenditures of public money required for shoreline stabilization.

Exceptions to this rule are the beaches near large metropolitan areas. The combination of extensive high-rise development and heavy beach use (100,000 or more people per day) affords ample economic justification for extensive and continuous shoreline stabilization projects. For example, to spend tax money for replenishing Coney Island, New York (or perhaps Fort Lauderdale, Florida), which accommodate tens of thousands of people daily, is more justifiable than spending tax dollars to replenish a beach that serves only a small number of private cottages or condos. In the case of the former, the beach maintenance is in the interest of the public that pays for it, whereas in the latter case the expenditures amount to a handout of public tax money to mostly well-off property owners. As our coastal population increases, however, and if the same mistakes continue to be made, the frequency of cases where large expenditures are required will only increase, as will the taxpayers' burden to underwrite these "eternal" projects.

Shoreline engineering destroys the beach it was intended to save. If this sounds incredible to you, drive to New Jersey and examine some of their shores. See the miles of "well-protected" shoreline along the northern New Jersey shore—shoreline without beaches (fig. 3.20)! If you do not want to drive to Sea Bright, New Jersey, try Palm Beach.

The cost of saving beach property through shoreline engineering is usually greater than the value of the property to be saved. Price estimates for shoreline engineering projects are often unrealistically low in the long run for a variety of reasons. Maintenance, repairs, and renourishment costs are typically underestimated because it is wrongly assumed that the big storm, capable of removing an entire beach replenishment project overnight, will somehow bypass the area. The inevitable hurricane or northeaster, moreover, is viewed as a catastrophic act of God or a sudden stroke of bad luck for which one cannot plan. The increased potential for damage resulting from shoreline engineering also is ignored in most cost evaluations. In fact, very few shoreline engineering projects would be funded at all if those controlling the purse strings realized that such "lines of defense" must be perpetual.

Once you begin shoreline engineering, you can't stop. This statement, made by the city manager of a community on Long Island sound, is confirmed by shoreline history throughout the world. Because of the long-range damage caused to the beach it "protects," this engineering must be maintained indefinitely. Its failure to allow the sandy shoreline to migrate naturally results in a steepening of the beach profile, reduced sand supply, and, therefore, accelerated erosion (see chapter 2). Thus, once man has installed a shoreline structure, "better"—larger and more expensive

Fig. 3.20. A New Jerseyized beach, Monmouth Beach, N.J. Photo by Orrin Pilkey, Jr.

—structures must subsequently be installed, only to suffer the same fate as their predecessors.

History shows us that there are two situations that may terminate shoreline engineering. First, a civilization may fail and no longer build and repair its structures. This was the case with the Romans, who built mighty seawalls and ports. Second, a large storm may destroy a shoreline stabilization system so thoroughly that people decide to stop trying. In the United States, however, such a storm is usually regarded as an engineering challenge and thus results in continued shoreline stabilization projects. As noted earlier, rubble from two or more generations of seawalls remains off some New Jersey beaches!

Our solutions are these:

1. Design to live with the flexible shoreline environment. Don't fight nature with a "line of defense."
2. Consider most man-made buildings near the shoreline to be temporary.
3. Base decisions affecting beach-front development on the welfare of the public at large rather than the minority of shorefront property owners.
4. Let the lighthouse, beach cottage, motel, or hot dog stand fall when its time comes.

4. Selecting a site on an East Florida beach

For the wary and wily coastal dweller, nature holds many clues that can reveal much about the safety of a lot, a cottage, or a condo. Of course, on some Florida islands such as Miami Beach there is not very much natural left except for the sea breeze. Nevertheless, you can do a lot of site evaluation yourself. Although it helps to be an expert in coastal processes, it is not at all necessary. All you need is common sense in most cases, since many of the indicators of site safety are simple to spot (fig. 4.1).

But there are some aspects of site choice that common sense alone will not really solve. For example, if one is examining a homesite on the bay side of an island, one is almost always there on a bright, sunny day. A gentle sea breeze is blowing, the bay is calm, and the waves are small to nonexistent. It is difficult in the extreme for most people to imagine what the same bay looks like with waves pounding the shore during an intense winter storm or summer hurricane.

Another aspect of site choice where common sense often fails is the long-range view of man's impact on the shoreline. For example, a newly constructed seawall in front of large buildings (say in Wilbur-by-the-Sea where such examples abound) may seem to coexist in perfect harmony with a broad beach, but 10 to 20 years from now the beach in front of that wall almost surely will be gone, and the original wall will be replaced by a much more im-posing structure.

The wise landowner knows that more than natural forces are at work. The politics of a community play a major role in determining how the community will interact with nature. Many American coastal communities with seasonal populations in the tens of thousands are controlled politically by a few dozen or a few hundred year-round residents. Therefore, it is important to understand the politics of a beach community.

Nature's clues to dangers at the beach

Why worry?

Just what are the dangers facing Florida coastal dwellers, especially those living near the beach front or on a barrier island? The fundamental problems of safety fall into three categories: (1) A storm may come and blow you and yours and your building away. (2) You and yours may drown because of high-water levels produced in a storm. (3) The shoreline may erode (with or without a big storm) and your building may fall in.

There are other important problems, less pressing than the loss of your life or property: (1) If poorly sited development results in construction of seawalls, etc., you may be in for a large and continuous tax bill. (2) Your poorly sited development may result in

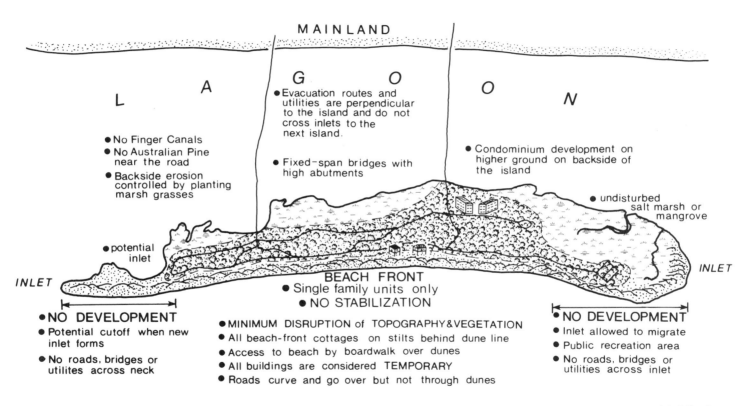

MAINLAND

L A G O O N

- No Finger Canals
- No Australian Pine near the road
- Backside erosion controlled by planting marsh grasses

- Evacuation routes and utilities are perpendicular to the island and do not cross inlets to the next island.

- Fixed-span bridges with high abutments

- Condominium development on higher ground on backside of the island

- undisturbed salt marsh or mangrove

- potential inlet

INLET

INLET

BEACH FRONT
- Single family units only
- **NO STABILIZATION**

- **NO DEVELOPMENT**
- Potential cutoff when new inlet forms
- No roads, bridges or utilites across neck

- **MINIMUM DISRUPTION** of **TOPOGRAPHY & VEGETATION**
- All beach-front cottages on stilts behind dune line
- Access to beach by boardwalk over dunes
- All buildings are considered **TEMPORARY**
- Roads curve and go over but not through dunes

- **NO DEVELOPMENT**
- Inlet allowed to migrate
- Public recreation area
- No roads, bridges or utilities across inlet

Fig. 4.1. The ideal way to develop a hypothetical barrier island. Since all barrier islands are different, the ideal plan would differ from island to island.

destruction of the beach that belongs to the rest of us, too. (3) You came for seclusion and quiet, but in a few years the condo developers may turn your village into a metropolis.

What to worry about

The principal factors noted in the danger category of our shoreline classification are (1) elevation, (2) erosion, (3) evacuation, and (4) dunes.

Elevation. Low areas are flooded when water rises during a storm. The back side or lagoon side of East Florida islands are particularly susceptible to this type of flooding (storm surges). It goes without saying: the higher the elevation the better. Much land on the back sides of Florida's islands has been artificially elevated by trucking or pumping in sand from elsewhere. Often this transfer involved covering up salt marsh or mangrove forests. Artificially elevated land is a better site for construction than lower elevations, but it is a poor substitute for naturally high land.

"High" elevations on the East Florida coast are of the order of 10 to 12 feet and sometimes more. Such sites are inevitably along the crests of sand dune ridges that parallel the present shoreline. You can purchase a U.S. Geological Survey map of an area to find out the natural elevation of your site. More important is the elevation of your site relative to predicted storm-flood levels. Storm-surge levels (fig. 4.2 and table 4.1) vary considerably from beach to beach and island to island because of a number of complex oceanographic factors, so elevation is meaningful only in the context of expected floods. Such information should be available in

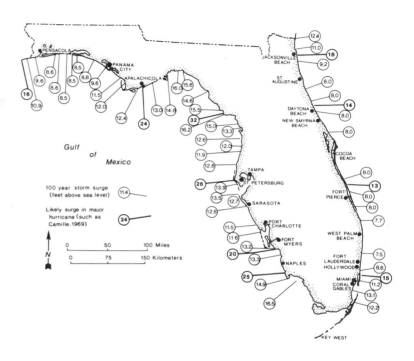

Fig. 4.2. The expected storm-surge levels for the 100-year storm at selected locations along Florida's coast. Courtesy of the National Oceanic and Atmospheric Administration.

Table 4.1. Worst probable storm tide ranges by county

Saffir-Simpson Scale	Elevation above sea level			
	Monroe	Dade	Broward	Palm Beach
1	5	5	4	4
2	7	7	5	5
3	10	10	7	6
4	13	13	9	8
5	15+	15+	11+	9+

Data from a Jacksonville District, U.S. Army Corps of Engineers, study in 1983 of hurricane evacuation problems.

virtually all city halls and county administrative buildings in the form of Federal Emergency Management Agency flood maps. In particular, ask to see the 100-year flood maps. They also are available to you by writing the nearest FEMA office.

Evacuation. The most prudent thing to do in the face of an approaching major hurricane is to get out. Perhaps the most appalling aspect of the Florida east coast's development patterns is the increasing difficulty of such evacuation. Many older buildings are sited well below flood levels, and it must be assumed that many condos are not well built. Most bridges to Florida's islands are drawbridges (fig. 4.3). It also must be assumed that the bridges will not be operable because of a power shutdown, or that they will be stuck in the open position, or that yacht traffic may take precedence over car traffic. Furthermore, almost all of East Florida's bridges have abutments at low elevations on the approaches to both drawbridges and fixed-span bridges. These can be expected

Fig. 4.3. A drawbridge open for repairs, Dania. Photo by Bill Neal.

to be under water early in the storm. Add to all of these woes the fact that early in the storm roads lined with Australian pines will almost certainly be blocked by fallen trees.

Successful evacuation not only requires safe escape from a beach-front community, but it also is necessary to have a safe place to go. From Palm Beach south the Florida peninsula is so low that rapid escape to a site above the 100-year flood level is

Table 4.2. Evacuation requirements for various coastal areas

Landfall location	Saffir-Simpson Scale	Time required for evacuation (hours)	Evacuation Order Time (hours)
Boca Chica	3 to 5	17.5	31.5
Marathon	3 to 5	12	25
Key Largo	3 to 5	6.5	18
Hollywood	4 to 5	9.5	16
Boynton Beach	4 to 5	6	17.5

Data furnished by the Jacksonville District of the U.S. Army Corps of Engineers.

nearly impossible. North of Palm Beach low ground is frequently a relatively narrow 4- to 5-mile-wide strip paralleling the shoreline.

Table 4.2 gives an estimate of times required for evacuation for several specific communities. The Saffir-Simpson Scale is discussed in chapter 2. *Evacuation order time* refers to the number of hours from the time an evacuation order must be given to the time when the eye of the storm actually passes over the community in question. The problem is that once gale-force winds arrive, evacuation becomes dangerous. For example, in Boca Chica it is assumed that evacuation will be dangerous 14 hours before the arrival of the eye as compared to 11.5 hours for Boynton Beach. The problem is obvious. How do you convince people to evacuate when a storm is still many miles offshore and when its exact track is still uncertain? Ironically, Civil Defense officials not only expect to have difficulty convincing the public to evacuate, but past experience has shown that many people drive *to* the beach to become eyewitnesses (and sometimes statistics).

Shoreline erosion. You should assume that all of Florida's east coast shoreline is eroding (fig. 4.4). This is almost, but not quite, true. The major exceptions to this statement are the shoreline stretches just north of jetties where sand has been halted in its slow trip south—to the detriment of beaches south of the jetties. The most common sign of recent erosion on a natural beach is a vertical or nearly vertical bluff on the seaward edge of the first dune row. Particularly spectacular examples of such bluffs are present on the south end of Amelia Island.

We note on our safety maps those communities that have particularly severe beach erosion. Solution: Do not live near an eroding beach. If you must, set way back and be prepared to move.

Dunes. Dunes are pretty and are worth saving for that reason alone. More important, perhaps, dunes furnish a reservoir of sand so the beach can respond properly to a storm. At the same time dunes absorb the impact of waves that could be hitting buildings.

Condominiums: friend or foe?

Increasingly, development along Florida's eastern shore is going the condo route (fig. 4.5). This is quite understandable since the price of shorefront property has skyrocketed.

There are some important problems stemming from this trend that should be considered by every potential shoreline dweller. High-rise condos instantly contribute to population density, thus increasing the evacuation hazard for all community inhabitants.

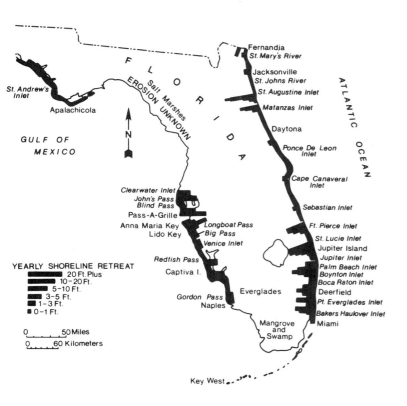

Fig. 4.4. Generalized erosion rates along Florida's shores. The "peaks" are almost always just south of jettied inlets. After Todd L. Walton.

Fig. 4.5. The top stories of a 38-story condo at Riviera Beach. Photo by Bill Neal.

A second problem created by high-rises concerns the community response to shoreline erosion. If a community has a rapidly eroding shoreline and its first row of buildings is threatened with collapse, the community can make a more flexible response if the threatened structures are beach cottages. Cottages can be moved or they can be allowed to fall in as their time comes. But few communities will allow a 20-story condo to crumble into the sea. Thus, the condo-lined shoreline is one that will inevitably require stabilization or engineering of some kind; the closer the condos are to the beach, the sooner the seawalls.

Florida and, for that matter, most of the nation could learn a lesson from North Carolina in this regard. North Carolina has a setback line for construction that is 30 times the annual erosion rate. The setback distance for condominiums is twice that for other structures. And unlike Florida, few exceptions to the setback rule are allowed.

North Carolina has gone a step further than this restriction. The state will allow no seawalls to be built for post-1980 construction. State officials even have ordered one individual to remove a nonconforming seawall from in front of his cottage!

There is a plus side to high-rise condominiums, especially on densely populated islands. If they are well-built, they can furnish a means of storm escape known as vertical evacuation. The idea is that neighbors from low-elevation buildings would prevail upon the neighborliness of nearby condominium dwellers and ride out the storm sitting in apartments on the third or fourth story or higher. The state of Florida toyed with the idea of organizing vertical evacuation on densely populated islands, but there was a hitch. As pointed out by Neil Frank, head of the National Hurricane Center, some condo construction has been substandard, and building inspection can be characterized as uneven. Hurricane Eloise, for example, revealed that an unfinished condominium torn apart by waves had not been properly attached to its pilings. Thus, the problem becomes, how can one designate vertical evacuation sites if the possibility of poor construction exists? For a vivid, worst-case scenario we recommend your reading John D. MacDonald's *Condominium*, a novel that is readily available in paperback.

In an ideal world, all condos would be on the back side of islands or well removed from the beach. They would all be well-constructed and located near a fixed-span bridge with approach roads at high elevations. Such, however, is seldom the case.

Finger canals: waterfronts for all

Finger canals (fig. 4.6) are the waterways or channels dug from the lagoon or bay side of an island into the island proper for the purpose of providing a large number of residents with waterfront lots. Canals can be made by excavation alone or by a combination of excavation and infill of adjacent low-lying salt marshes and mangrove swamps.

Finger canals can be beautiful to live alongside, providing they do not begin to have fish kills and providing a storm does not come by. By its very nature, land along such canals is at low elevation and susceptible to flooding. Problems often associated with finger

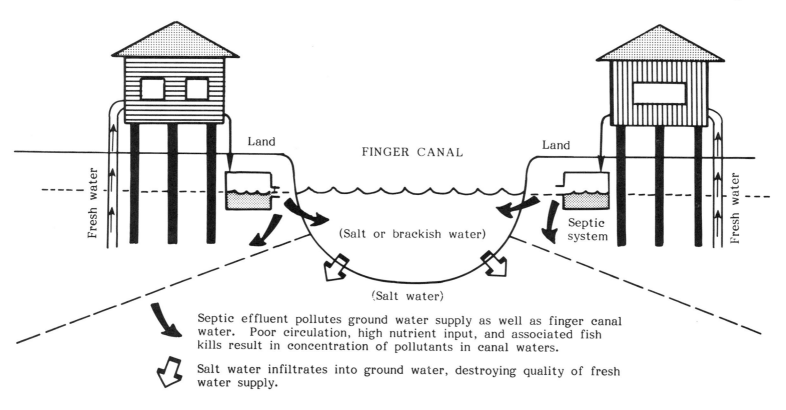

Septic effluent pollutes ground water supply as well as finger canal water. Poor circulation, high nutrient input, and associated fish kills result in concentration of pollutants in canal waters.

Salt water infiltrates into ground water, destroying quality of fresh water supply.

Fig. 4.6. The Septic Tank Saga.

canals are (1) lowering of the groundwater table, (2) pollution of groundwater by seepage of salt or brackish canal water into the groundwater table, (3) pollution of canal water by septic seepage, (4) pollution of canal water by stagnation due to lack of tidal flushing or poor circulation or exchange with bay waters, (5) fish kills generated by higher canal water temperatures, and (6) fish kills generated by nutrient overloadings (algal blooms) and deoxygenation of water.

Bad odors, flotsam of dead fish, and algal scum and contamination of adjacent shellfishing grounds are symptomatic of polluted canal water. Thus, finger canals often become health hazards, and the homesites near them become unpleasant places to live.

Florida has far more finger canal pollution problems than any other state simply because the state has the most and largest canal systems. Florida's experience shows that the problems do not appear until 5 to 10 years after development has occurred. Tributary canals are much more likely to experience pollution than main canals. Short canals are generally less likely to become polluted than long ones.

If you must live by a finger canal, *think short*.

The safety classification—quantifying the subjective

The maps in this chapter are the most important part of this book. They are intended to provide a basis for anyone who is interested to understand the good and bad aspects of any site on a Florida east coast barrier island. For many reasons, these classifications are subjective. Two of the authors of this book independently classified the entire shoreline of east Florida; we sometimes differed, especially in our judgment as to what should be classified as low risk and what was moderate risk. We rarely differed, however, as to which stretches of the shoreline offer high risk to development. The final decisions regarding classification were made on the scene amid swaying palms, booming surf, and honking car horns.

On each of the site-specific classification maps in this chapter is a list of *dangers* and *cautions*. If a problem facing a beach community is severe (for example, high erosion rate, high potential for flooding), it is listed as a danger. If a problem exists but is not severe, the problem falls into the caution category. Three "dangers" result in a high-risk classification. Two "cautions" are considered to be equivalent to a single "danger." Thus, a listing of two dangers and two cautions also results in a high-risk classification. Two "dangers" lead to a moderate-risk classification. Additional comments, usually of a positive nature, also are listed on the maps. Table 4.3 is a summary of the risk classification categories for various eastern Florida counties.

It can be argued that such a classification into three simple categories does not do complete justice to systems as complex as barrier islands. For example, Fernandina Beach is largely in the high-risk category because of the very severe erosion and flood risk of beach-front property. Yet the old town of Fernandina Beach, well behind the beach, may be the safest community on any Florida barrier island because of its high elevation. Another common

Table 4.3. Risk classification breakdown for beachfronts of Florida East Coast counties

County	High risk Miles	High risk Percentage	Moderate risk Miles	Moderate risk Percentage	Low risk Miles	Low risk Percentage	Total miles
Nassau	3.6	29.25	5.1	41.5	3.6	29.25	12.3
Duval	6.9	73.4	2.5	26.6	0	0	9.4
St. Johns	23.8	59.8	8.6	21.6	7.4	18.6	39.8
Flagler	8.2	44.8	10.1	55.2	0	0	18.3
Volusia	28.6	75.7	3.5	9.2	5.7	15.1	37.8
Brevard	27.4	81.1	6.4	18.9	0	0	33.8
Indian River	5.8	20.2	22.9	79.8	0	0	28.7
St. Lucie	18.0	84.5	3.3	15.5	0	0	21.3
Martin	8.5	5.6	6.8	4.4	0	0	15.3
Palm Beach	7.9	20.0	25.8	65.5	5.7	14.5	39.4
Broward	13.3	64.3	7.5	35.7	0	0	21.0
Dade	4.8	32.7	9.9	67.3	0	0	14.7
Total	157.0	53.8	112.4	38.5	22.4	7.7	291.8

problem is exemplified by Vitano Beach. This community is still at a stage of relatively light development, and its moderate classification could change to high risk if beach-front construction of poor quality is allowed.

There are other ways by which the classifications could well change with time. If a 2-lane drawbridge is replaced by a new 4-lane road and a fixed-span bridge, the evacuation risk in case of a storm could be eased. On the other hand, construction of a row of condominiums in any area will increase the congestion and make evacuation more difficult. Politics enter into the classification as well. If a community has a strong emergency plan and will likely enforce early evacuation to a safe place, it will be a better community in which to live. Perhaps even more important for a potential property buyer to consider is how well the setback and hurricane construction regulations have been and will be enforced by local officials.

Even your age will play a role in using this classification as a basis for property purchase. If you are young and energetic, your chances of successful evacuation are better than if you are in the "golden years."

To sum up, we have produced a classification of Florida's east coast shoreline based on a geologic view of the natural hazards of beaches and islands. You will have to insert your own priorities into the classification to make it work for you. In chapter 1 we noted that if we were looking for a homesite for our parents, we would apply extremely stringent standards, and only a couple of sites on the Florida coast would meet our approval. We urge you to see for yourself if we are correct in our assessment of hazards in your particular community; and, most of all, we again urge you to take a long trip on Highway A1A before you settle down.

Nassau County

Amelia Island is the northernmost island on the east coast of Florida (fig. 4.7). St. Marys Entrance at the north end of the island marks the Florida-Georgia border. Unfortunately, the entrance is protected by a very long pair of U.S. Navy-built jetties that are bound to cause erosion problems for the island in the long run. The southern tip of Amelia Island ends at St. George Inlet in Nassau Sound, down the center of which runs the boundary with Duval County. The island is more than 13 miles long and covers 16,500 acres.

Of the shoreline capable of being developed on Amelia Island, we classify 3.6 miles as low risk, 5.1 miles as moderate risk, and 3.6 miles as high risk.

Amelia Island is an island of paradoxes. In some regards it may be Florida's safest island for development. Much of the old town of Fernandina Beach on the back side of the island against the Amelia River is above 20 feet in elevation. None but the most disastrous of storms could possibly flood the high areas of town. As a consequence, the storm evacuation problem for this island is almost nonexistent; at least prudent homeowners should be able to easily escape to high ground.

On the other hand, serious beach erosion occurred during the winter of 1983 on both the northern third and southern third of the island. Amelia Island Plantation to the south often has been cited as an environmentally sound development because many of its condos are nestled in maritime forests at relatively high elevations. But if the beach continues to erode at the same high rates of the past few years (fig. 4.8), some of the most shoreward buildings will soon be threatened. On northern Fernandina Beach, shorefront houses sit almost astride the surf zone. South of state Highway 108, however, two rows of dunes are usually present between the houses and the surf, and homesites are *much* safer as a result.

American Beach is the last of a vanishing kind of community in the American South (fig. 4.9). This small community is owned almost exclusively by blacks, most of whom come from nearby Jacksonville. The town is suffering some beach erosion, but most buildings sit well back from the beach at high elevations.

Between 1837 and 1945, more than 60 storms of hurricane intensity affected Amelia Island's beaches. The most notable hurricanes occurred in September 1896, October 1898, October 1944, October 1950, August 1964 (Cleo) and September 1964 (Dora). Northeasters that inflicted major damage include those of November 1932, September–October 1947, March 1962 (Ash Wednesday storm), February 1973, as well as winter storms in 1981 and 1983. These hurricanes and northeasters have caused extensive damage to local property by flood and erosion due to high tides, storm surge, wave action, and strong winds. More than 200 feet of beach width and more than 5 to 10 feet of beach/dune elevations have been eroded in a single storm. The 100-year storm-surge levels are 12 to 15 feet above mean sea level. The highest dune on Amelia Island is 47 feet above mean sea level.

The northern portion of the island at the mouth of St. Marys Entrance has been changing rapidly since the first jetty was built in 1881–1890. The area south of the jetty built seaward along the northern 3,500 feet between 1843 to 1943. However, since 1950 there has been a gradual erosion along this section (fig. 4.10) as well as the section south of Atlantic Boulevard. The average erosion rate is about 2 feet per year.

The central section of the island is generally stable and high, but 4 identifiable storm washovers can be seen on recent aerial photographs. The southern section of the island has experienced severe erosion, and as much as 15 feet of beach per year disappears at the mouth of St. George Inlet. Three major washover sites are identifiable in this zone.

After Hurricane Dora in 1964, the state of Florida's Office of Emergency Preparedness provided funds for 3.6 miles of revetment for Fernandina Beach. In 1979 a beach nourishment project followed, using the dredged material from St. Marys Inlet maintenance. Most of this sand has long since disappeared.

In summary, if you really want a safe building site, look to the portion of Fernandina Beach on the lagoon side where high elevations prevail. Otherwise, the safest sites are atop high dune ridges paralleling the shoreline. Probably it would be most prudent to stay away from sections of the shoreline where revetments have been placed. Adjacent property owners may have large tax assessments in the future for wall construction and repair.

Amelia Island offers an abundance of relatively safe (and beautiful) home sites for the discerning property owner. Watch out, however, for the eroding shoreline on the northern and southern sections of the island.

Duval County

Here in Duval County is the northernmost extension of a type of development that characterizes much of South Florida: high-density, high-rise condominiums (fig. 4.11). Duval County also is the northernmost example of one of Florida's most serious hazards affecting beach-front development: the problem of storm evacuation. Evacuation will be necessary along much of the Duval shoreline because a major storm will cause widespread flooding. Because the Duval shoreline is served by narrow drawbridges with approach roads at low elevations, we consider evacuation to be a real danger here.

We classify 6.9 miles of Duval County's developable shoreline as high risk and 2.5 miles as moderate risk for development (fig. 4.12). We find no shorefront areas in the low-risk category.

Duval County's 16 miles of Atlantic beach front is entirely a barrier island shoreline. The county is bounded to the north by

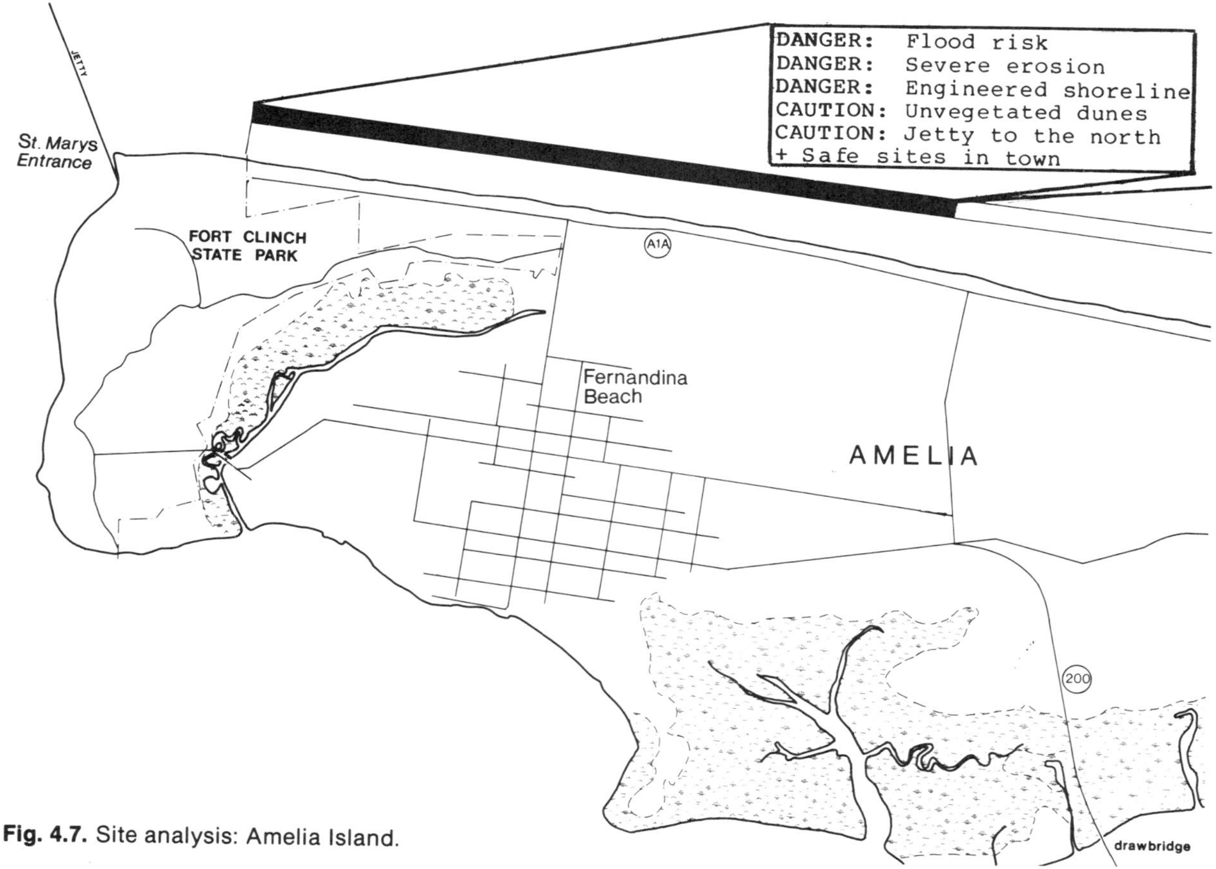

Fig. 4.7. Site analysis: Amelia Island.

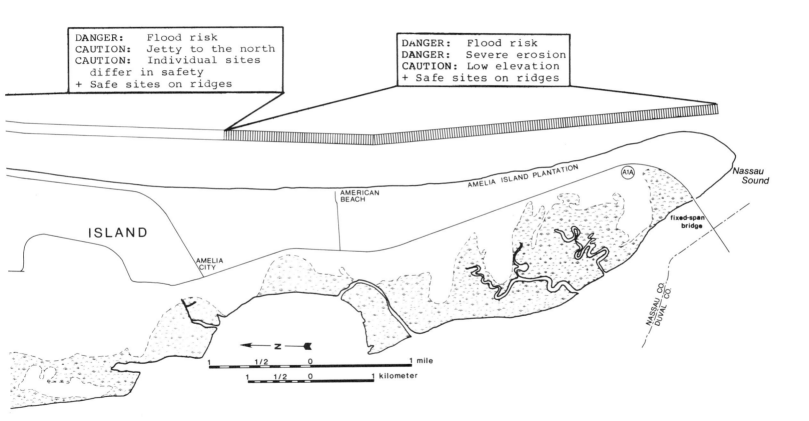

DANGER: Flood risk
CAUTION: Jetty to the north
CAUTION: Individual sites
  differ in safety
+ Safe sites on ridges

DANGER: Flood risk
DANGER: Severe erosion
CAUTION: Low elevation
+ Safe sites on ridges

ISLAND

AMERICAN
BEACH

AMELIA ISLAND PLANTATION

A1A

Nassau
Sound

AMELIA
CITY

fixed-span
bridge

NASSAU CO.
DUVAL CO.

← N →

1   1/2   0   1 mile

1   1/2   0   1 kilometer

Fig. 4.8. Dune scarp indicating severe recent erosion near Amelia Island Plantation development. Photo by Barb Gruver.

Fig. 4.9. A small row of rocks has failed to halt shoreline retreat at American Beach, Amelia Island. Photo by Bill Neal.

Nassau Sound and is interrupted by Fort George Inlet at the mouth of the St. Johns River. North of the St. Johns River jetty is Little Talbot Island, which is entirely in state hands and will not be developed for private use. South of the St. Johns River jetty, development is intense. The barrier island (Guano Island) ranges in width from 3,000 to 13,000 feet and in elevation from 10 to 15 feet above the low water mark; the island continues, uninterrupted, for 10 miles in Duval County and another 23 miles in St. Johns County to St. Augustine Inlet.

The St. Johns River navigation channel is maintained at a depth

Fig. 4.10. Cottages on Fernandina Beach "protected" by a revetment. Photo by Barb Gruver.

Fig. 4.11. A condo at Pelican Point behind the artificial beach. Beach nourishment may unduly encourage rapid shorefront development. Photo by Dinesh Sharma.

of 40 feet. The jetties are of "rubble mound" construction. The north jetty is 14,200 feet long, and the southern jetty is 11,192 feet in length. These jetties have a profound effect on "downdrift" beaches, that is, beaches to the south. They increase the natural erosion or recession rate by trapping sand.

Hurricanes and tropical storms, as well as northeasters, cause beach erosion and property damage along the barrier islands. Between 1870 and 1972 more than 20 hurricanes passed within a 50-mile radius of Duval County; that is an average of 1 hurricane every 5 years. With the exception of Hurricane Dora in 1964 and

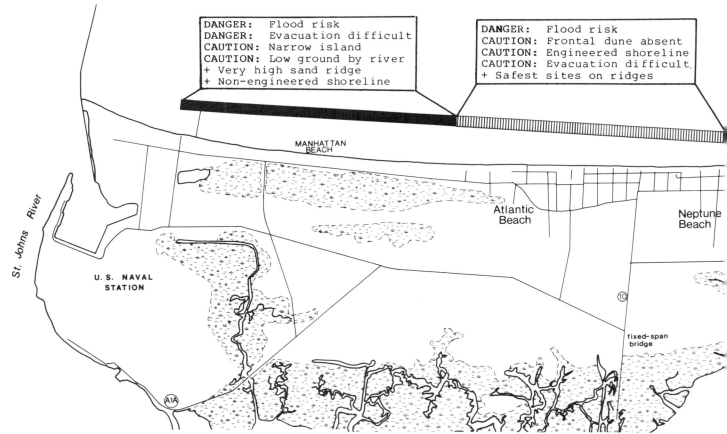

DANGER: Flood risk
DANGER: Evacuation difficult
CAUTION: Narrow island
CAUTION: Low ground by river
+ Very high sand ridge
+ Non-engineered shoreline

DANGER: Flood risk
CAUTION: Frontal dune absent
CAUTION: Engineered shoreline
CAUTION: Evacuation difficult
+ Safest sites on ridges

MANHATTAN
BEACH

St. Johns River

Atlantic
Beach

Neptune
Beach

U. S. NAVAL
STATION

fixed-span
bridge

A1A

Fig. 4.12. Site analysis: St. Johns River to Ponte Vedra Beach.

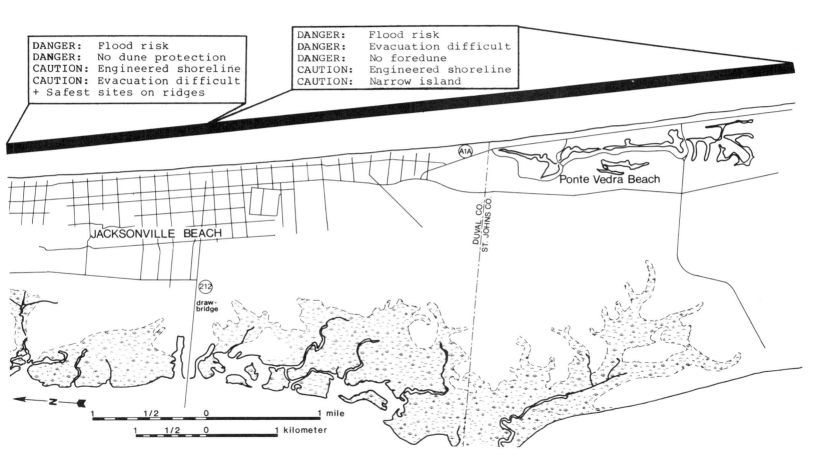

DANGER: Flood risk
DANGER: No dune protection
CAUTION: Engineered shoreline
CAUTION: Evacuation difficult
+ Safest sites on ridges

DANGER: Flood risk
DANGER: Evacuation difficult
DANGER: No foredune
CAUTION: Engineered shoreline
CAUTION: Narrow island

A1A

Ponte Vedra Beach

JACKSONVILLE BEACH

DUVAL CO.
ST. JOHNS CO.

212

draw-
bridge

N

1   1/2   0   1 mile
1   1/2   0   1 kilometer

Hurricane David in 1979, northeasters have been more damaging to Duval County barrier beaches than hurricanes. Particularly severe northeast storms occurred in 1925, 1932, 1947, 1962, and 1981. Memorable and damaging hurricanes occurred in 1926, 1944, 1964 (Dora), 1968 (Gladys), and 1979 (David). The federal government estimates 100-year flood tides to be 11.0 feet above mean sea level in Duval County. The storm surge could add another 5 to 7 feet to this flood level along some embayments behind the island. In 1898 a hurricane produced water levels 8 to 10 feet above normal in Mayport. The 1944 hurricane produced 11- and 12-foot floods, respectively, in Atlantic Beach and Jacksonville Beach. Twenty years later Hurricane Dora left behind 6-foot waters in the same communities. Waves of 20 to 30 feet were reported striking the beaches during the 1944 and 1964 hurricanes. The mean tidal range of the Atlantic here is just over 5 feet. This tidal range is sufficiently large that storms which strike at high tide may do much more damage than those which hit at low tide.

Beach erosion was noted as early as 1834 in Duval County. When Manhattan Beach and Neptune Beach were first laid out, there was another tier of lots seaward of the present concrete bulkheads. These oceanfront lots were 150 to 175 feet deep, but all became property of King Neptune by the mid-1930s due to natural recession of the shoreline. The present-day concrete bulkhead and the public right-of-way in these communities are located on the back side of the earlier "oceanfront" lots. Since the 1920s, construction of seawalls, bulkheads, and riprap revetments has been carried out to protect property and "control" erosion. Timber bulk-

heads were built in the 1920s and were destroyed in the 1925 storm. They were rebuilt to be destroyed again in the 1932 storm. After the 1932 storm Neptune Beach, Atlantic Beach, and Jacksonville Beach constructed a concrete seawall with federal aid. These seawalls were seriously damaged in 1947, 1956, 1962, 1964, and 1968 storms (fig. 4.13). After the 1962 storm, granite revetments were emplaced to reinforce the damaged seawalls, and about 320,000 cubic yards of sand also was placed on the beaches. After Hurricane Dora in 1964 more than 25,750 linear feet of granite revetment reinforcement were placed on Jacksonville Beach, Neptune Beach, and Atlantic Beach, and protective beach nourishment was provided at Mayport Naval Station.

Contour maps of the seafloor off beaches here show that the nearshore zone is steepening. For example, the 18-foot contour in front of Manhattan Beach receded 1,000 feet between 1874 and 1963. This effect is probably due to the various walls and revetments that have been placed there. The same effect has been observed on beaches in New Jersey where stabilization structures such as seawalls have been in place for many years.

Largely as a result of the damage caused by the Ash Wednesday storm (1962), planning began in 1964 for a beach nourishment project along 10 or 11 miles of Duval County, south of the St. Johns River jetty. It was planned to place 3.75 million cubic yards of sand from offshore borrow sites at an estimated cost of $4.145 million initially, plus $565,000 annually, to provide a beach 60 feet wide and 11 feet above mean low water. The project was finally initiated in 1977 and completed in 1980. The total cost for

Fig. 4.13. Revetment in front of a destroyed seawall, Jacksonville Beach. Photo by Bill Neal.

2,250,000 cubic yards of beach nourishment on 10 miles of beach exceeded $18.0 million. (That is, when the project was completed, it had cost *4 times* the original dollar estimate to emplace *60 percent* of the sand originally estimated to be needed. Such escalations in cost are almost sure to continue.)

The new beach provides much-improved recreational opportunities and protects structures behind the planted dunes from some storms. However, the new beach has given developers and potential residents a false sense of security, and many small beachfront cottages and motels are being replaced with very expensive high-density/high-rise residential and commercial buildings on the beach. It has increased the potential for greater loss of property during a major hurricane, and it has created hurricane evacuation problems due to the narrow bridges linking the barrier island to the mainland. The new beach is eroding; even now the beach is very narrow to absent at high tide in some areas south of the jetty.

A continuous sand ridge, more than 10 feet in elevation, runs about 100 feet back of the midtide shoreline south of the jetty to the county line, with the exceptions of automobile access points where the elevations have been lowered. There were several areas where 20-foot dunes were present before development activities leveled them, making the island more vulnerable to flood and erosion damage. Automobile access points and street endings will provide access for the sea during the next storm.

St. Johns County

St. Johns County still has miles of beautiful, unspoiled beaches and barrier islands. But the future is arriving fast; development is increasing in intensity almost on a daily basis. How well the county controls the development will determine how safe shoreline habitation will be for future homeowners. As things stand at present, the St. Johns shoreline has examples of very dangerous homesites south of Summer Haven (fig. 4.14), and examples of low-risk development in areas such as Butler Beach. In fact, the stretch of Anastasia Island south of St. Augustine Beach has some of the best-sited shorefront buildings to be seen in any heavily developed area along the east coast of Florida. Many buildings along Butler Beach and Crescent Beach, including condominiums, stand behind two rows of dunes! A notable exception to this excellent development trend is a cluster of condos just south of St. Augustine Beach that are built out virtually on the beach. Probably a "rich" political story stands behind these condos.

The well-sited development of southern Anastasia Island stands in stark contrast to the very dangerous construction patterns south of Daytona Beach, an area at a similar stage of development. There is a fly in the ointment on Anastasia Island, however. At the south boundary of Anastasia State Park a short stretch of shoreline has been seawalled, and the beach has disappeared. The long-range prognosis is that the lack of a beach front in front of this short stretch of seawall will stop beach sand transport to the south, allowing increased erosion rates to ensue.

The St. Johns County shoreline consists of more than 41 miles of barrier beach with tidal marshes and lagoons behind it. For the northern 6 miles the barrier island is about 3 miles wide with 15-

Fig. 4.14. Beach to the left may soon merge with marsh to the right. This narrow stretch of land just north of Marineland is a very unsafe location to build. Photo by Barb Gruver.

to 25-foot dunes. For the next 12 miles the barrier island has 2 major dune ridges separated by 2 low marshes. The shorefront sand dune ridge is about 500 to 1,500 feet wide, with 15-foot to 44-foot elevations along its length. The back side of the island is bordered by a salt marsh, 3,000 to 9,000 feet wide, along the

Tolomato River and the Intracoastal Waterway. The Tolomato River and Guano River meet 18 miles south of the Duval County–St. Johns County line. For the next 7 miles to Vilano Beach and St. Augustine Inlet the barrier beach is about 1,000 to 2,000 feet wide with dunes of around 15 feet in height. Some of the description of island widths can be misleading. From the county line south to St. Augustine Inlet the area presently being developed is a single narrow sand ridge, and many buildings are being sited too close to the beach.

South of St. Augustine Inlet is Conch Island, which was formed by the coalescing of several small islands after inlet stabilization with rocks in 1940. Conch Island is now about 3 miles long and 500 to 4,000 feet wide. The old, natural St. Augustine Inlet was temporarily reopened across Conch Island by a northeaster in 1962 (the Ash Wednesday storm). The opening has now closed again. Anastasia Island exists south of Salt Run for a distance of about 11 miles to Matanzas Inlet. The width of the island varies from about 2 miles at the northern end to less than 1,000 feet at the southern end, and the elevations range from 10 to 30 feet above midtide. The beach ridge south of Matanzas Inlet to the Flagler County line, a distance of 3 miles, is very narrow and only 5 to 10 feet in elevation.

The various communities along the barrier islands from north to south are Ponte Vedra Beach, South Ponte Vedra Beach, Usina Beach, Vilano Beach (St. Augustine Inlet), Anastasia State Park, St. Augustine Beach, Coquina Gables, Butler Beach, Crescent Beach (Matanzas Inlet), and Summer Haven.

The barrier islands of St. Johns County are composed of unconsolidated sand and shell material. Underlying this sand and shell in some places is a type of coquina or shelly rock in various stages of consolidation, known as the Anastasia Formation, formed during the ice ages. These coquina outcroppings are found sporadically from St. Augustine to Palm Beach; the most prominent outcrops in this county are at Anastasia Island and at Matanzas Inlet. Rocks generally occur in thin layers and are easily eroded by wave action, thereby contributing large quantities of shell fragments to the beaches.

St. Johns County barrier islands are subject to frequent northeasters during winters and tropical storms and hurricanes during summers. The northeaster storms have been, with a few exceptions, the more damaging of the two for this county. This is because hurricane-generated winds and waves are usually of short duration and affect localized areas, whereas a northeaster may cause high winds and waves over a larger area for a longer duration, slowly nibbling away the beaches. The granddaddy of all northeasters to affect St. Johns County was the 1962 Ash Wednesday storm. An idea of the size of this storm can be gained from the fact that the Ash Wednesday storm did most of its damage along the New Jersey shore.

Between 1830 and 1982, 20 hurricanes passed within 50 miles of the St. Johns County shoreline, an average hurricane frequency of 1 every 7.5 years. During the same period 48 hurricanes passed within 150 miles of the shoreline, an average of 1 hurricane every 3 years.

The most damaging hurricanes and northeasters to strike the county were the following ones. The October 1944 hurricane caused 50 to 150 feet of beach erosion and a 3 to 4 feet vertical drop in beach profile at Summer Haven. The October 1956 northeaster caused tides 4 feet above normal, damaged Highway A1A, and dropped the beach profile 3 feet in some places with severe erosion. Hurricane Greta (October 1956) followed on the heels of the previous storm and caused more flooding and erosion. The Ash Wednesday storm of March 1962 was followed by another storm in November 1962, causing extensive damage from high tides and the reopening of old St. Augustine Inlet, known as Salt Run. Hurricane Dora in September 1964 caused 125 mph winds, tides 12 feet above normal along Anastasia Island, and waves 20 to 30 feet high along the island's beaches! The shoreline at St. Augustine Beach receded more than 100 feet, and 15-foot dune scarps (a sure sign of severe erosion) appeared at Crescent Beach. Damage to structures was estimated at $1.8 million in St. Johns County and $200 to $300 million in all of Florida. A northeaster in February 1973 caused 60 to 70 feet of beach recession at St. Augustine Beach and a 3-foot drop in the beach profile at Crescent Beach. According to the federal government, 100-year flood tide levels along St. Johns County are 8.5 feet above midtide along the northern half and about 8.0 feet above midtide along the southern half of this stretch. However, these estimates do not include the wave height on top of the still-water elevations.

The St. Johns County shoreline is characterized by recession of the shoreline and dunes, lowering of beach profiles, and in a few places accretion or building out due to long-term natural processes. The problems of erosion were noted as early as 1887. Beach erosion has become a much more critical problem where man-made structures like buildings, parking lots, seawalls, bulkheads, revetments, groins, or jetties have been placed on the shifting and unstable beaches and dunes.

Various structures have been placed to stabilize St. Johns County's inlets and beaches, but they have had limited success and incurred great costs. The Corps of Engineers placed three groins on Anastasia Island and Vilano Beach in 1889 (private interests built four additional groins at Vilano Beach) to stabilize the inlet for navigation. Since 1892 various types of seawalls and bulkheads were placed along the developed coast of Anastasia Island and St. Augustine Beach. After the Ash Wednesday storm the Federal Office of Emergency Planning authorized 50,000 cubic yards of sand fill and 450 linear feet of granite revetment for St. Augustine Beach at a cost of $95,000 as well as 1,800 feet of granite revetment and 1,130 linear feet of road pavement at Summer Haven. After Hurricane Dora in 1964 federal emergency funds were provided for more stabilization of both St. Augustine Beach and Summer Haven. Now at St. Augustine Beach (fig. 4.15) there is a concrete seawall 800 feet in length and 13.5 feet in elevation with an 18-foot-wide boardwalk. North of this seawall is a 580-foot timber seawall. At Ponte Vedra Beach a 2-mile-long concrete seawall with a height of 13.5 feet was built in 1934.

The most severe erosion problems in St. Johns County during storms occur in the St. Augustine Beach and Summer Haven areas

Fig. 4.15. Seawall reinforcement, St. Augustine Beach. Photo by Bill Neal.

due to a combination of natural conditions and the impact of man-made structures on the beach. These two areas project seaward and act as headlands where wave energy is concentrated, causing more erosion as compared to a perfectly straight shore. In addition, man-made structures like seawalls, bulkheads, and con-

crete revetments contribute to greater wave scouring, lowering of the beach profiles, higher velocities of the littoral currents, and higher erosion rates.

Automobiles on the beaches create a major problem along the county shoreline. The automobile access points create weak spots where overwash and erosion are magnified during storms. The use of automobiles on the beaches (in the opinion of some) interferes with tranquility, peace, and recreational enjoyment; disrupts the nesting of sea turtles and shore birds; and most significantly interferes with the stabilization by beach grasses that help to build new dunes by trapping sand.

Evacuation difficulty is a major hazard for residents along the St. Johns County shoreline. There are 5 roads leading off county islands to higher ground. The situation is complicated by the fact that most of the escape routes are over drawbridges that may be inoperable because of power failure in times of need. State Highway 312 is a safer fixed-span bridge. People evacuating Ponte Vedra Beach will have to drive through the congestion of Jacksonville Beach or alternatively drive down long stretches of flood-prone Highway 210. Evacuees from Vilano Beach, St. Augustine Beach, Crescent Beach, and Summer Haven will have to evacuate into the congestion and chaos of St. Augustine. Plan your escape route (and your destination) ahead of time.

For long stretches of St. Johns County the highway runs along the crest of the most seaward dune, giving developers the choice of siting buildings between the road and the sea or behind the road. Do not live in the narrow areas between sea and road, for example, near South Ponte Vedra. It makes sense to keep the road between you and the sea.

According to our classification scheme, shorefront development is high risk along 23.8 miles of St. Johns County shoreline; 8.6 miles is of moderate risk; and 7.4 miles is classified as low risk (figs. 4.16, 4.17, and 4.18).

Flagler County

Flagler County has only 18 miles of open ocean shoreline. From Matanzas Inlet to just north of the county line and then to Ponce de Leon Inlet to the south, the barrier island extends uninterrupted for a length of 50 miles, making it the longest barrier island in Florida. In Flagler County the barrier island varies considerably in width. The island is about a mile wide in the northern 9 miles of the county and between 800- and 2,000-feet wide in the southern 9 miles. A continuous dune ridge with 10- to 15-foot elevations runs along the entire county shoreline. Along the southern half of the Flagler County shore some secondary dune ridges are found. The barrier island is separated from the mainland by the Matanzas River to the north, Smith Creek to the south, and the Intracoastal Waterway in the middle section of Flagler County. Marineland, Painters Hill, Beverley Beach, Silver Lake, and Flagler Beach are the developed communities, while the rest of the coast remains undeveloped at this time.

Beaches along the northern 3 miles of Flagler County are quite narrow, 30 to 50 feet wide at low tide, as well as steep and soft because of high shell content. Much of the shell is derived from a large offshore coquina outcrop, known as "The Rocks," about 1 mile south of the northern county line. This coquina outcrop contributes shells for the beaches all the way to Flagler Beach and Ormond Beach in Volusia County. Although beaches along Flagler County are 100 to 150 feet wide above low tide, there are several locations where erosion scarps at the toes of dunes are pronounced (indicating severe erosion).

Information on other characteristics of the Flagler shoreline, such as storm history, are given in the next section on Volusia County.

We consider 8.2 miles of the Flagler shoreline to be high risk for development and 10.1 miles to be moderate risk (fig. 4.19). Over most of Flagler County a single ridge line next to the beach is the only developable land of reasonable safety. The best sites are those with the highway (A1A) between them and the beach. In many areas building sites have been carved out of an overly narrow strip, with sites crowded against the beach by the highway. There is very little beach stabilization in Flagler County, which is a definite plus for the future. A notable exception is Marineland where shoreline recession is threatening the buildings. Evacuation difficulty is a serious problem and will become more so as development proceeds and population increases.

Flagler County citizens will decide the safety of shoreline development by their future action. Lots of future options remain open for sound shoreline management.

Volusia County

Volusia County has about 49 miles of shoreline along the Atlantic Ocean. North of Ponce de Leon Inlet the Volusia shoreline is part of the 50-mile barrier island extending through Flagler County and into St. Johns County. The barrier islands in Volusia County generally should have been relatively safe for development, but poor development practices have negated the natural advantages of the islands.

The prevailing winds here are from the northeast during the winter months and from the east during spring, summer, and fall. Wave heights average 4 to 9 feet. The mean tide range at Daytona Beach pier is 4.1 feet, with a spring tide range of 4.9 feet. The ocean swells approach the coast predominantly from the northeast and contribute to the net southerly littoral drift of beach sand, except during June, July, and August when the prevailing winds and swells are from the southeast and south and the littoral drift of sand is temporarily to the north.

The barrier islands of this coast are subject to attack by frequent northeasters during winter and hurricanes and tropical storms during summer. The records indicate that a hurricane will pass within 50 miles of Matanzas Inlet once every 7 years, and within 50 miles of Ponce de Leon Inlet once every 8 years. Northeasters, which are typically caused by a low-pressure system located off the coast, may occur several times during each winter, causing more chronic beach erosion problems. Some of the more damaging northeasters and hurricanes occurred in 1848, 1932, 1947, 1956, 1962, 1964, 1973, and 1979. The September 1848 hurricane came ashore near the Flagler County–Volusia County line and caused 11 shipwrecks along the Florida coast, including 3 in Volusia County. In July 1926 a hurricane came ashore near Ponce de Leon Inlet and wrecked the Inlet Terrace, a million-dollar hotel under construction in Ponce Park. The foundations of this wrecked hotel can still be seen from the beach. In the October 1944 hurricane the tides were 8.4 feet above mean sea level at Daytona Beach, and property damage along the beaches was in the millions of dollars; total damage in Florida was $60 million. An October 1947 northeaster caused 100 feet of beach retreat and 10-foot dune scarps between Ormond Beach and New Smyrna Beach. More than a dozen houses disappeared into the ocean, and roads and seawalls were destroyed along the developed barrier island. Hurricane "King" in October 1950 caused tides 8 feet above normal along the coast from Daytona Beach to St. Augustine and in the Halifax River, flooding many homes. The winter storm of 1962 (the famous Ash Wednesday storm) caused extensive beach erosion in Volusia, Flagler, and St. Johns counties, which were declared federal disaster areas. Seawalls were destroyed along Daytona Beach, and Highway A1A was overwashed and required revetment reinforcement. Hurricane Dora in September 1964 caused extensive flooding along the beach and up the Halifax River; beach erosion near the Coast Guard Lighthouse at Ponce Inlet exceeded 100 feet. A northeast storm in February 1973 washed away a seawall at the Ponce Inlet Club South condominium, dislodged a rubble mound portion of the north jetty at Ponce de Leon Inlet, and breached a channel on the north side of the inlet. Tropical Storm "Gilda" in October 1973 caused substantial dune erosion north of Ponce Inlet.

The Federal Emergency Management Agency and NOAA estimate 100-year flood levels along this coast at about 8.0 feet above

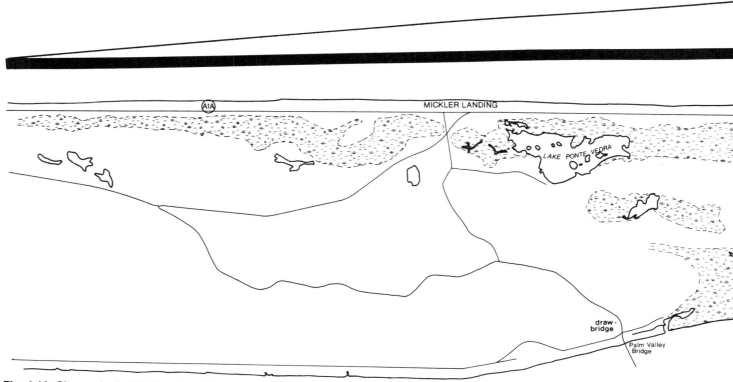

Fig. 4.16. Site analysis: Micklers Landing and vicinity.

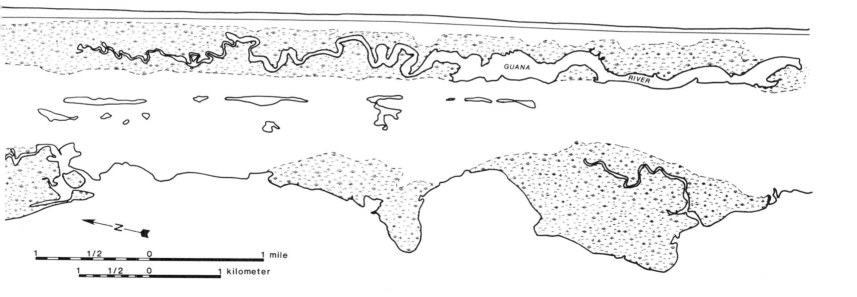

DANGER: Flood risk
DANGER: Evacuation difficult
DANGER: No foredune
CAUTION: Engineered shoreline
CAUTION: Narrow island

GUANA

RIVER

N

1   1/2   0   1 mile

1   1/2   0   1 kilometer

mean sea level at the north Flagler County line and 8.0 feet above msl in Volusia County along the open coast. However, these estimates do not include wave height, that is, the height of the storm waves which are on top of the water flooding the beach areas.

Detailed information on shoreline and offshore depth contour changes over historic periods is not available for the entire Flagler County and Volusia County shoreline. However, information from the U. S. Army Corps of Engineers' studies and the University of Florida Coastal and Oceanographic 'Laboratories' studies at Matanzas Inlet, Ponce de Leon Inlet, and Daytona Beach reveal that in the last century most of the shoreline has retreated and offshore depth contours have steepened.

It is fair to say that some of the communities in Volusia County have not done a good job of promoting safe shorefront development. An indication of this can be gained by comparing the locations of old buildings with those of more recently developed towns such as Daytona Beach Shores, Halifax Estates, and Wilbur-by-the-Sea (fig. 4.20). Buildings of about 20 years ago are usually set back a prudent distance from the beach. It is apparent that some of the development in Volusia County is unsafe, unsound, environmentally damaging, and in violation of at least the spirit of the state's present setback regulations. The next big storm someday will demonstrate the lack of wisdom in ignoring the power of the sea.

Ironically, most of the barrier island area in Volusia County is relatively wide and high, with multiple ridges of sand dunes that make good building sites (figs. 4.21 and 4.22). Citizens living one

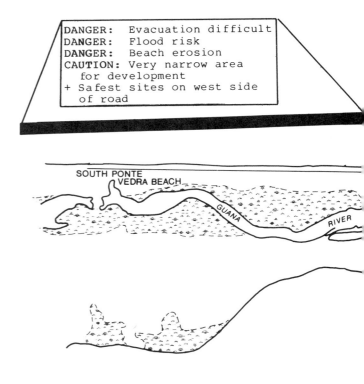

```
DANGER:   Evacuation difficult
DANGER:   Flood risk
DANGER:   Beach erosion
CAUTION:  Very narrow area
     for development
+ Safest sites on west side
  of road
```

Fig. 4.17. Site analysis: South Ponte Vedra Beach to St. Augustine Inlet

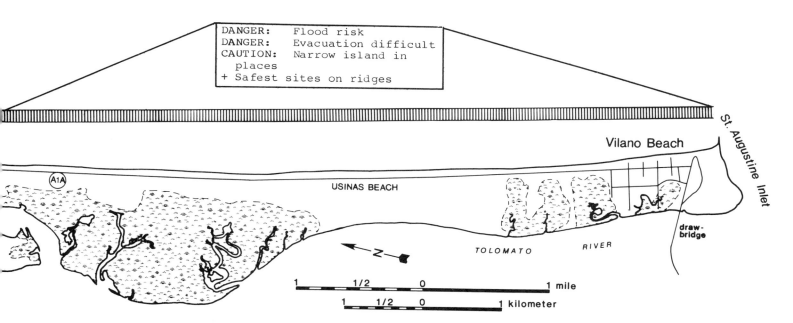

DANGER: Flood risk
DANGER: Evacuation difficult
CAUTION: Narrow island in
   places
+ Safest sites on ridges

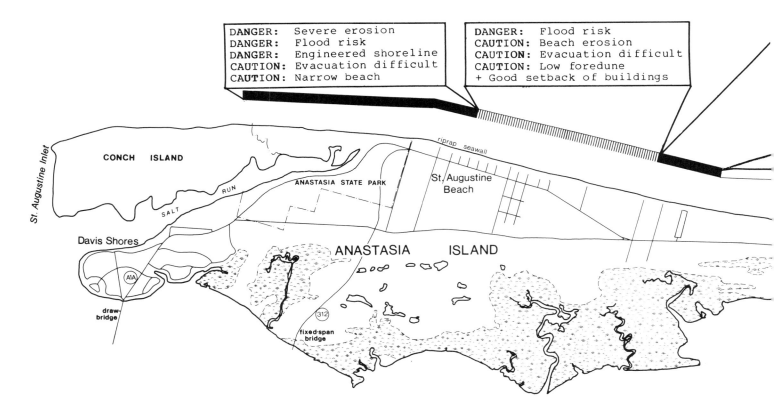

DANGER: Severe erosion
DANGER: Flood risk
DANGER: Engineered shoreline
CAUTION: Evacuation difficult
CAUTION: Narrow beach

DANGER: Flood risk
CAUTION: Beach erosion
CAUTION: Evacuation difficult
CAUTION: Low foredune
+ Good setback of buildings

CONCH ISLAND

St. Augustine Inlet

SALT RUN

ANASTASIA STATE PARK

riprap seawall

St. Augustine Beach

Davis Shores

ANASTASIA ISLAND

A1A

312

draw-bridge

fixed-span bridge

Fig. 4.18. Site analysis: St. Augustine Inlet to Matanzas Inlet.

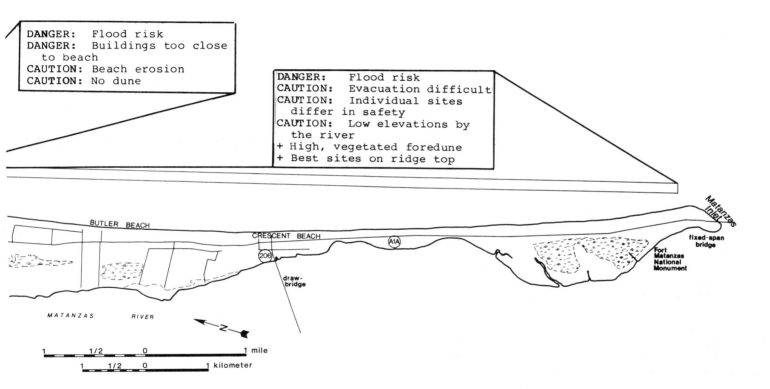

DANGER: Flood risk
DANGER: Buildings too close
  to beach
CAUTION: Beach erosion
CAUTION: No dune

DANGER: Flood risk
CAUTION: Evacuation difficult
CAUTION: Individual sites
  differ in safety
CAUTION: Low elevations by
  the river
+ High, vegetated foredune
+ Best sites on ridge top

Matanzas Inlet

BUTLER BEACH

CRESCENT BEACH

(A1A)

(206)

draw-bridge

fixed-span bridge

Fort Matanzas National Monument

MATANZAS   RIVER

N

1   1/2   0   1 mile

1   1/2   0   1 kilometer

or more blocks from the beach should remember that someday they may be asked to pay to halt the beach erosion caused by imprudent beach-front development.

The use of automobiles on beaches of Volusia County is an old and important tradition—an American tradition. Daytona Beach (fig. 4.23) has the unique characteristics of a wide, flat, compact beach with little or no shell material. These attributes created conditions suitable for automobile races, the first of which was the Daytona 500 in 1906. The name of Daytona Beach has become synonymous with car speed—which exceeded 200 miles per hour by 1930. However, because of natural storm events and possibly excessive use of the beach, shell pockets began to appear in early 1932. These pockets created hazards for drivers, and the races were moved to new quarters inland.

Storm evacuation problems are severe for Volusia County. Evacuation routes on the island north of Ponce de Leon Inlet will be relatively safe because most routes are above 11 feet in elevation. The problem stems from the low elevation (4 feet) of bridge approaches on both the island and mainland sides of the Halifax River. Most of the bridges are drawbridges, which adds to the evacuation problem, but Fairview Main Street Bridge and the Florida Highway 20 bridge are fixed spans. New Smyrna Beach evacuation should not pose an insurmountable problem because two bridges (both drawbridges) serve a relatively small population.

In all, 28.6 miles of the Volusia County shoreline are considered high risk for coastal development. Moderate-risk and low-

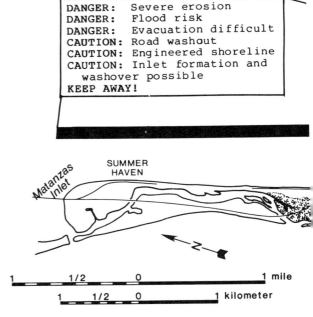

Fig. 4.19. Site analysis: Summer Haven to Marineland

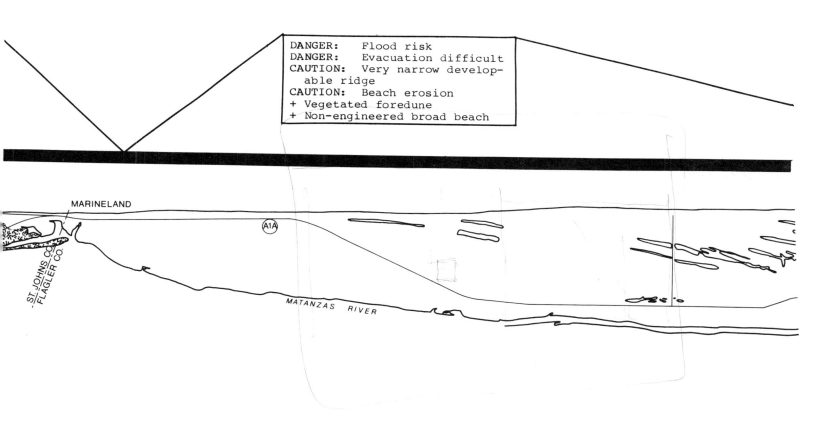

DANGER: Flood risk
DANGER: Evacuation difficult
CAUTION: Very narrow develop-
          able ridge
CAUTION: Beach erosion
+ Vegetated foredune
+ Non-engineered broad beach

MARINELAND

A1A

ST. JOHNS CO.
FLAGLER CO.

MATANZAS   RIVER

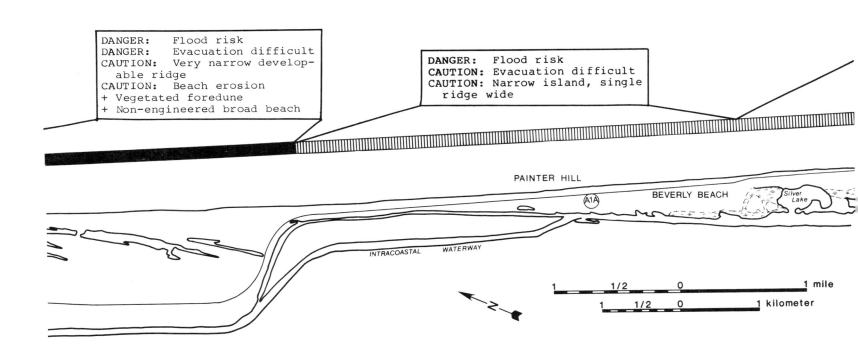

DANGER: Flood risk
DANGER: Evacuation difficult
CAUTION: Very narrow develop-
     able ridge
CAUTION: Beach erosion
+ Vegetated foredune
+ Non-engineered broad beach

DANGER: Flood risk
CAUTION: Evacuation difficult
CAUTION: Narrow island, single
     ridge wide

PAINTER HILL

BEVERLY BEACH

Silver Lake

A1A

INTRACOASTAL   WATERWAY

1   1/2   0   1 mile
1   1/2   0   1 kilometer

Fig. 4.20. Site analysis: Flagler Beach.

DANGER: Flood risk
CAUTION: Evacuation difficult
CAUTION: Beach erosion
CAUTION: Low elevation on the
riverside of island
+ Road between beach and
development
+ Best sites on ridges

Flagler   Beach

Silver Lake

100

draw-
bridge

SMITH   RIVER

FLAGLER CO.
VOLUSIA CO.

Fig. 4.21. The primary dune was removed to site this house in Wilbur-by-the-Sea. Photo by Barb Gruver.

Fig. 4.22. Homes in Ormond-by-the-Sea set back a relatively safe distance. Photo by Bill Neal.

Fig. 4.23. New house at the north end of New Smyrna Beach set well behind the second row of dunes. Photo by Barb Gruver.

risk developments, respectively, span 3.5 and 5.7 miles of shoreline (figs. 4.24, 4.25, and 4.26).

Brevard County

The Brevard County shoreline includes Cape Canaveral, one of the world's most publicized pieces of coastal real estate, thanks to the space program. Cape Canaveral also is one of the world's largest cuspate forelands. It is a body of sand very similar in shape and origin to Cape Hatteras, Cape Fear, and Cape Lookout in North Carolina and Cape San Blas in West Florida. The origin of these features and the large shoal of sand extending seaward from each of them remain enigmas to coastal geologists.

A widely held idea is that all the Carolina capes are basically river deltas, formed when the sea level was lower during the ice ages. That does not explain Cape Canaveral, however, because there is no river here. Perhaps Cape Canaveral owes its origin to wave bending (refraction) around some large sand bars on the continental shelf. Waves striking the beach and pushing sand to a "nodal point" from both the north and south could have formed the cape.

The ocean shoreline of Brevard County extends for 72 miles from Volusia County in the north to Indian River County in the south. South of the Canaveral Barge Canal the coastline consists of a single barrier island separated from the mainland by Mosquito Lagoon and the Banana and Indiana rivers, all of which are shallow tidal lagoons.

The northern 32 miles of county shoreline is in federal owner-

Fig. 4.24. High-rise condos and seawalls, Daytona Beach. Photo by Barb Gruver.

ship, including Cape Canaveral National Seashore, Merritt Island National Wildlife Refuge, and Kennedy Space Center. Patrick Air Force Base occupies about 4 miles of shoreline south of Cocoa Beach. The beach communities along the Atlantic include the cities of Cape Canaveral, Cocoa Beach (fig. 4.27), Satellite Beach, Indian Harbour Beach, Indialantic, Melbourne Beach, and Floridana Beach. Sebastian Inlet State Recreation Area occupies the southern 1 mile of the barrier island.

We have classified 6.4 miles of the privately owned Brevard County shoreline as moderate risk, and we consider 27.4 miles to be in the high-risk category (figs. 4.28, 4.29, and 4.30).

Brevard County's long barrier island is made up of unconsolidated sand and shell. Elevations are not high, but a more or less continuous 10-foot dune runs along the front of most of the island. Underlying the island and cropping out offshore is a shelly (coquina) rock that formed thousands of years ago and is presently breaking up and furnishing shells to Brevard beaches.

The most common winds along the coast are from the east, while the strongest winds are from the north. Swells approaching from the north and northeast are predominant during winter and spring and produce southerly littoral drift of beach sand; from June through August the prevailing and predominant swells are from the south and southeast, creating northerly littoral drift of beach sand. The net annual drift of sand is to the south. The average tidal range at Cape Canaveral is about 3.5 feet, with a spring tide range of 4.1 feet. Peak water levels could exceed 9 to 11 feet above mean low water during a major hurricane. The mean tide range at Sebastian Inlet is estimated to be 3.8 feet along the open ocean beach.

The forces of wind, waves, and tides as well as hurricanes and storms cause drastic changes in Brevard County barrier island morphology, and, of course, they also cause property damage. Between 1871 and 1982, 6 hurricanes passed within a 50-mile radius of Cape Canaveral, or an average of 1 hurricane every 18 years. This is a low rate of hurricane landfall relative to most of Florida's east coast, but Brevard seems to get enough northeasters to make up for the lack of hurricanes.

The storm history of Brevard County is long and "exciting." Most of the early storm-related floods did little damage to buildings or people and caused little loss of life. The situation is different today with hundreds of buildings crowding the shore adjacent to a narrowing beach. A repeat of the storms of the 1920s (discussed below) would be a disaster for Brevard County.

Brevard's storm history begins with the July 31, 1715, hurricane that wrecked the Spanish treasure fleet off the east coast of Florida near present-day Sebastian Inlet. McLarty State Museum was constructed in 1970 at the site of an old Spanish ship salvage camp. The October 1910 hurricane demolished a yacht club and other docks at Titusville. The October 1921 storm caused extensive flooding along the Indian River at Titusville, and the August 24, 1924, storm opened the shoaled (sand-choked) Sebastian Inlet. In July and August 1926 a storm caused extensive flooding and wave damage along the Indian River.

The September 1928 hurricane generated tides 7 feet above normal and 60-mph winds in Melbourne. The September 1948 hurricane once again caused extensive flooding along the Indian River, and an October 1950 storm caused flooding in the Titusville area, breaching the sand dike at Old Sebastian Inlet. Hurricane Donna in 1960 caused beach erosion and damaged seawalls at Patrick Air Force Base. The March and November 1962 storms caused extensive erosion along all Brevard beaches. The Lincoln's Birthday storm in February 1973 caused dune overtopping and 5 to 25 feet of horizontal beach retreat along the county beaches accompanied by tides 4 to 6 feet above normal. The October 1974 storm caused severe flooding and beach erosion because of tides 3 to 5 feet above normal and gale-force winds. Finally, the winter storms of 1981 and 1983 caused continuing severe beach and dune retreat.

It needs to be pointed out that northeasters during the fall and winter actually cause more serious beach erosion than do winds and waves from other directions during the rest of the year. If northeasters occur when tides are highest (spring tides), the erosion is spectacular. The impact of large waves from the northeast during high tides for several days appears to cause more sand movement than the average hurricane, probably due to the short duration of hurricanes. According to the Federal Emergency Management Agency, 100-year flood levels range from 7 feet at the north county boundary to 8 feet at the south county line.

The general trend of shoreline changes along the Brevard County barrier beaches is that of beach and dune recession and lowering and steepening of the offshore beach profiles. Data compiled by

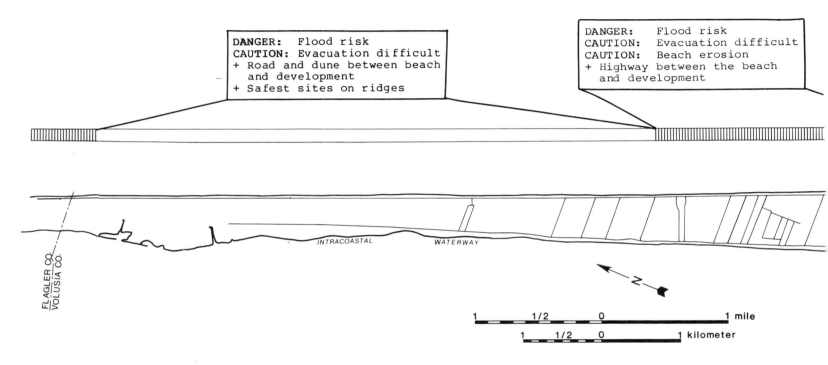

DANGER: Flood risk
CAUTION: Evacuation difficult
+ Road and dune between beach
  and development
+ Safest sites on ridges

DANGER: Flood risk
CAUTION: Evacuation difficult
CAUTION: Beach erosion
+ Highway between the beach
  and development

INTRACOASTAL WATERWAY

FLAGLER CO.
VOLUSIA CO.

N

| 1 | 1/2 | 0 | 1 mile |
| 1 | 1/2 | 0 | 1 kilometer |

Fig. 4.25. Site analysis: Ormond Beach.

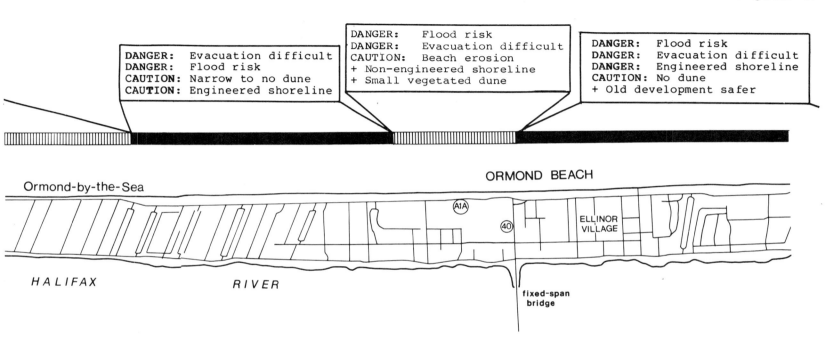

DANGER: Evacuation difficult
DANGER: Flood risk
CAUTION: Narrow to no dune
CAUTION: Engineered shoreline

DANGER: Flood risk
DANGER: Evacuation difficult
CAUTION: Beach erosion
+ Non-engineered shoreline
+ Small vegetated dune

DANGER: Flood risk
DANGER: Evacuation difficult
DANGER: Engineered shoreline
CAUTION: No dune
+ Old development safer

ORMOND BEACH

Ormond-by-the-Sea

A1A

40

ELLINOR
VILLAGE

HALIFAX   RIVER

fixed-span
bridge

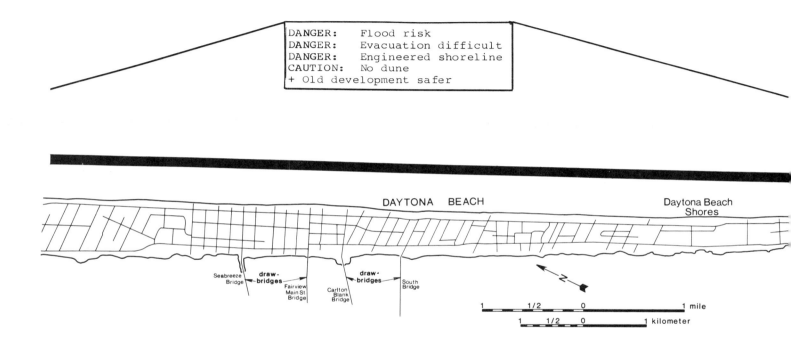

DANGER: Flood risk
DANGER: Evacuation difficult
DANGER: Engineered shoreline
CAUTION: No dune
+ Old development safer

DAYTONA BEACH

Daytona Beach
Shores

Seabreeze
Bridge

draw-
bridges

Fairview
Main St
Bridge

Carlton
Blank
Bridge

draw-
bridges

South
Bridge

1   1/2   0   1 mile

1   1/2   0   1 kilometer

Fig. 4.26. Site analysis: Daytona Beach to Ponce de Leon Inlet.

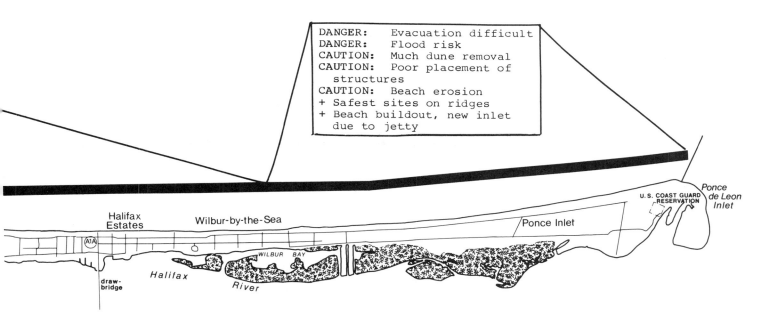

DANGER: Evacuation difficult
DANGER: Flood risk
CAUTION: Much dune removal
CAUTION: Poor placement of
          structures
CAUTION: Beach erosion
+ Safest sites on ridges
+ Beach buildout, new inlet
  due to jetty

Halifax
Estates

Wilbur-by-the-Sea

Ponce Inlet

U.S. COAST GUARD
RESERVATION

Ponce
de Leon
Inlet

A1A

WILBUR BAY

Halifax
River

draw-
bridge

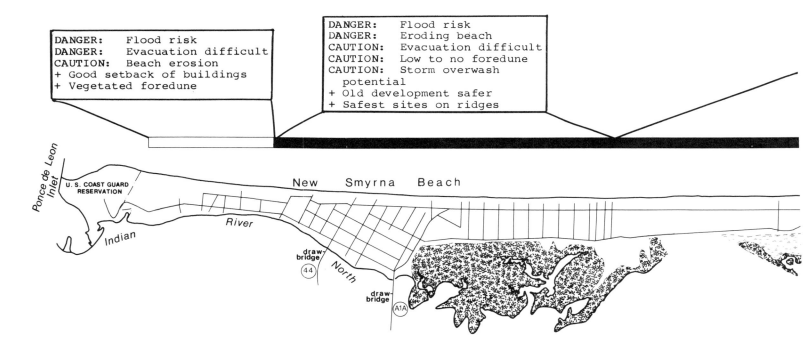

DANGER: Flood risk
DANGER: Evacuation difficult
CAUTION: Beach erosion
+ Good setback of buildings
+ Vegetated foredune

DANGER: Flood risk
DANGER: Eroding beach
CAUTION: Evacuation difficult
CAUTION: Low to no foredune
CAUTION: Storm overwash
  potential
+ Old development safer
+ Safest sites on ridges

Fig. 4.27. Site analysis: New Smyrna Beach.

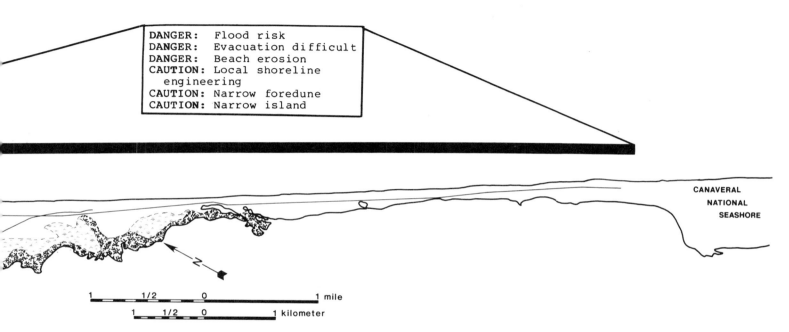

DANGER: Flood risk
DANGER: Evacuation difficult
DANGER: Beach erosion
CAUTION: Local shoreline
           engineering
CAUTION: Narrow foredune
CAUTION: Narrow island

CANAVERAL
NATIONAL
SEASHORE

Fig. 4.28. Condo Row, Cocoa Beach. Photo by Bill Neal.

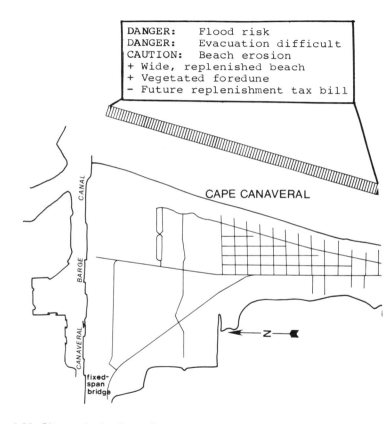

Fig. 4.29. Site analysis: Cape Canaveral to South Cocoa Beach.

the U.S. Army Corps of Engineers and the University of Florida indicate that between 1878–81 and 1965 the shoreline just north of the tip of Cape Canaveral receded 896 feet, or an average of 10 feet annually, while south of the cape the shoreline advanced 345 feet, or an average of 4 feet annually. During this same period the shoreline between Canaveral Harbour and Eau Gallie (Canova Beach) advanced 98 feet, or an average of 1 foot per year, while an

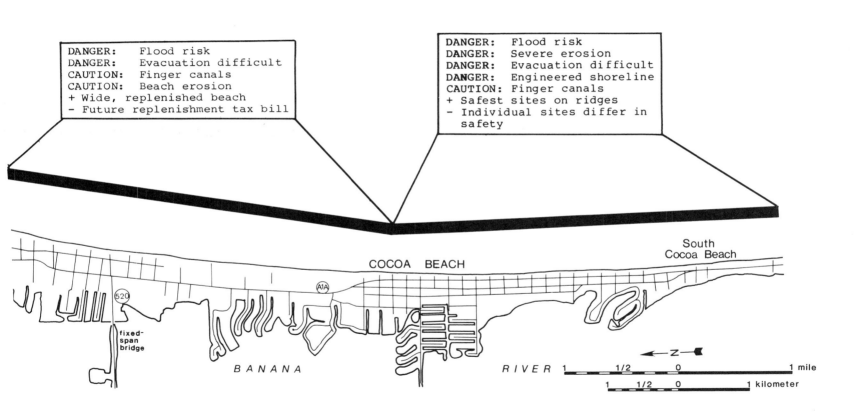

DANGER: Flood risk
DANGER: Evacuation difficult
CAUTION: Finger canals
CAUTION: Beach erosion
+ Wide, replenished beach
- Future replenishment tax bill

DANGER: Flood risk
DANGER: Severe erosion
DANGER: Evacuation difficult
DANGER: Engineered shoreline
CAUTION: Finger canals
+ Safest sites on ridges
- Individual sites differ in
  safety

COCOA   BEACH

South
Cocoa Beach

520

fixed-
span
bridge

A1A

BANANA

RIVER

N

1   1/2   0   1 mile
1   1/2   0   1 kilometer

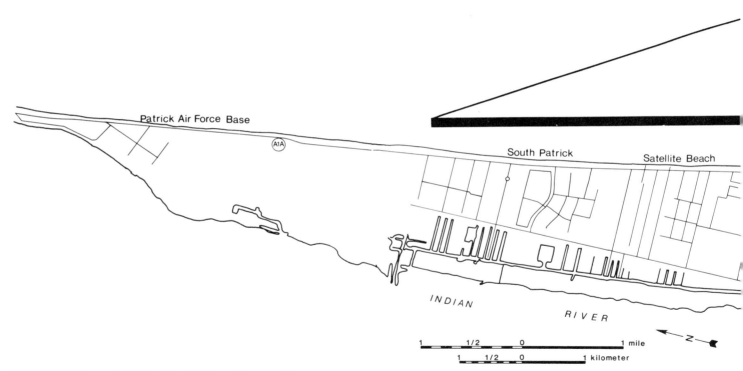

Fig. 4.30. Site analysis: Patrick Air Force Base to Melbourne Beach.

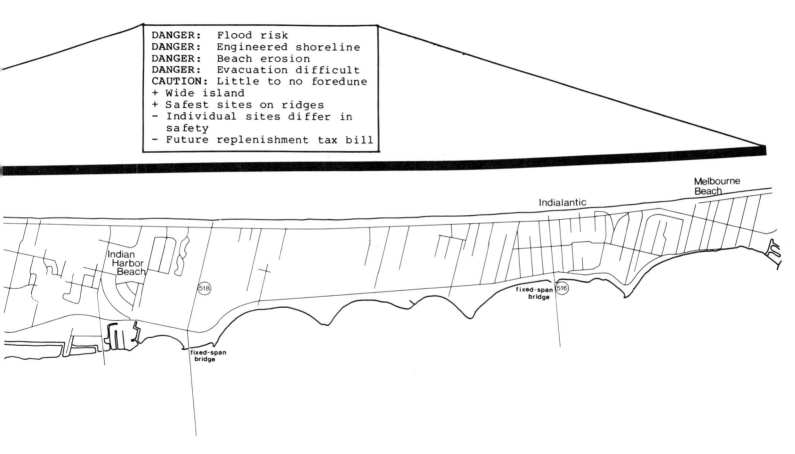

DANGER: Flood risk
DANGER: Engineered shoreline
DANGER: Beach erosion
DANGER: Evacuation difficult
CAUTION: Little to no foredune
+ Wide island
+ Safest sites on ridges
- Individual sites differ in
  safety
- Future replenishment tax bill

Melbourne Beach

Indialantic

Indian Harbor Beach

518

fixed-span bridge

516

fixed-span bridge

unstable area immediately south of Canaveral Harbour receded an average of 1 foot per year. Looking at shoreline movement over a shorter time reveals a different picture. Following the construction of Canaveral Harbour jetties in 1954, the shoreline of the reach between Canaveral Harbour and Eau Gallie (Canova Beach) has retreated an average of 5 feet per year. The construction of Sebastian Inlet jetties caused shoreline buildup north of the inlet for a distance of about 4 miles and retreat of the beaches for approximately 4 miles south of the inlet; the maximum retreat was about 0.5 miles south of the inlet. Cape Canaveral Harbour and Sebastian Inlet are two classic examples of jetties on the shoreline causing seaward advance of beaches on the updrift (north) side and erosion of the shoreline on the downdrift (south) side of the inlets along all of Florida's east coast.

Also in the files of the Corps of Engineers and the University of Florida are data indicating that the entire inner continental shelf (commonly called the shoreface) has become steeper. Between Canaveral Harbour and the southern county line, between 1928 and 1965, the 12-, 18- and 30-foot depth contours receded (moved landward) averages of 197, 319, and 394 feet, respectively. Geologists do not completely understand why this steepening occurs, but it does make the beaches more vulnerable to erosion in the future. The point is that even without the rising sea level, beach erosion in Brevard County probably can be expected to continue— and at accelerating rates.

As in most of the shoreline areas of Florida, evacuation is a major hazard for island dwellers. Immediate evacuation at the first recommendation of local officials is essential. The prudent island dweller will evacuate even before official warnings to do so. A storm heading your way, even if still many miles at sea, is a good excuse to visit the inland-dwelling aunt you haven't seen for a long time. Most mainland areas adjacent to the lagoons behind the Brevard County island are at high elevations and should be relatively safe. Towns such as Palm Bay, Sebastian, and Cocoa have large areas of high elevation. The Bennett (Highway A1A) and Merritt (state Highway 520) causeways that lead to the mainland from Cocoa Beach and Cape Canaveral both have sections that are only 5 feet in elevation. However, the Merritt Causeway is a fixed-span bridge that is an advantage. The Pineda Expressway is the evacuation route with the highest elevation in the county. Residents of Floridana Beach and the rest of southern Brevard County will be forced to drive long distances along narrow islands to the nearest bridge. If residents drive south over Sebastian Inlet, they will have to traverse stretches of low-elevation island and cross the lagoon via Highway 510, which has elevations as low as 4 feet along bridge approaches. The evacuation route north of the Melbourne Causeway is along a high sand ridge, seldom less than 12 feet high. The increased safety of this route, however, is partly negated by the congestion of Melbourne Beach and Indialantic.

Shoreline stabilization is fairly common in Brevard County. Seawalls and revetments abound in South Cocoa Beach and in Melbourne Beach. Several beach nourishment projects have been carried out, but the replenished sand disappears quickly on most Brevard beaches (fig. 4.31).

The best choice of a homesite near the beach would be one at high elevation back from the beach on a wide portion of the island. Finger canals, here as elsewhere, increase the danger of flooding and evacuation. Essentially all of Brevard's developed shoreline is in a state of erosion; increasing assessments from the tax collector, both county and local, can be expected to pump up more sand and build more walls. Simultaneously, the quality of beaches in front of the more heavily developed beach areas can be expected to degrade.

Indian River County

Indian River County's 28 miles of ocean coastline are low and narrow barrier islands. The northern 3 miles are very narrow, averaging 300 to 500 feet in width, and low with mostly 6- to 8-foot elevations. The beach in this section also is narrow and steep. In the middle section from the South Hole Cove area through Wabasso Beach and Indian River Shores, the island width varies from about 1,000 feet to more than 5,000 feet. The elevations in this section range from 8 to 15 feet, with the high point at 24 feet north of Wabasso Beach. Within the Vero Beach city limits, the barrier island is about 1 mile wide, narrowing to the south. In this area the elevations are low, with a 10-foot dune running along the beach.

The northern 1.8 miles of the Indian River barrier island is part of the Sebastian Inlet State Recreation Area. The City of Vero Beach has more than 3,350 feet of oceanfront in public parks, and the county owns another 500 feet of ocean frontage in public parks in the northern section. The section of the island south of the state park to the northern boundaries of Indian Rivers Shores (across from Barkers Island) has been designated as an undeveloped barrier island unit under the Federal Barrier Resources Protection Act of 1982. In this section of the island, federal flood insurance and other federal assistance for construction of new structures are not available. The remaining shoreline is in private ownership.

The beaches of Indian River County are characterized by high shell contents and coarse grain size when compared to Daytona Beach or Jacksonville Beach to the north. This coarseness results in steep and narrow beaches. In the northern section of the county the beach width varies from 80 to 100 feet at mean low water, while at Vero Beach the beach width ranges between 20 and 60 feet. Along the southern section, beach width varies from 50 to 60 feet. Scarp erosion is quite common, and ordinary high tides reach all the way to the vegetation line or toe of the dunes. Longshore currents in the surf zone move sands from north to south along the coast most of the time. The predominant wave direction is from the north through the east, and the largest waves approach from the northeast. Average wave height just seaward of the surf is about 2 feet. The mean tide range and spring tide range are estimated to be 3.3 feet and 3.8 feet, respectively.

The forces of winds, waves, currents, and tides in conjunction with occasional hurricanes and northeasters cause constant changes in barrier island shape and size. Between 1830 and 1980, 19 hurricanes passed within 50 miles of the Vero Beach area, or 1 hurricane every 8 years. One of the most remarkable and damag-

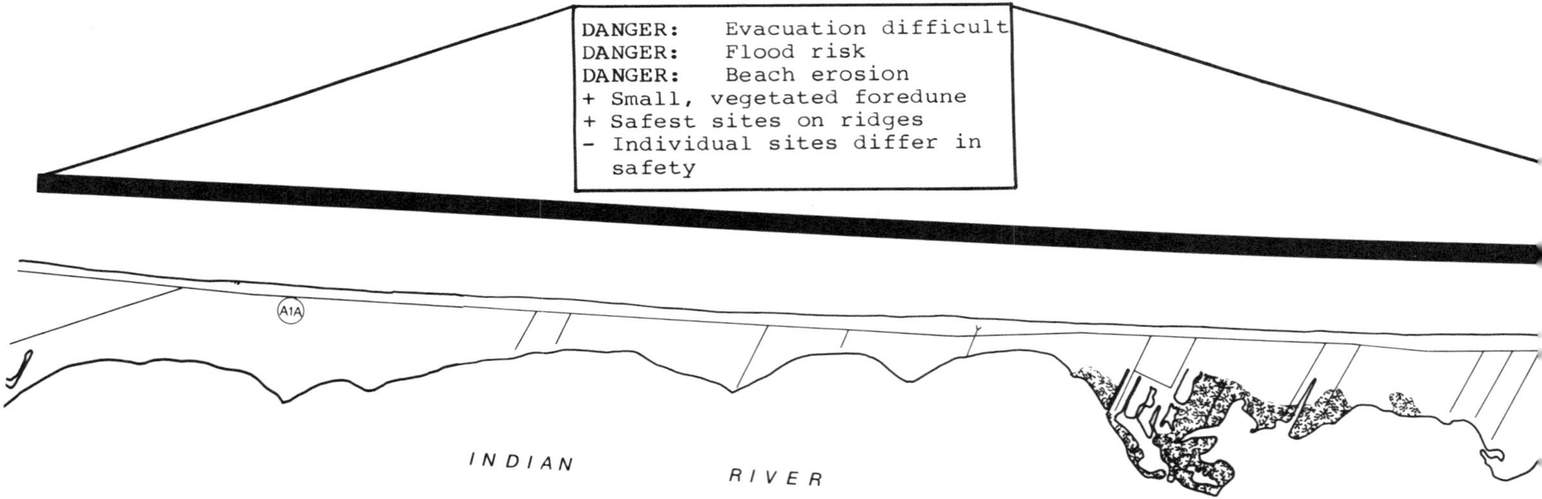

DANGER: Evacuation difficult
DANGER: Flood risk
DANGER: Beach erosion
+ Small, vegetated foredune
+ Safest sites on ridges
- Individual sites differ in
  safety

A1A

INDIAN   RIVER

Fig. 4.31. Site analysis: Melbourne Beach to Sebastian Inlet.

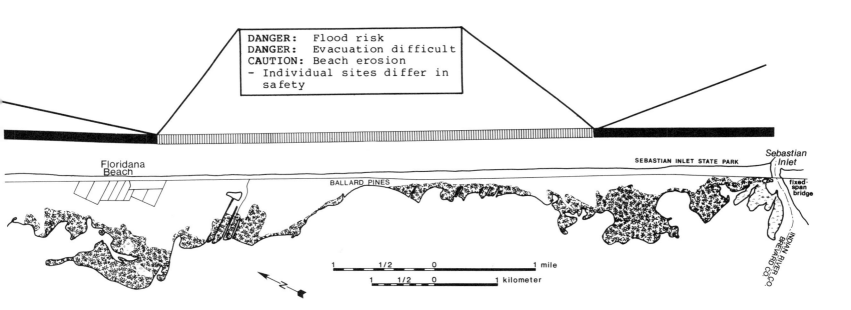

DANGER: Flood risk
DANGER: Evacuation difficult
CAUTION: Beach erosion
- Individual sites differ in
  safety

Floridana Beach

SEBASTIAN INLET STATE PARK

Sebastian Inlet

BALLARD PINES

fixed-span bridge

INDIAN RIVER CO.
BREVARD CO.

1   1/2   0   1 mile
1   1/2   0   1 kilometer

ing hurricanes was the September 1928 storm that breached the Lake Okeechobee levees, killing more than 2,000 people, and caused the failure of most wooden beach structures with high tides and winds in Indian River County. Tropical storm "Gilda" in October 1973 caused 5 to 25 feet of beach erosion. Hurricane David in 1979 caused extensive beach and dune erosion along Vero Beach. Since northeasters are most frequent and last longer than hurricanes, beach erosion is an annual phenomenon in the Vero Beach area. The great Ash Wednesday storm of March 1962 produced tides of 6.5 feet at Fort Pierce, south of the Indian River County line. The Lincoln's Birthday storm of February 1973 caused 5 to 10 feet of beach erosion at Vero Beach.

The general shoreline trend along the Indian River is that of beach and dune retreat and lowering of the offshore depth profile for much of the ocean front. Average retreat of the shoreline between 1930 and 1972 was 3.2 to 3.7 feet per year for the northern 4 miles of Indian River County. For the next 6 miles the erosion rate ranged from between 1 and 2 feet per year. For the 3-mile section around Indian River Shores, the shoreline was stable during a period from 1930 to 1972. At Vero Beach the average recession rate is estimated at just under 1 foot per year. The southern 5.5 miles of county shoreline experienced 1 to 5 feet of annual seaward advance.

Vero Beach has stabilized its shoreline over the years with a series of walls, groins, and revetments (fig. 4.32). The September 1983 issue of *Discover* magazine featured a photograph of a Vero Beach shorefront dune with two junked cars sticking out of it.

Fig. 4.32. Erosion scarp on the beach at Patrick Air Force Base. The nourished beach is disappearing rapidly here.

Obviously the dune was an artificial one that was given some "backbone" by throwing in old cars. As a result of the various stabilization schemes, Vero Beach's beach is narrowing and will soon disappear. Plans afoot to pump up new sand on the beach will cost local citizens a bundle. The possibility of future beach replenishment costs should be a factor in the decision of anyone

Fig. 4.33. A very unusual revetment on Vero Beach. Photo by Dinesh Sharma.

to build and buy in Vero Beach (or for that matter in any of Florida's shoreline communities with degrading beaches).

Along much of Indian River County, one or more sand dune ridges parallel the shoreline and afford relatively high elevations. In some areas a heavy forest remains, and future development will be made much safer if the forest is left as intact as possible. Besides elevation and forest cover, a third factor that should be considered by potential homeowners is island width—the wider the better. Wide islands may be less susceptible to flood and overwash, providing their elevation is not low. Overall, development in Indian River County is still light enough that the safety of future development here is in the hands of those who will enforce setback and other regulations. Things do not look good for Vero Beach, but in the southern part of Indian River County the setback line seems to be observed.

Evacuation is a problem here. Highway 510 near Wabasso Beach has elevations of only 4 feet in the approaches to the fixed-span bridge. However, the bridges to the Vero Beach mainland have higher elevation abutments. From southern Indian River County through Vero Beach, Highway A1A runs through flood-prone zones. The lowest points are around 2 feet, according to the National Ocean Survey's flood maps; these elevations are not nearly as low as on Hutchinson Island to the south. Australian pines are a problem in Indian River County. Where they line the highway, it should be assumed that once the winds start, they will fall across the road and block the only escape routes.

We have classified 22.9 miles of this county as moderate risk for development and 5.8 miles as high risk (figs. 4.33 and 4.34).

St. Lucie County

St. Lucie County's Atlantic Ocean barrier island coast stretches for about 22 miles. The county's open ocean shoreline consists

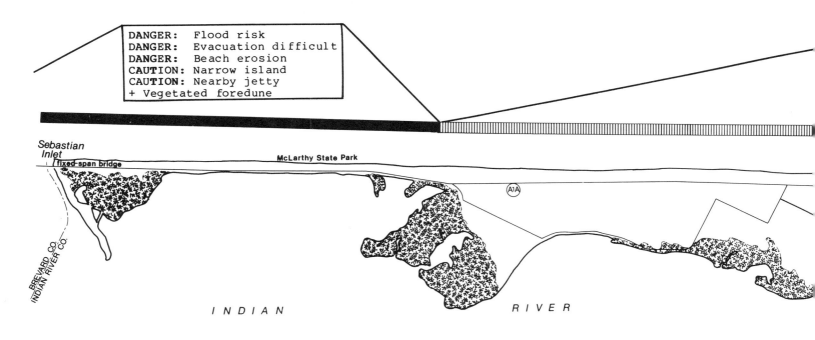

DANGER: Flood risk
DANGER: Evacuation difficult
DANGER: Beach erosion
CAUTION: Narrow island
CAUTION: Nearby jetty
+ Vegetated foredune

Sebastian
Inlet
fixed-span bridge   McLarthy State Park

A1A

BREVARD CO.
INDIAN RIVER CO.

I N D I A N   R I V E R

Fig. 4.34. Site analysis: Sebastian Inlet to Wabasso Beach.

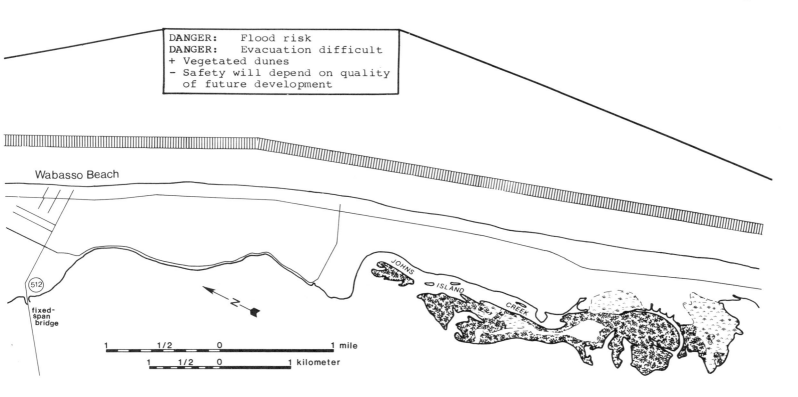

DANGER: Flood risk
DANGER: Evacuation difficult
+ Vegetated dunes
- Safety will depend on quality
  of future development

Wabasso Beach

512

fixed-
span
bridge

N

JOHNS
ISLAND
CREEK

1   1/2   0   1 mile

1   1/2   0   1 kilometer

entirely of barrier islands with a single break, Fort Pierce Inlet. The islands range in width from 700 to 3,000 feet, and a single or sometimes double dune line extends along the beach front. This dune line is widest and highest north of Fort Pierce Inlet. As usual, the safest sites for building or purchasing are at high elevations.

Hutchinson Island, the barrier island south of Fort Pierce Inlet, has what we assume to be the world's only nuclear power plant located on a barrier island. Hutchinson Island also is the northernmost island on the east coast of Florida with extensive stands of mangrove trees on its back side.

St. Lucie County's barrier islands are subject to frequent winter storms as well as tropical storms and hurricanes. Between 1900 and 1962 a total of 17 hurricanes passed within a 50-mile radius of Fort Pierce, with no hurricane passing close by during the last two decades. This is a hurricane frequency of 1 in 3.6 years.

Northeasters are almost an annual event during winter months and cause considerable erosion of the beaches. The available storm information indicates that the most memorable and damaging storms affected the area in September 1928, September 1933, September 1947, August 1949, and Hurricane Isabell in October 1964. The Ash Wednesday northeaster of March 1962, and to a lesser extent the winter storm of 1981, caused the most severe beach erosion in this century.

The Federal Emergency Management Agency estimates 100-year flood tides of 8 feet above midtide along the open ocean shoreline of St. Lucie County. With the addition of waves atop the flooding waters, floodwater elevations could reach up to 12 feet above midtide along the moderately steep beach slopes. During the 1947 hurricane, water level was 5.8 feet above mean sea level in Fort Pierce.

Not much is known about shoreline change rates in St. Lucie County. It is apparent that during the last few years erosion has been occurring along Hutchinson Island at a rapid rate. The incontrovertible evidence of this erosion is the widespread presence of tree stumps and clay beds on the beach. Take a look for yourself.

Since the dominant direction of sand movement along the shoreline is from north to south, the beach on the north side of Fort Pierce has built out, while south of the jetty the beach has receded. In the immediate vicinity of the jetties this beach retreat is as much as 8 feet per year, and 3 miles away the retreat is 3 feet per year. In 1971, 1.3 miles of the shoreline south of Fort Pierce was replenished. Subsequently, the erosion rate of the man-made beach has been higher than it ever was for the natural beach. A second beach replenishment project was carried out by the Corps of Engineers in 1981. This later project cost $5.4 million for 1.3 miles of beach. The sand was obtained during dredging operations to maintain this inlet, which developers originally opened in 1921. More than a third of this sand was lost in a single winter storm in 1982.

Evacuation is a major problem from St. Lucie County islands. All bridges are drawbridges, and the escape road along the island's length (Highway A1A) is frequently at elevations of less than 5 feet and within a few feet of the lagoon (Indian River) shoreline. Flooding will occur from the lagoon side of the island during major storms.

At the present time development is relatively light, but as "condomania" arrives the evacuation problem will become more severe.

During a severe storm there is a strong likelihood that new inlets will break through some of the narrow portions of the islands. New inlets, of course, add to the problem of post- and prestorm evacuation of St. Lucie County. It should be assumed that Australian pines, when adjacent to a road, will block that road at an early stage of the storm.

In summary, we have classified 3.3 miles of the St. Lucie County shoreline as moderate risk and 18.0 miles as high risk (fig. 4.35).

Martin County

Martin County's ocean shoreline consists of about 21 miles of barrier islands—approximately 7 miles of Hutchinson Island from the northern county line to St. Lucie Inlet, and 14 miles of Jupiter Island to the southern county line. Hutchinson Island is low and narrow, ranging in elevations from 5 to 10 feet and in width from 200 to 4,000 feet. Jupiter Island varies in width from 200 feet near Peck Lake in the north to 3,600 feet near the Jupiter Island Country Club. The northern 5 miles of Jupiter Island are below 5 feet in elevation, while south of this section the elevations range between 10 to 15 feet, with the highest point at 24 feet. Thus, on the basis of physical island characteristics alone, the southern third of Martin County's shore is probably the safest.

Down the length of Hutchinson Island is a single sand dune ridge that is the safest area for development. Just north of Seminole Shores is a stretch of island that is probably the narrowest in all of Florida. This section would appear to be a highly probable site of overwash and new inlet formation and a major obstacle to

evacuation for Seminole Shores. However, this thin neck (100 to 200 feet) has existed for over 100 years because it is protected by well-cemented rocks that crop out on the beach (fig. 4.36). The northern 3 or 4 miles of Jupiter Island are being eroded at a very rapid rate as a result of jetty construction on the north side of St. Lucie Inlet. The jetty has blocked the natural north-south flow of sand and has starved Jupiter Island beaches. It is likely that this sand starvation is affecting Jupiter Island over its entire length.

Martin County beaches are subject to both hurricanes and winter storms. More than 15 hurricanes passed within a 50-mile radius of Martin County between 1830 and 1982, at an average of 1 hurricane every 10 years. Damaging storm floods occurred in 1928, 1933, 1947, 1949, and 1964. During September 1933, winds of 125 mph were estimated at Jupiter Inlet just south of the Martin County line. During the August 26, 1949, hurricane, winds of up to 153 mph were recorded in the Stuart-Jupiter area. A high-water mark of 8.5 feet was observed in the St. Lucie River on the railroad bridge near Stuart, and the town suffered the worst damage in its history. Five hundred people were left homeless, but the same storm today would destroy many more hundreds of homes. During Hurricane Isabell winds reached 80 to 100 mph, and the Hobe Sound area was severely flooded. The effect of hurricanes on beaches has not been as serious as that resulting from many northeasters. The most severe northeast winter storms occurred in 1925, 1932, 1947, 1962, 1981, and 1983.

The Federal Emergency Management Agency estimates that 100-year flood levels along the oceanfront would range between 7 and 8 feet above mean sea level. Besides the measured storm surge

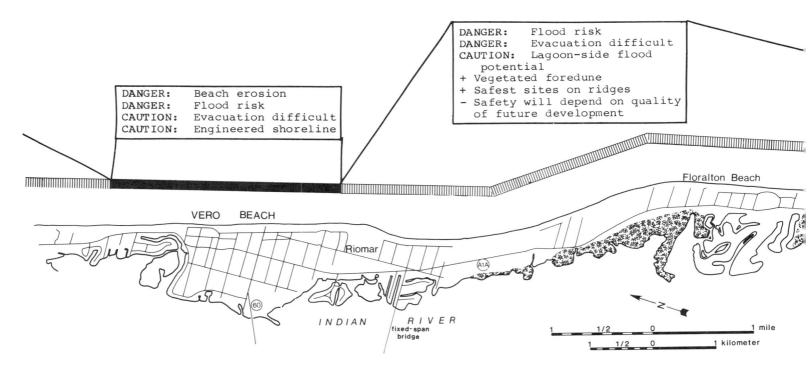

DANGER: Beach erosion
DANGER: Flood risk
CAUTION: Evacuation difficult
CAUTION: Engineered shoreline

DANGER: Flood risk
DANGER: Evacuation difficult
CAUTION: Lagoon-side flood
            potential
+ Vegetated foredune
+ Safest sites on ridges
- Safety will depend on quality
  of future development

Floralton Beach

VERO   BEACH

Riomar

A1A

60

INDIAN   RIVER
fixed-span
bridge

N

1   1/2   0   1 mile
1   1/2   0   1 kilometer

Fig. 4.35. Site analysis: Vero Beach to Fort Pierce Inlet.

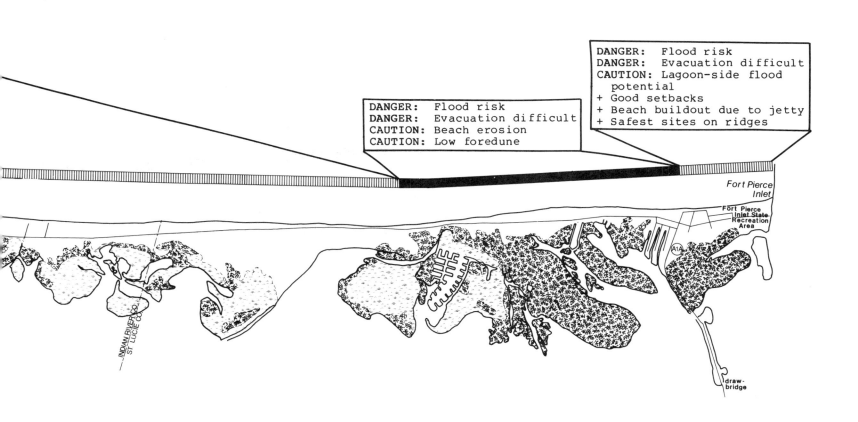

DANGER: Flood risk
DANGER: Evacuation difficult
CAUTION: Lagoon-side flood
   potential
+ Good setbacks
+ Beach buildout due to jetty
+ Safest sites on ridges

DANGER: Flood risk
DANGER: Evacuation difficult
CAUTION: Beach erosion
CAUTION: Low foredune

Fort Pierce
Inlet

Fort Pierce
Inlet State
Recreation
Area

A1A

INDIAN RIVER CO.
ST. LUCIE CO.

draw-
bridge

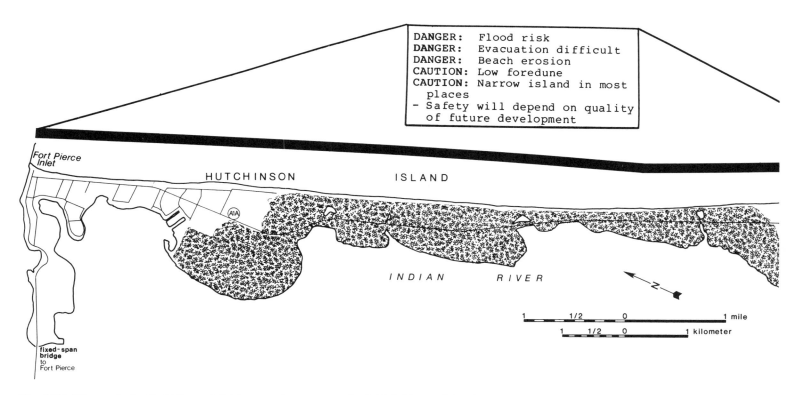

DANGER: Flood risk
DANGER: Evacuation difficult
DANGER: Beach erosion
CAUTION: Low foredune
CAUTION: Narrow island in most
         places
- Safety will depend on quality
  of future development

Fort Pierce
Inlet

HUTCHINSON   ISLAND

A1A

INDIAN   RIVER

fixed-span
bridge
to
Fort Pierce

1   1/2   0   1 mile
1   1/2   0   1 kilometer

Fig. 4.36. Site analysis: Fort Pierce Inlet to a nuclear power plant, Hutchinson Island.

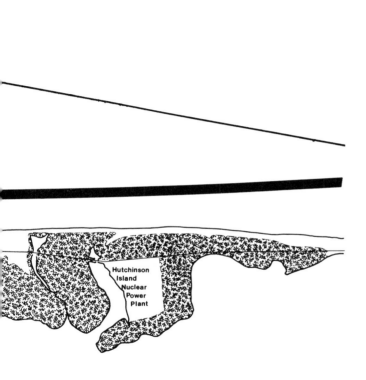

of 8.5 feet at Stuart, still water levels of 7 and 6.5 feet were noted during hurricanes at Jupiter Inlet (1945) and at St. Lucie Locks (1947), respectively.

The beach over most of the area is 50 to 100 feet wide at low water, and the slopes are rather steep. At several locations the mean high water reaches the toe of the dunes, upland trees, or the seawalls. The entire shoreline here has a history of retreat since the 1880s, with the exception of the aforementioned rocky beach on Hutchinson Island. The opening of an artificial inlet, St. Lucie Inlet, in 1892 and construction of the north jetty (1930), which acted as a littoral barrier for the movement of sediments to the south, are 2 events that greatly increased shoreline retreat.

The U.S. Army Corps of Engineers' beach erosion control study of Martin County indicates that between 1882 and 1964 there was general retreat of the shoreline for the area south of St. Lucie and Jupiter inlets and accretion of the shoreline north of the jettied inlets. Between 1882 and 1964 the 16 miles of shoreline south of St. Lucie Inlet receded 490 feet, or an average of 6 feet per year, with the greatest retreat immediately south of the inlet. The recession for the undeveloped northern part of Jupiter Island was 1,502 feet for this period.

Natural shoreline retreat and storm damage provided the reasons for the property owners and communities to install seawalls, sloping revetments, and groins, and to support beach nourishment. Many of these structures have helped to protect upland property but caused the loss of beaches and lowering of the profiles (steepening of the beach) in front of the erosion control structures. Hobe Sound on Jupiter Island had at least 3 major beach nourishment projects in 1973, 1974, and 1978 involving 2.3 million, 1.0 million, and 1.0 million cubic yards of fill. There were 3 earlier nourishment projects in 1956, 1963, and 1967. Another beach renourishment project was completed in 1983. The length of beach being nourished is 5 miles. The average life of the beach nourishment projects on Hobe Sound is about 5 years. In all cases local property owners paid for the beach nourishment (fig. 4.37) or other corrective action without any federal or state funding because of the lack of adequate public beach access. Hobe Sound is one of Florida's most exclusive beach communities, and in Florida that says a lot (fig. 4.38).

Evacuation is a problem in Martin County. Most of the developed areas will be flooded during a major storm, and the roads lined with beautiful Australian pines will prove impassable. Australian pines have shallow root systems, and it is safe to assume that these trees will be toppled across the road in the earliest winds to strike the already rain-soaked island at the onset of the next hurricane. All Martin County beaches are connected to the mainland by drawbridges, which increases the hazard of evacuation. The heavy forests in some developed areas are a plus because trees will partially protect houses from wave and wind impact (although splintered branches may leave a few holes in the roof). As yet condo development is not heavy on Hutchinson Island and Fisher Island, at least in comparison to other South Florida communities. As condo development increases, evacuation hazards will increase in direct proportion. Martin County evacuees should

Fig. 4.37. Limestone outcrop in front of the house of refuge on Hutchinson Island. Photo by Bill Neal.

drive to the high (greater than 20 feet) ridge on the mainland immediately behind the island.

We consider 8.5 miles of the Martin County open ocean shoreline to be of high risk to development and 6.8 miles to be of moderate risk (figs. 4.39 and 4.40).

Fig. 4.38. Beach replenishment project, 1983. Hobe Sound on Jupiter Island. Photo by Bill Neal.

Fig. 4.39. A house snuggled behind the low frontal dune on Jupiter Island. Photo by Bill Neal.

Palm Beach County

Just about everybody in the western world has heard about Palm Beach, the crown jewel of Palm Beach County's 45 miles of open ocean shoreline. Only slightly less famous are such names as Delray Beach and Boca Raton. It seems as if everybody wants a piece of the Palm Beach shoreline, and the closer the piece is to the beach the better. As a result, this county has one of the most extensively developed barrier systems in the world, and beach-front property prices here are astronomical by anybody's standard.

The quality of this much sought after environment is highly variable. For example, only a small amount of beach remains in front of the seawalls at Palm Beach, but that seems to have little

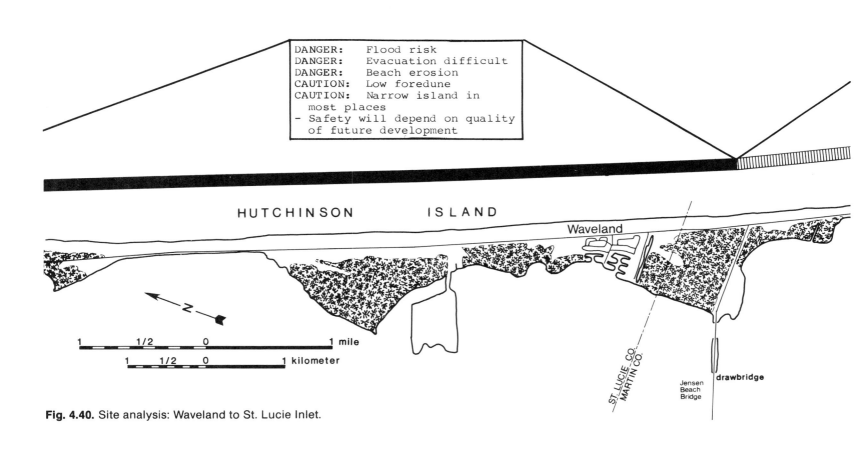

DANGER: Flood risk
DANGER: Evacuation difficult
DANGER: Beach erosion
CAUTION: Low foredune
CAUTION: Narrow island in
   most places
- Safety will depend on quality
   of future development

HUTCHINSON ISLAND

Waveland

1   1/2   0   1 mile

1   1/2   0   1 kilometer

ST. LUCIE CO.
MARTIN CO.

Jensen
Beach
Bridge

drawbridge

Fig. 4.40. Site analysis: Waveland to St. Lucie Inlet.

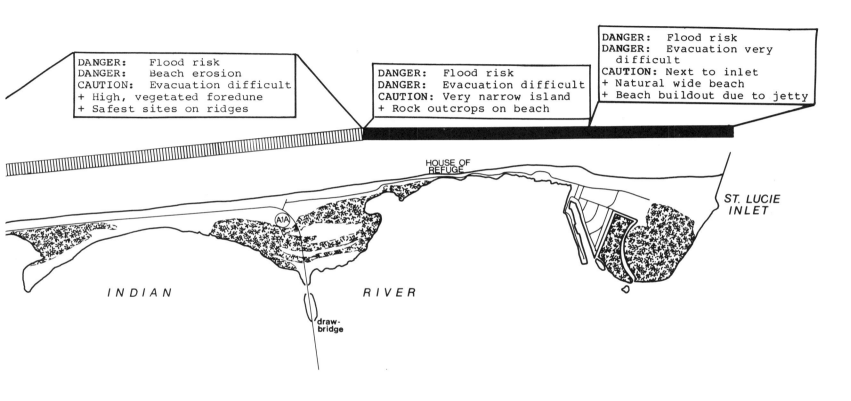

DANGER: Flood risk
DANGER: Beach erosion
CAUTION: Evacuation difficult
+ High, vegetated foredune
+ Safest sites on ridges

DANGER: Flood risk
DANGER: Evacuation difficult
CAUTION: Very narrow island
+ Rock outcrops on beach

DANGER: Flood risk
DANGER: Evacuation very
   difficult
CAUTION: Next to inlet
+ Natural wide beach
+ Beach buildout due to jetty

HOUSE OF
REFUGE

A1A

ST. LUCIE
INLET

INDIAN   RIVER

draw-
bridge

impact on the quality of life of the community. In fact, many Palm Beach residents oppose replenishing the beach because a broad new beach might bring in an influx of people from the outside world. At the other end of the spectrum are some of the beaches off Boca Raton that are relatively broad and relatively "unspoiled." The aesthetic quality of development varies as well, ranging from the spectacularly beautiful hedge-lined streets of Palm Beach, to the endless condo rows fronting South Palm Beach and Delray Beach, to the lightly developed maritime forest at the north end of Lake Worth. Safety is variable as well. We classify 5.7 miles of Palm Beach County's shoreline as low risk, 25.8 miles as moderate risk, and 7.9 miles as high risk (figs. 4.41, 4.42, and 4.43).

We rank 3 areas in the county as low-risk sites for development. In chapter 1 we asked the question (of ourselves) where would we want our parents to live along Florida's east coast, and the Juno Beach area turns out to be one of those locations. Although there is a flood risk, evacuation from this area should be reasonably safe for anyone with a modicum of prudence and common sense. Two other areas, near Delray Beach and Boca Raton, also were classified as low risk, but here evacuation poses somewhat more of a hazard. The section of shoreline classified low risk near Boca Raton has a public park fronting the beach, and the park along with the highway act as a good natural buffer to the forces that ravage the shoreline. The 2 areas in Palm Beach County classified as high risk are Highland Beach and the area south of Lake Worth Inlet. Among other problems, both beach-front areas have particularly severe erosion.

The northern 2 miles of barrier island (south end of Jupiter Island) in the county range in width from 700 feet to about 2,300 feet near Jupiter Inlet. Jupiter Inlet Colony is located north of the inlet. The beach width in this section varies from 20 to 70 feet at mean low water and has steep slopes in the nearshore. The frontal dune elevations (which have been partially built upon) range from 15 to more than 20 feet.

From Jupiter Inlet to Lake Worth Inlet (artificially cut in 1918) the barrier island is 11.7 miles long. The towns of Juno Beach and Palm Beach Shores (Singer Island) are located on this island. In different sections the island width varies from 600 feet to about 1 mile. Frontal dunes, with elevations of 15 to 20 feet, occur for most of the reach. The natural dunes are particularly well developed on the northern half of this island, and at Juno Beach a 53-foot dune has been mapped. The southern 3-mile section of the island (Singer Island) has average elevations of only 10 feet above the low-tide mark.

It is worth mentioning here one of the most startling examples of unwise development we have seen on East Florida's beach front (fig. 4.44). This is the Jupiter Reef Condo between Juno Beach and Jupiter Inlet. It has been built virtually on the beach. It not only endangers its own inhabitants, but the structure will act as a groin and will cause erosion of beaches to the south. Somehow this folly has occurred in a community where the setback line is generally observed.

The barrier island between Lake Worth Inlet and South Lake Worth Inlet (another man-made inlet cut in 1927) stretches for

15.6 miles. Palm Beach and South Palm Beach are the towns on this island. The width of the island varies from about 600 feet to about 4,500 feet. The elevation of the first row of dunes (primary dunes) is less than 13 feet within the Palm Beach city limits and increases to 27 feet on the southern portion of the island. The dunes are steep, and the offshore profiles in this section also are steep. Often Australian pines cover these dunes, and as discussed earlier these pines do not retain or protect the dune sand very well.

The barrier island between South Lake Worth Inlet and Boca Raton Inlet (fig. 4.45) stretches for 14.5 miles. The barrier width varies from 750 feet to about 2,000 feet, and the primary dune elevations range from 15 to 23 feet above mean low water. The beaches are narrow and steep.

South of Boca Raton Inlet is about a 1-mile section of island in Palm Beach County. This stretch is about 700 to 800 feet wide. The elevations are relatively low, about 12 feet above mean low water, and the beach is narrow and steep.

The bay side of the barrier islands was originally lined with mangrove trees. However, along much of the county's shoreline mangroves were leveled and the area filled; the estuarine and Intracoastal Waterway shoreline is now lined with bulkheads.

Palm Beach County has one of the most urbanized barrier island shorelines in Florida. However, almost 9 miles of the county's total of 45 miles of beach front is in public ownership, and an additional 4 miles or so is being acquired by state and county agencies to meet public recreation demands and to minimize public hazards and losses from hurricanes and shoreline erosion.

The forces of wind, waves, current, sea-level rise, and tides continually affect the barrier beaches. The predominant winds are from the southeast, but the strongest winds are from the northeast. The highest recorded storm tide in Palm Beach was 11.2 feet above sea level during the 1928 hurricane. The predominant littoral currents are from north to south during winter and spring and from south to north during the summer and fall, with the net annual movement from north to south.

Hurricanes and winter storms with winds from the northeast cause rapid changes in the beaches and dunes and cause property damage and evacuation problems. Between 1900 and 1982 a total of 15 major hurricanes passed within a 50-mile radius of Palm Beach County, a frequency of 1 every 5.5 years. The storm of October 1910 brought severe rain and a 5-foot rise in the Loxahatchee River and Hobe Sound, causing extensive flooding on the bay side. The storm of September 1926 caused considerable damage and loss of beach material. The most severe storm to hit Palm Beach was the September 1928 hurricane, the eye of which passed right over the county. Winds of over 100 mph, a barometric pressure of 27.43 inches, and a storm surge or tide of 11.2 feet were recorded. The property damage in the Palm Beach–Lake Worth area was estimated at $11 million (it would be about 6 times that amount in 1984 dollars), and various sections of Highway A1A and State Road 707 were damaged. The storm of September 11–19, 1947, with over 100-mph winds, caused severe erosion of the beaches and washed out a 1-mile section of Highway A1A in Del-

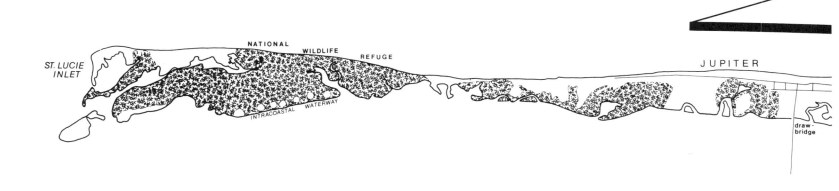

Fig. 4.41. Site analysis: Jupiter Island to Jupiter Inlet Colony.

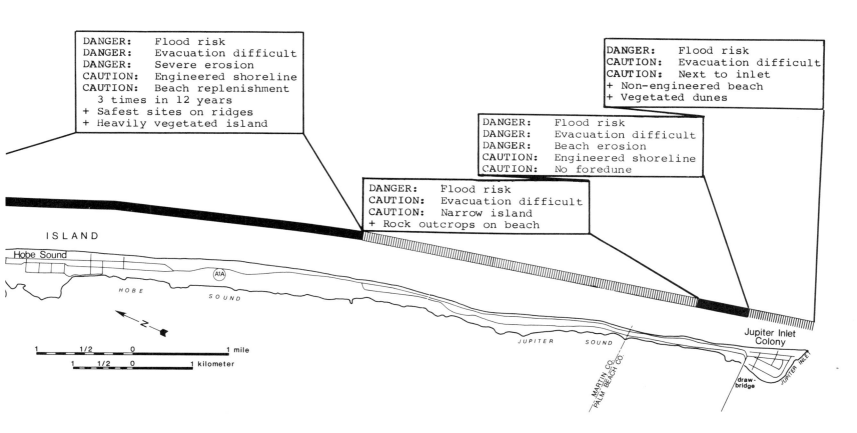

DANGER: Flood risk
DANGER: Evacuation difficult
DANGER: Severe erosion
CAUTION: Engineered shoreline
CAUTION: Beach replenishment
    3 times in 12 years
+ Safest sites on ridges
+ Heavily vegetated island

DANGER: Flood risk
CAUTION: Evacuation difficult
CAUTION: Next to inlet
+ Non-engineered beach
+ Vegetated dunes

DANGER: Flood risk
DANGER: Evacuation difficult
DANGER: Beach erosion
CAUTION: Engineered shoreline
CAUTION: No foredune

DANGER: Flood risk
CAUTION: Evacuation difficult
CAUTION: Narrow island
+ Rock outcrops on beach

ISLAND

Hobe Sound

HOBE   SOUND

A1A

N

1   1/2   0   1 mile
1   1/2   0   1 kilometer

JUPITER   SOUND

MARTIN CO.
PALM BEACH CO.

Jupiter Inlet
Colony

draw-
bridge

JUPITER INLET

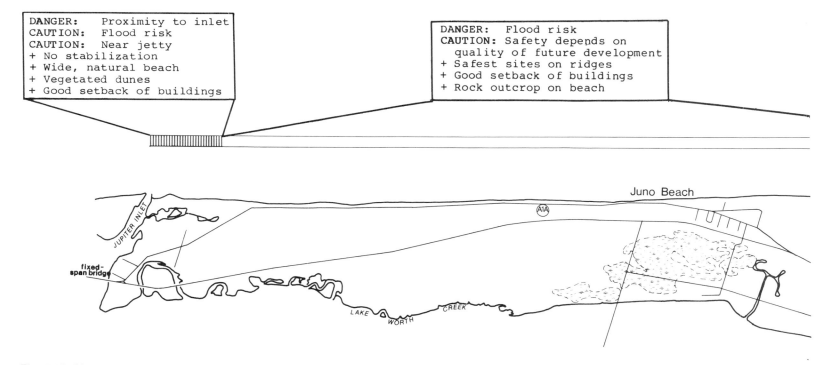

DANGER: Proximity to inlet
CAUTION: Flood risk
CAUTION: Near jetty
+ No stabilization
+ Wide, natural beach
+ Vegetated dunes
+ Good setback of buildings

DANGER: Flood risk
CAUTION: Safety depends on
   quality of future development
+ Safest sites on ridges
+ Good setback of buildings
+ Rock outcrop on beach

Fig. 4.42. Site analysis: Jupiter Inlet to Palm Beach Shores.

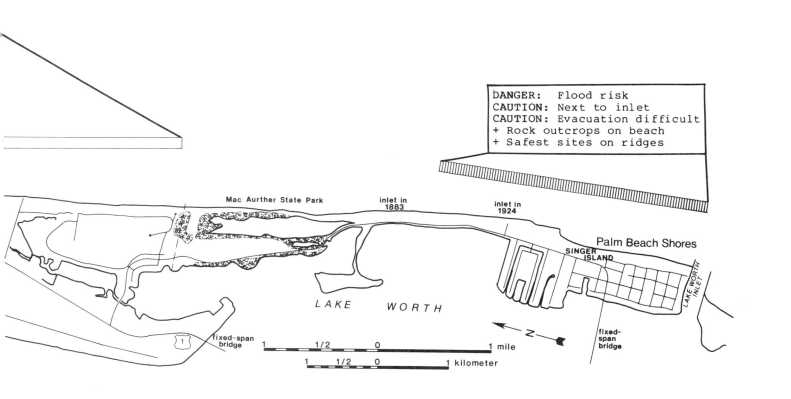

DANGER: Flood risk
CAUTION: Next to inlet
CAUTION: Evacuation difficult
+ Rock outcrops on beach
+ Safest sites on ridges

Mac Aurther State Park

inlet in
1883

inlet in
1924

Palm Beach Shores

SINGER
ISLAND

LAKE   WORTH

LAKE WORTH INLET

fixed-span
bridge

fixed-span
bridge

1   1/2   0   1 mile

1   1/2   0   1 kilometer

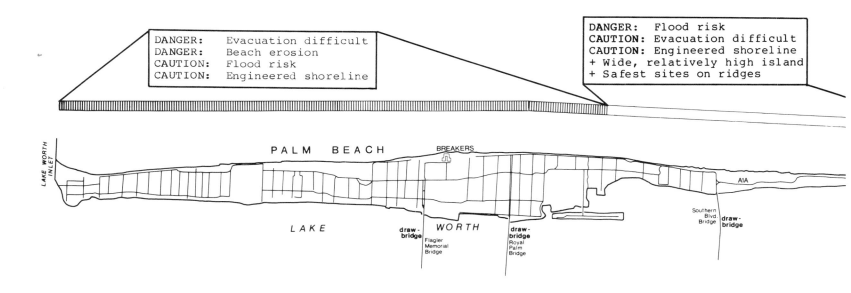

DANGER: Evacuation difficult
DANGER: Beach erosion
CAUTION: Flood risk
CAUTION: Engineered shoreline

DANGER: Flood risk
CAUTION: Evacuation difficult
CAUTION: Engineered shoreline
+ Wide, relatively high island
+ Safest sites on ridges

LAKE WORTH INLET

PALM BEACH

BREAKERS

A1A

LAKE   WORTH

draw-bridge
Flagler
Memorial
Bridge

draw-bridge
Royal
Palm
Bridge

Southern
Blvd.
Bridge

draw-bridge

Fig. 4.43. Site analysis: Palm Beach Shores to South Lake Worth Inlet.

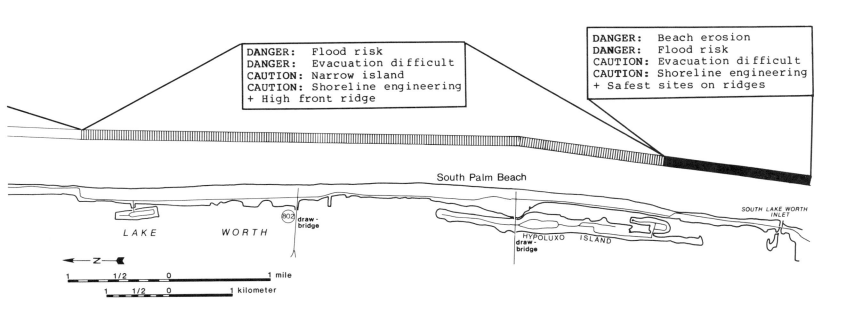

DANGER: Flood risk
DANGER: Evacuation difficult
CAUTION: Narrow island
CAUTION: Shoreline engineering
+ High front ridge

DANGER: Beach erosion
DANGER: Flood risk
CAUTION: Evacuation difficult
CAUTION: Shoreline engineering
+ Safest sites on ridges

South Palm Beach

LAKE   WORTH

802 draw-
bridge

N

1   1/2   0   1 mile
1   1/2   0   1 kilometer

SOUTH LAKE WORTH
INLET

HYPOLUXO   ISLAND
draw-
bridge

ray Beach along with the municipal pavilion. The storm of August 1949 pounded Palm Beach with 130-mph winds and washed out a 3-mile section of Highway A1A from Lantana to Lake Worth. Other highway sections from Boynton Beach to Delray Beach also were damaged. If a hurricane struck Palm Beach now, the damage to shorefront property would be greater than ever because there is no natural beach buffer.

The annual northeasters have caused the most severe and lasting changes along the shoreline. The winter storms of 1957, 1962, and 1981–82 were particularly notable for the considerable damage they did to bulkheads and beach dune profiles.

Over much of the county shoreline from 1883 to 1983 the beaches have generally retreated—but at varying rates. As a general rule, stretches of 1 to 1.5 miles in length north of the inlets and their associated jetties have either remained stable or have built seaward. The areas immediately south of the inlets have experienced severe retreat due to the blocking of the littoral drifts at the jetties and shoaling of the inlet bars. The beaches of Palm Beach Island experienced erosion landward of the 30-foot depth contour, amounting to 8,000,000 cubic yards between 1929 and 1955. The beaches south of South Lake Worth Inlet have experienced both retreat and buildout, but retreat exceeds buildout for the entire section in spite of a sand transfer plant at the inlet. The Army Corps of Engineers estimates that Palm Beach County is subject to annual losses of 190,000 cubic yards of sand.

The shoreline of Palm Beach County has been extensively engineered with seawalls, groins, revetments, jetties, and beach nour-

ishment. There have been several beach nourishment projects on Palm Beach Island and at Delray Beach. Sand bypass systems on Lake Worth Inlet and South Lake Worth Inlet place an annual average of 63,000 cubic yards and 80,000 cubic yards of sand, respectively, on the south side of the inlet. However, the fixed-boom type of sand transfer system at South Lake Worth Inlet is inefficient and at times pumps water instead of sand. Delray Beach was nourished in 1973 with 1.6 million cubic yards of sand placement; the same was done in 1978–79. There are currently active projects to nourish Ocean Ridge Beach south of the South Lake Worth Inlet and to renourish Delray Beach. In 1974 Palm Beach County conducted a study that recommended a beach nourishment program for 33.9 miles of beaches at a cost of $17.5 million. The Corps of Engineers study recommended improvement for 12.2 miles of beaches at a cost of $22.98 million. These projects have not been carried out as yet.

Evacuation is a serious problem for Palm Beach County. Most areas on the barrier islands are well below the 100-year flood level. Jupiter Inlet Colony residents must escape via Highway 707, which has low-elevation approaches to a drawbridge. From the vicinity of Juno Beach to the Seminole Golf Club may be one of the safest areas on the east coast of Florida in terms of evacuation. Palm Beach has three routes of evacuation to the mainland, all via drawbridges. Australian pines line most of the streets in Northern Palm Beach and should be expected to blow down and block evacuation routes. Much of the evacuation route in South Palm Beach lies below a 5-foot elevation along the back side of the island and is very susceptible to flooding. The 2 closest routes to the mainland are drawbridges. On the Delray Beach, Gulf Stream, and Ocean Ridge segment of the Palm Beach County shoreline, Highway A1A is on fairly high ground. However, roadways back to the mainland lie below 5 feet in elevation and are therefore susceptible to flooding. Florida Highway 804 has a drawbridge over the Intracoastal Waterway. Highway 806 has a fixed-span bridge. The Boca Raton area is best evacuated by the 4-span stationary bridges to the north over Lake Rogers.

Broward County

Broward County has about 24 miles of open ocean shoreline. Two inlets break the Broward barrier chain. These are Hillsboro Inlet north of Pompano Beach and Port Everglades Harbor south of Fort Lauderdale. All of Broward's open ocean coast is fronted with barrier islands. Where natural sounds and lagoons do not exist, the Intracoastal Waterway cuts through behind the shoreline isolating the beach-front strip of land. Width of the islands in Broward County ranges from a mere 300 feet or so north of Hillsboro Inlet to 4,500 feet near Fort Lauderdale. Elevations of the Broward County islands are usually less than 15 feet and reach maximums of a little more than 20 feet. There is a more or less continuous ridge of sand down the length of the Broward shore, but it is generally lower and less well-developed than the ridge of the Palm Beach County shore. Of the 24 miles of county shore- ont, a little more than 8 miles is in public hands, that is, owned the government.

The county's beach-front communities are, from north to south, Deerfield Beach, Hillsboro Beach, Pompano Beach, Lauderdale by-the-Sea, Fort Lauderdale, Dania, Hollywood, and Hallandale. Broward County is highly developed. Thousands of buildings hug the shoreline, and more and bigger structures go up every day. Unfortunately this shoreline has a long history of erosion that has resulted in emplacement of a great deal of shoreline stabilization structures: seawalls, groins, revetments, etc. The natural erosion rates are high but have been pushed even higher in some cases by jetties and other structures. For example, prior to 1960 the Corps of Engineers estimated that the annual shoreline recession rate of the stretch between the county line and Hillsboro Inlet was 4 feet per year. During the sixties and seventies the rate accelerated to more than 10 feet per year. Part of the acceleration may be due to jetties at Boca Raton Inlet in southern Palm Beach County. Between Hillsboro and Port Everglades Inlet the recession rates have been much smaller, although Pompano Beach is an exception with its rates of 4 to 8 feet per year. On a shoreline as heavily stabilized as Broward, perhaps present-day recession rates are rather meaningless. Much of the shoreline retreat now affects replenished or nourished beaches (fig. 4.47). Almost every community in the county has, or plans to have, some sort of beach nourishment project. The experience so far indicates that replenished beaches here disappear very quickly (3 to 5 years), and replenishment and re-replenishment are required. In some cases the reason for the quick loss of sand may be poor choice of siting for the offshore dredging. During the summer of 1983 we observed

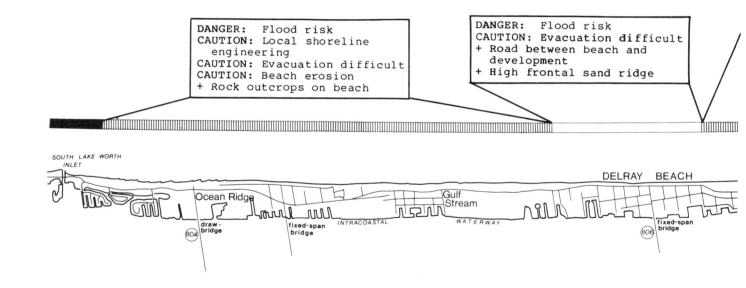

Fig. 4.44. Site analysis: Ocean Ridge to Boca Raton Inlet.

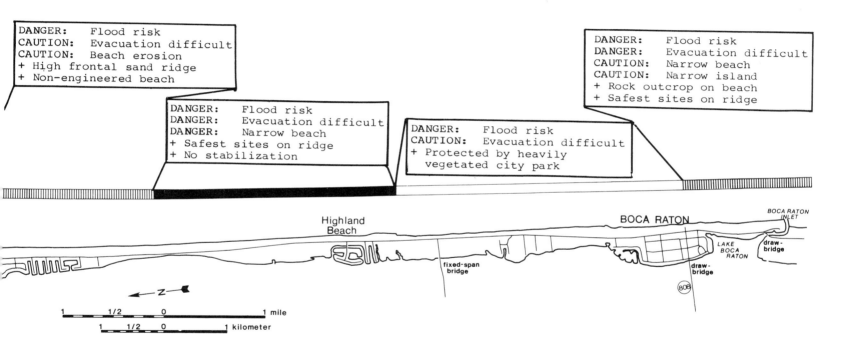

DANGER: Flood risk
CAUTION: Evacuation difficult
CAUTION: Beach erosion
+ High frontal sand ridge
+ Non-engineered beach

DANGER: Flood risk
DANGER: Evacuation difficult
DANGER: Narrow beach
+ Safest sites on ridge
+ No stabilization

DANGER: Flood risk
CAUTION: Evacuation difficult
+ Protected by heavily
  vegetated city park

DANGER: Flood risk
DANGER: Evacuation difficult
CAUTION: Narrow beach
CAUTION: Narrow island
+ Rock outcrop on beach
+ Safest sites on ridge

Highland
Beach

BOCA RATON

BOCA RATON
INLET

LAKE
BOCA
RATON

draw-
bridge

fixed-span
bridge

draw-
bridge

808

N

1   1/2   0   1 mile

1   1/2   0   1 kilometer

Fig. 4.45. Seawall and groin in front of a too-close-to-the-beach development. Juno Beach south of Jupiter Inlet. Photo by Bill Neal.

Fig. 4.46. Shorefront condos, Boca Raton. Photo by Bill Neal.

brown-stained sand on newly replenished beaches (for example, Hollywood Beach and Pompano Beach). Since brown staining of shells probably occurs on the beach while material is exposed to air, the fact that brown shells are being pumped up means that a hole is being dug in the lower beach. Replenished sand may simply fall back into the old hole, which could account for the very rapid disappearance of some of the artificial Broward beaches.

Prudent potential Broward beach-front property owners should snoop around and find out what their future tax bills may be like because of the community's beach stabilization projects.

Fig. 4.47. Repienished beach at Hollywood Beach. This beach is experiencing high rate of erosion. Photo by Bill Neal.

Broward County has had an active storm history. Between 1870 and 1970 the eyes of 7 storms passed through Broward County. Four of these storms exited—that is, passed from land to sea—and 3 storms made a landfall. The exiting storms can cause severe wind damage, but as a rule they do not cause major flooding. The flooding problems are much greater when a storm moves on to land from the sea. Expected 100-year flood levels from such storms along the open ocean shoreline are in the range of 7 to 12 feet. Maximum hurricane water levels actually recorded at Fort Lauderdale include a high of 12.6 feet above sea level in the 1926 storm and 8 feet in the Yankee storm (1935). The 1947 storm produced a 9.8-foot storm surge at Hillsboro Inlet. The Yankee storm, by the way, was so named because it actually moved ashore from the north.

A third type of hurricane affecting Broward County is called an "alongshore hurricane." These storms do not come ashore near the county but pass along offshore and parallel to the coastline. The last alongshore hurricane was David (1979).

Of the 24 miles of Broward County shoreline, we consider about 65 percent to be in the high-risk category and 35 percent in the moderate-risk category (figs. 4.48, 4.49, and 4.50). We found no shoreline segments here that we would classify as low risk.

Evacuation is a major problem in Broward County and is one of the reasons so much of the shore is considered to be high risk. There are 12 bridges across the Intracoastal Waterway to the mainland here, but all are drawbridges and hence are risky to depend on in a storm crisis. A large number of people live in low-elevation, high flood-risk zones, the most important of which are the extensive finger canal developments. There will be many thousands of people trying to simultaneously escape the Broward shore if a big one threatens. Perhaps you might consider choosing a

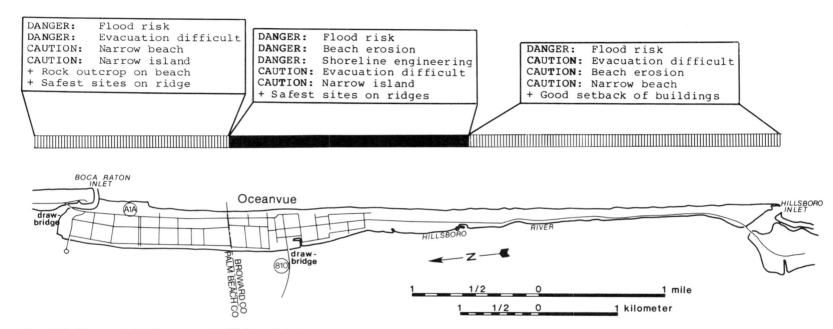

DANGER: Flood risk
DANGER: Evacuation difficult
CAUTION: Narrow beach
CAUTION: Narrow island
+ Rock outcrop on beach
+ Safest sites on ridge

DANGER: Flood risk
DANGER: Beach erosion
DANGER: Shoreline engineering
CAUTION: Evacuation difficult
CAUTION: Narrow island
+ Safest sites on ridges

DANGER: Flood risk
CAUTION: Evacuation difficult
CAUTION: Beach erosion
CAUTION: Narrow beach
+ Good setback of buildings

Fig. 4.48. Site analysis: Oceanvue to Hillsboro Inlet.

high-rise building that you know is well-built and use a friend's condo for shelter.

Wide beach-front areas offer the least risk. In Broward County these can be found at the south end of Fort Lauderdale and Dania. Dania, an anomalous community of single-family dwellings, is almost surrounded by high-rises. The beach is relatively broad here, but the low elevation of the island dictates a need for storm evacuation. Another rather striking anomaly in beach-front development in Broward County is the Marriott Hotel in Fort Lauderdale. For some reason the motel chain was given a variance to the coastal setback line, and the building sits far out on the beach relative to adjacent, more prudently sited buildings. It is predictable that the seawall in front of the Marriott Hotel will soon be reducing the sand supply and causing erosion of downstream (southerly) beaches.

Dade County

Dade County has about 35 miles of open ocean shoreline, of which 15 miles are made up of barrier islands. In this discussion we will restrict ourselves to the barrier beach communities. Much important information concerning Key Biscayne, Virginia Key, and Miami Beach is included in the field trip guide at the end of the book and will not be repeated here. Hence this discussion of Dade County is somewhat abbreviated.

The main beach-front communities on the Dade County shore are, from north to south, Golden Beach, Sunny Isles (fig. 4.51), Bal Harbor, Surfside, Miami Beach, and Key Biscayne. Here in Dade County and especially in Miami Beach is one of the world's most densely developed barrier island shorelines. Also here are some of the world's most famous luxury hotels.

The barrier islands range from 0.2 miles to 1.5 miles in width. Elevations are generally quite low. A more or less continuous sand ridge parallels the beach, with elevations ranging from 5 to 12 feet. Behind the narrow frontal sand ridges the islands tend to be flat and low, much of the area being less than 5 feet in elevation.

Miami Beach and Bal Harbor occupy the same island that is bordered to the north by Bakers Haulover Cut and to the south by Government Cut. Both inlets are jettied, and Government Cut is the main channel for the Port of Miami. The dominant direction of sand movement along the beaches of Dade County is from north to south; hence, beaches to the south of jetties have suffered erosion. Essentially no sand escapes to the south of the Government Cut jetties.

Although the shoreline elsewhere in Dade County has generally retreated, the Miami Beach strandline has more or less remained stationary since 1920. The recent $6 million per mile nourishment project has widened the beach to 300 feet (fig 4.52). That Miami Beach had no beach during the sixties and seventies was due not so much to erosion as to the fact that buildings were constructed right on the beach. During most of this century the shoreface, or lower beach, to a depth of about 30 feet has become gradually steeper along much of the Dade shoreline. Waves approaching the shore are greatly influenced by the bottom; that is, when an approaching wave "feels the bottom" it breaks. If the shoreface is steep, a wave will not feel the bottom and break until it is closer to shore. Therefore, larger waves on the average are hitting the beach today than 50 years ago.

During the last 100 years or so, 12 hurricanes have passed through Dade County, 8 of which made landfall in the county and 4 of which exited back out to sea. A number of other hurricanes brushed by the Dade coast on their way north. Hurricanes that caused significant damage to Dade County occurred in 1903, 1906, 1926 (the big one), 1929, 1935 (2 storms), 1941, 1945, 1947 (2 storms), 1948, 1949, 1950, 1964, 1965, and 1966. Since 1966

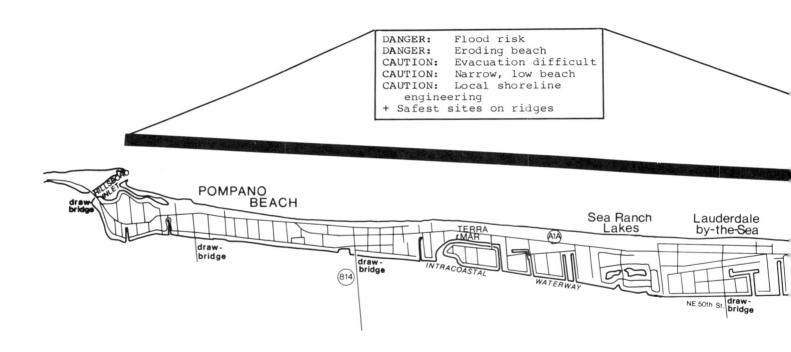

DANGER: Flood risk
DANGER: Eroding beach
CAUTION: Evacuation difficult
CAUTION: Narrow, low beach
CAUTION: Local shoreline
          engineering
+ Safest sites on ridges

Fig. 4.49. Site analysis: Pompano Beach to Harbor Heights.

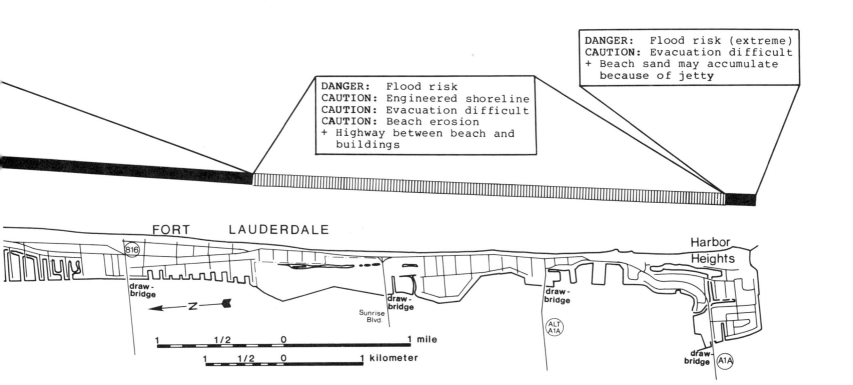

DANGER: Flood risk (extreme)
CAUTION: Evacuation difficult
+ Beach sand may accumulate
  because of jetty

DANGER: Flood risk
CAUTION: Engineered shoreline
CAUTION: Evacuation difficult
CAUTION: Beach erosion
+ Highway between beach and
  buildings

FORT   LAUDERDALE

Harbor
Heights

816

draw-
bridge

N

Sunrise
Blvd.

draw-
bridge

draw-
bridge

ALT
A1A

draw-
bridge

A1A

| 1 | 1/2 | 0 | | 1 mile |

| 1 | 1/2 | 0 | | 1 kilometer |

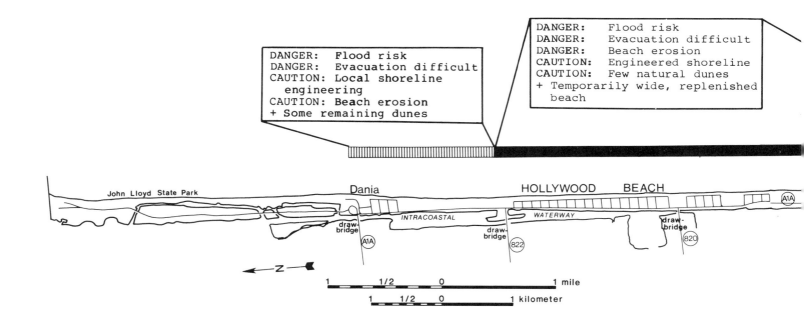

DANGER: Flood risk
DANGER: Evacuation difficult
CAUTION: Local shoreline
    engineering
CAUTION: Beach erosion
+ Some remaining dunes

DANGER: Flood risk
DANGER: Evacuation difficult
DANGER: Beach erosion
CAUTION: Engineered shoreline
CAUTION: Few natural dunes
+ Temporarily wide, replenished
  beach

John Lloyd State Park

Dania

HOLLYWOOD   BEACH

INTRACOASTAL   WATERWAY

draw-bridge

A1A

draw-bridge

822

draw-bridge

820

A1A

← N

1   1/2   0   1 mile
1   1/2   0   1 kilometer

Fig. 4.50. Site analysis: Dania to Bakers Haulover Cut.

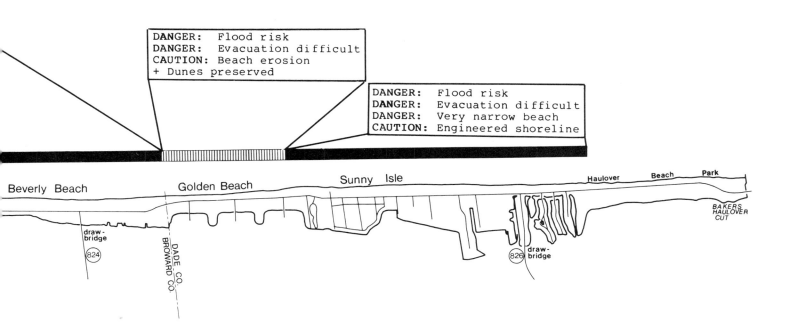

DANGER: Flood risk
DANGER: Evacuation difficult
CAUTION: Beach erosion
+ Dunes preserved

DANGER: Flood risk
DANGER: Evacuation difficult
DANGER: Very narrow beach
CAUTION: Engineered shoreline

Beverly Beach   Golden Beach   Sunny Isle   Haulover   Beach   Park

draw-
bridge

824

DADE CO.
BROWARD CO.

826 draw-
bridge

BAKERS
HAULOVER
CUT

Fig. 4.51. Sunny Isle beach. Note remnants of groins. Photo by Bill Neal.

Fig. 4.52. Construction of the new (1983) Miami beach boardwalk on th
new $68 million beach. Photo by Bill Neal.

there have been some close calls but no really damaging storms. Interestingly, a recent Corps of Engineers evacuation study indicated that numerous South Florida citizens think they have survived an important hurricane, even though no such storms have occurred since their arrival in the sunny south. The problem is that such people may treat the next *real* storm with undue contempt.

Hurricanes are not the only storms that cause shoreline damage. Winter storms, often from the northeast, cause both damage (fig. 4.53) and erosion.

Evacuation is, as usual in South Florida, a major problem.

Fig. 4.53. Miami Beach after the October 31, 1969, storm. Photo by the Miami *Herald* from the University of Florida coastal engineering archives.

Seven bridges connect the beach-front communities of Dade County to the mainland, but only 1 is a fixed-span bridge (the Julia Tuttle Causeway, which is also federal Highway 195 and state Highway 112). Besides being the only fixed-span bridge, the Julia Tuttle Causeway has a relatively high abutment elevation of 8 to 10 feet and is definitely the safest way off Miami Beach. The Venetian, MacArthur, and North Bay causeways have minimum elevations of 4 feet and can be expected to flood early. The approaches to the Rickenbacker Causeway, the only escape route from Key Biscayne, are 3 feet in elevation and are lined by massive Australian pines that should be expected to totally block escape from this low-elevation island early on in a major storm.

Adding to the problem is the fact that once you have escaped to the mainland, your troubles are not over. Much of Miami is very low in elevation and in the next big storm can expect to be flooded. Therefore, it is very critical for all residents of the Dade shoreline to plan ahead. Find out from your local city hall what the evacuation plan is. What shelters can you reach in time? We think the best advice is to leave your island abode more than 24 hours before the storm strikes. (At that stage, of course, you cannot even be certain that the storm will strike your community.) Next, drive inland and visit Aunt Sue in Orlando or see the museums and colonial homes in Tallahassee or go to the coastal engineering library in Gainesville and read about Florida's shoreline problems.

For the barrier island stretch of the Dade County shoreline we consider 33 percent to be high risk for development and 67 percent to be moderate risk (figs. 4.54 and 4.55). Most of the stretch

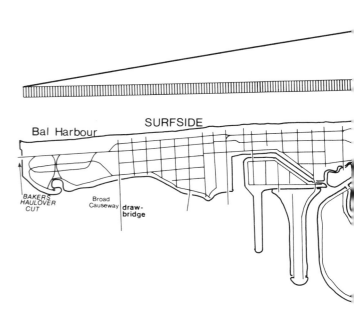

Fig. 4.54. Site analysis: Miami Beach.

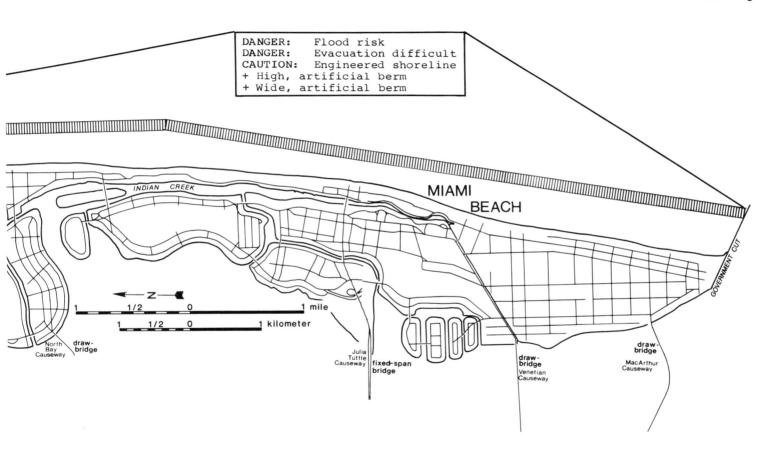

DANGER: Flood risk
DANGER: Evacuation difficult
CAUTION: Engineered shoreline
+ High, artificial berm
+ Wide, artificial berm

INDIAN   CREEK

MIAMI
BEACH

GOVERNMENT CUT

N

| 1 | 1/2 | 0 | 1 mile |
| 1 | 1/2 | 0 | 1 kilometer |

North
Bay
Causeway

draw-
bridge

Julia
Tuttle
Causeway

fixed-span
bridge

draw-
bridge
Venetian
Causeway

draw-
bridge

MacArthur
Causeway

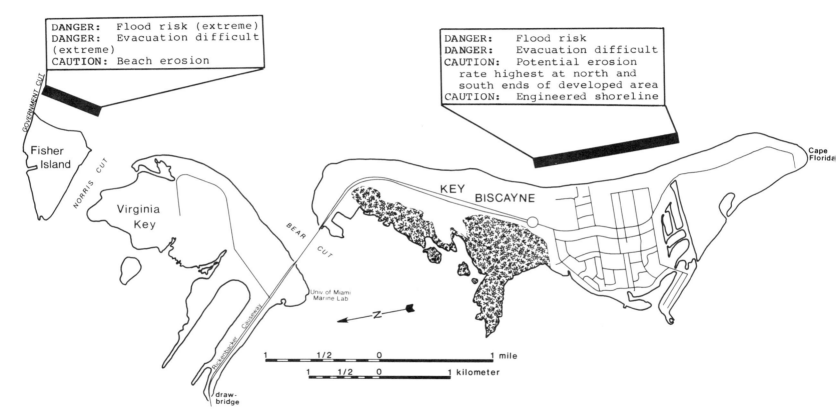

DANGER: Flood risk (extreme)
DANGER: Evacuation difficult (extreme)
CAUTION: Beach erosion

DANGER: Flood risk
DANGER: Evacuation difficult
CAUTION: Potential erosion rate highest at north and south ends of developed area
CAUTION: Engineered shoreline

GOVERNMENT CUT

Fisher Island

NORRIS CUT

Virginia Key

BEAR CUT

Rickenbacker Causeway

Univ. of Miami Marine Lab

draw-bridge

KEY BISCAYNE

Cape Florida

N

1   1/2   0   1 mile

1   1/2   0   1 kilometer

Fig. 4.55. Site analysis: Fisher Island through Key Biscayne.

of barrier island fronted by the replenished Miami Beach falls in the moderate-risk category because of the shock-absorbing effect of the new beach.

Monroe County/Florida Keys

"Key" comes from the Spanish word *cayo*, meaning small, low-lying island. The Florida Keys are quite different from the beach and barrier island systems that we have been discussing. They are a chain of 97 low-lying, limestone islands extending in an arc around the tip of the Florida peninsula from about Miami to a point 235 miles south, then southwest to the Dry Tortugas (fig. 4.56). The islands and some barely submerged banks between are composed of 2 formations of limestone named Key Largo Limestone and Miami Oolite, both formed during the ice ages. The Key Largo formation is an old coral reef built upon unconsolidated quartz and carbonate sand. It is a typical coral reef with the expected variety of fossil coral heads and the shells of many different snails and clams. The Miami Oolite formation is composed of fragments of shells and of particles called oolites, sand-sized spherules of calcium carbonate that precipitate out of seawater in a shallow-water environment subject to lots of wave activity.

The environment. The natural environment of the Florida Keys, where it still exists, is breathtakingly beautiful. This beauty is due to many unique and fragile interelated ecosystems. Figure 4.57 is a typical but generalized cross section of a part of the Florida Keys.

On the seaward edge of the limestone platform are the barrier reefs. Landward of the these reefs are small, more or less circular features called patch reefs. These 2 types of reef make up the only large living reef systems of the continental United States. The beautiful reefs can best be viewed at John Pennekamp Reef State Park. Besides providing beauty for all to enjoy, the reefs, especially the barrier reefs, provide protection from waves.

Mixed among the patch reefs (fig. 4.57) are shifting shoals of calcareous sand made up mostly of fragments of the reefs broken up during storms.

The islands themselves are the high points of the old barrier reef systems. There are few natural beaches in the Keys; usually the shoreline is bare limestone. Most beaches on the Keys are artificial, the beach at Key West being an example. Before 1926 a small beach was present at Key West, but construction of a seawall behind the beach caused its rapid disappearance. The artificial beach, made up of crushed limestone and dredged sand, was emplaced in 1960 for $285,000. Most of it disappeared within a decade.

Good examples of small natural beaches in the Keys still exist on Marathon Key and in Bahia Honda State Park.

Often instead of beaches, mangroves grow along all the margins of the islands. The mangrove community is a very important one in that it provides a nursery for the larvae of many forms of marine life. Red mangrove lies at the edge of the shore and has roots that are capable of being permanently submerged in seawater. Black mangrove trees grow on slightly higher elevations with roots submerged by every high tide, while the third species of the mangrove

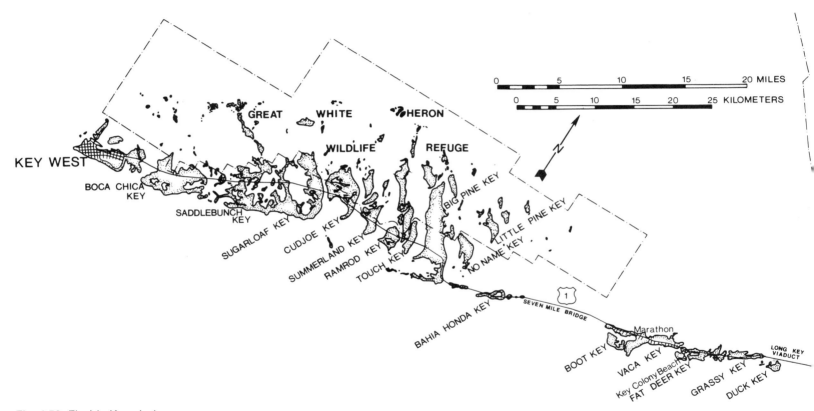

Fig. 4.56. Florida Keys index map.

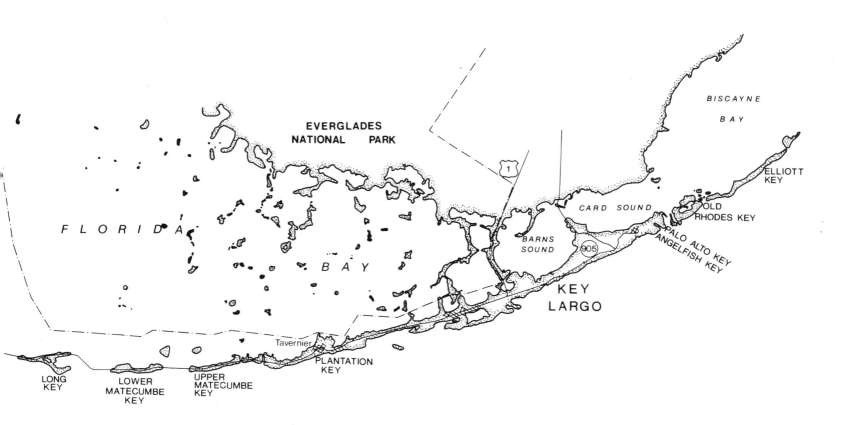

EVERGLADES
NATIONAL PARK

BISCAYNE
BAY

FLORIDA

BAY

BARNS
SOUND

CARD SOUND

ELLIOTT
KEY

OLD
RHODES KEY

PALO ALTO KEY
ANGELFISH KEY

KEY
LARGO

Tavernier

PLANTATION
KEY

LONG
KEY

LOWER
MATECUMBE
KEY

UPPER
MATECUMBE
KEY

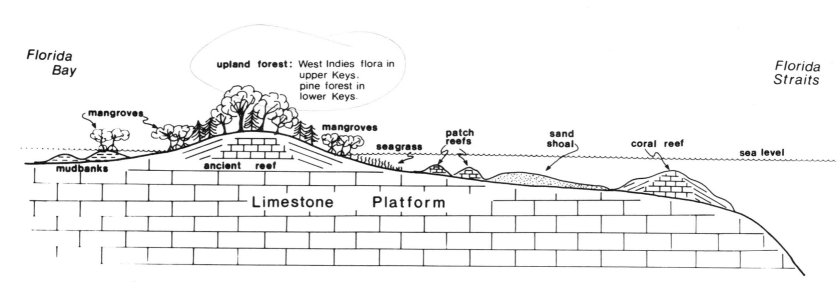

Fig. 4.57. Generalized cross section across the Florida Keys.

troika, the white mangrove, has roots that are flooded only by storms or spring tides.

The islands are crowned with a forest (fig. 4.57) called a "tropical hammock," which is a typical West Indies assemblage of exotic trees and bushes found nowhere else on mainland America. The tropical hammock assemblages are found on the northern Keys, while on the southern Keys the native forest is dominated by pines, thatch palms, palmettos, and shrubs and grasses typical of nearby mainland areas. Behind the Keys is Florida Bay (fig. 4.57), a shallow bay dotted with numerous mud banks. Some of the mud banks have mangroves on them and others do not. Florida Bay is an important nursery area for commercial species of shrimp.

Look what they've done to our Keys! People have moved to the Florida Keys for many reasons, but foremost among them is the natural beauty of this delicate ecosystem. Unfortunately, but certainly not surprisingly, development is rapidly destroying the very environment that people are moving to the Keys to enjoy. Development has been especially heavy in the northern Keys. Parcels of land have been stripped of their unique West Indian vegetation, built up, flattened, and relandscaped, often unsuccessfully. Introduced plants often do poorly in the poor to nonexistent soils; thus, fertilizers and topsoil from elsewhere must be introduced.

Most new residents have septic tank systems. Combined septic tank effluent and fertilizer seep into the porous and permeable limestone, causing these pollutants to be rapidly introduced into the adjacent marine environment. Some pollutants also may be transported south from the Miami area. Unfortunately, develop-

ment also is accompanied by dredging and filling that muddies the adjacent waters.

Drinking water, by the way, arrives via pipeline from the mainland—a long, tenuous lifeline.

There is a possibility that pollution may be killing the barrier reefs. It is not always easy to distinguish natural from man-made effects, but the Florida Department of Natural Resources estimates that 85 percent of Hen and Chicken Reef off Key Largo is dead. Adding to the problem are souvenir-hunting tourists who remove coral heads and allow anchors to drag. Loss of the reefs would be a great natural disaster. Among other effects, storm-wave intensity will be much increased without the protection of the reef, a phenomenon observed in the Virgin Islands where sugarcane production killed offshore reefs.

Some of this discussion about the Keys comes from a 1975 book, *Environmental Quality by Design: South Florida*, by A. R. Veri and others. We highly recommend this book to the reader interested in learning more about the Keys and other marine environments of South Florida (see full entry in appendix C).

The storm threat. Hurricanes pose an enormous threat to people on the Florida Keys. Perusal of the index map (fig. 4.56) shows why. There is a single highway, recently expanded to four lanes, that connects the Keys all the way from Key West to the mainland. There is no other land connection. Complete evacuation before a big storm will be virtually impossible because Route 1 in the Keys is low and crosses numerous bridges. Flooding will close the escape road early, and you can be sure there will be fender benders,

Fig. 4.58. Repair of the old Florida Keys highway 3 days after the passage of Hurricane Donna (1960). The new highway also is vulnerable to such breakthroughs in future hurricanes, making the evacuation problem particularly critical. Photo furnished by Harold R. Wanless.

jackknifed trucks, and other smashups blocking the escape route.

Compounding the dangers is the fact that many residents of the Keys live in mobile homes that can be destroyed by even a modest hurricane.

Finally, the Keys themselves provide no place to hide. Average elevation is only 3 feet, and *maximum* elevation in the whole chain is only about 18 feet. More than 99 percent of the land area of the Keys is below the 100-year flood level, and 90 percent of the land is less than 5 feet. Many residents have been lulled into a false sense of security because the Keys have not suffered a direct hit since Hurricane Donna ravaged the area in 1960. The worst storm occurred on September 2, 1935, when a hurricane with sustained winds estimated at 200 mph struck the Keys, caused massive damage, and killed 400 people. The strip of maximum damage was only 40 miles wide. In 1846 a hurricane destroyed Key West. Water was 5 feet deep in the main street, and survivors clustered at the highest point in the area (only about 17 feet) were nearly washed away by waves.

Of 17 Red Cross shelters listed for the Keys, every one would be flooded in a hurricane of strength "5," and many would be inundated in hurricanes of Saffir-Simpson class "3" (table 2.1). A recent, previously discussed study of hurricane evacuation risks (see tables 4.1 and 4.2) shows that a serious misconception exists among South Florida and Florida Keys residents. Many of them think they have been through a hurricane, when the records show that they have not. No wonder that Civil Defense and officials involved with evacuation are concerned that many people will not heed their warning until it is too late.

We consider the entire Florida Keys to be high risk for development. There are several reasons for this classification but the principal one is the *evacuation difficulty*.

5. The coast, land use, and the law

The previous chapters demonstrate that the coastal zone is a dynamic area where land, wind, wave, and organisms interact. The resulting rapid changes are especially apparent on barrier islands. We cannot build and live in this zone without some level of interference, or without risking the negative impacts brought about by natural changes.

Coastal dynamics preclude shoreline and island development patterned after traditional inland styles. A 1-story, ranch-style house at the back of the beach will block wind transport of sand, interfere with overwash, and ultimately behave as a seawall before being destroyed in its turn by storm waves and flooding. This traditional design in this dynamic zone would have a much shorter life expectancy than the same house in an inland location. The services for this house and many like it (for example, electric lines, gas mains, water lines), the sewage generated, and the roads, bridges, and service structures required for such development will exceed the carrying capacity of a barrier island much quicker than for a similar inland community. The resulting damage to the environment through pollution, loss of habitat, stabilization structures, and the like removes the amenities that most shore dwellers originally came to enjoy. Not only aesthetic value is lost, but the risk from coastal hazards is increased.

Wise land-use planning, environmental maintenance, and conservation of the coastal zone are necessary to protect the environment. But just as significant, they are necessary to protect ourselves. The ecosystem is as important to the human population as it is to a population of pelicans or a stand of sea oats. Curiously, laws are passed to protect the latter with the goal of protecting the former—sometimes from ourselves.

Population growth, affluence, and migration to the Sun Belt will necessitate increased regulation of the coastal zone. Florida's coastal population is expected to approach 10 million by the year 2000! By analogy, as the traffic increases, more traffic laws and regulations are required to avoid the certainty of traffic jams.

The best philosophy on shoreline development is that land use should be in harmony with the natural environments and processes that constitute the system. Of course, various segments of society view the coastal zone differently. The extreme views range from untouched preservationism to unplanned, uncontrolled urbanization. Increasingly, decisions on land use are made by governments under the pressure of various special interest groups. Existing legislation is often that of compromise, satisfying the various federal, state, and local levels of the political infrastructure. We can expect that regulations will continue to be established and modified with the intention of ensuring reasonable, multiple land use of the coastal zone, while attempting to protect both inhabitants and the natural environment. Developers have had this expectation in the past, and in some cases it has spurred unwise development.

That is, buildings have been constructed before tighter restrictions could go into effect. Current and prospective owners of coastal property, especially on barrier islands, should be aware of their responsibilities under current law and expect additional regulation with respect to development and land use.

A trip along Highway A1A demonstrates the inconsistency with which communities have approached coastal development. Like the New Jersey shore, southeast Florida's coast is nearly continuous urban-suburban development. The same trend is apparent along most of Florida's Atlantic coastline. One often does not need signs to denote community boundaries; they are apparent by the sharp contrasts in types of buildings and their position with respect to beach and dunes (if the latter are still present). A county ordinance limiting buildings to 4 stories is of little consolation if you live on the last lot next door to the county line, across which are clusters of high-rise buildings! The same is true for beach protection. It is not a curiosity of nature that the character of the beach and associated dunes often changes at or near community boundaries. Such changes reflect differences in land-use policy and regulations.

A partial list of relevant current land-use programs and regulations applicable to the Florida coast follows. The explanations provided are general and introductory in nature; appendix B lists the agencies that will supply more specific and detailed information. The regulations listed here range from federal laws that protect the interests of the larger society to state and local laws and ordinances that serve the interests of Florida citizens and the local community. A review of these regulations before investing in or undertaking property development anywhere on the coast will be in your best interest. We recommend that you contact your local county or municipal planning, zoning, or building departments to determine state and federal permit requirements.

Coastal Barrier Resources Act of 1982

Recognizing the serious hazards, costs, and problems with federally subsidized development of barrier islands, the U.S. Congress passed the Coastal Barrier Resources Act (Public Law 97-348) in October 1982. The purpose of this federal law is to minimize loss of human life and property, wasteful expenditure of federal taxes, and damage to fish, wildlife, and other natural resources from incompatible development along the Atlantic and Gulf coasts. The act covers 190 designated areas, covering 700 miles of undeveloped barrier beaches in the United States.

Specifically, the act prohibits the expenditures of federal funds, including loans and grants, for the construction of infrastructures that encourage barrier island development; these infrastructures include roads, bridges, water supply systems, waste water treatment systems, and erosion control projects. Any new structure built on these designated barrier islands after October 1, 1983, is not eligible for federal flood insurance. Certain activities and expenditures under the act are permissible. The act does not prohibit private development on the designated barrier islands, but it passes the risks and costs of development from taxpayers to owners. All applicable federal, state, and local permits still must be obtained before any development begins in the designated areas.

The Coastal Barrier Resources Act affects all or part of 33 of Florida's barrier islands covering 110 miles of ocean beaches (table 5.1). For exact boundaries of the designated areas, contact local city or county planning departments or the Florida Coastal Zone Management Program Office (appendix B).

National Flood Insurance Program (NFIP)

Florida's barrier beaches are prone to flood damage from hurricanes and tropical storms. The probability of a hurricane striking Florida's coastline is very high, up to 1 hurricane every 1.5 years. During hurricanes, storm surge and wave heights reach 12 to 20 feet above normal, and winds of 100 to 150 miles per hour are not uncommon. Between 1900 and 1980, hurricanes inflicted approximately $1.5 billion worth of damage in the Florida coastal zone. However, this figure is misleading because it is not in terms of today's inflated dollar. Given the present heavily developed Florida coasts, a *single* moderate hurricane could match or exceed this level of destruction!

The National Flood Insurance Act of 1968 (P.L. 90-448) as amended by the Flood Disaster Protection Act of 1973 (P.L. 92-234) was passed to encourage prudent land-use planning and to minimize property damage in flood-prone areas like barrier beaches. Local communities must adopt ordinances to reduce future flood risks in order to qualify for the National Flood Insur-

Table 5.1. East Florida's barrier islands affected by the Coastal Barrier Resources Act

East Florida island	Miles of beach
Bird/Talbot Island	3
Usinas Beach	0.5
Conch Island	2
Mantanzas River	1.75
Ormond-by-the-Sea	3
Ponce Inlet	1.5
Coconut Point	3.25
Vero Beach	0.75
Blue Hole Unit	6
Hutchinson Island	9.75
Hobe Sound	1
North Beach	0.75

Source: Public Law 97-348.

ance Program. The NFIP provides an opportunity for property owners to purchase flood insurance that generally is not available from private insurance companies.

The initiative for qualifying for the program rests with the community, which must contact the Federal Emergency Management Agency (FEMA). FEMA will provide the community with a Flood Hazard Boundary Map (FHBM). Any community may join the National Flood Insurance Program provided that it requires development permits for all proposed construction and other development within the flood zone and ensures that construction materials and techniques are used to minimize potential flood damage. At this point the community is in the "emergency phase" of the NFIP. The federal government makes a limited amount of flood insurance coverage available, charging subsidized premium rates for all existing structures and/or their contents, regardless of the flood risk.

FEMA may provide a more detailed Flood Insurance Rate Map (FIRM) indicating flood elevations and flood-hazard zones, including velocity zones (V-zones) for coastal areas where wave action is an additional hazard during flooding. The FIRM identifies Base Flood Elevations (BFEs), establishes special flood-hazard zones, and provides a basis for floodplain management and the establishing of insurance rates.

To enter the regular program phase of the NFIP, the community must adopt and enforce floodplain management ordinances that at least meet the minimum requirements for flood-hazard redution as set by FEMA. The advantage of entering the regular program is that increased insurance coverage is made available, and new development will be more hazard-resistant. All new structures will be rated on an actual risk (actuarial) basis, which may mean higher insurance rates in coastal high-hazard areas but generally results in a savings for development within numbered A-zones (areas flooded in a 100-year coastal flood, but less subject to turbulent wave action).

FEMA maps commonly use the 100-year flood as the BFE to establish regulatory requirements. Persons unfamiliar with hydrologic data sometimes mistakenly take the 100-year flood to mean a flood that occurs once every 100 years. In fact, a flood of this magnitude could occur in successive years, or twice in one year, and so on. The flooding in Jackson, Mississippi, that has occurred over the last few years illustrates this point. If we think of a 100-year flood as a level of flooding having a 1 percent probability of occurring in any given year, then during the life of a house within this zone that has a 30-year mortgage, there is a 30 percent probability that the property will be flooded. The chance of losing your property becomes 1 in 4, rather than 1 in 100. Having flood insurance makes good sense.

In V-zones, new structures will be evaluated on their potential to withstand the impact of wave action, a risk factor over and above the flood elevation. Elevation requirements are adjusted, usually 3 to 6 feet above still-water flood levels, for structures in V-zones to minimize wave damage, and the insurance rates also are higher. When your insurance agent submits an application for a building within a V-zone, an elevation certificate that verifies the post-construction elevation of the first floor of the building must accompany the application.

The insurance rate structure provides incentives of lower rates if buildings are elevated above the minimum federal requirements. General eligibility requirements vary among pole houses, mobile homes, and condominiums. Flood insurance coverage is provided for structural damage as well as contents. Table 5.2 presents Florida's coastal counties that are participating in the National Flood Insurance Program as of August 1981. Almost all coastal communities with barrier beaches are now covered under the regu-

Table 5.2. Flood insurance policies in coastal counties of Florida (as of August 31, 1981)

County	Regular (R) or emergency (E) program	Policies in effect	Dollar value of policies	County	Regular (R) or emergency (E) program	Policies in effect	Dollar value of policies
Counties with barrier islands and beaches				*Counties without barrier islands and beaches*			
Bay	R	4,005	222,805,400	Citrus	E	1,358	47,419,600
Brevard	R	18,294	1,419,068,800	Dixie	E	176	4,284,000
Broward	R	111,354	7,075,675,400	Hernando	E	625	20,663,600
Charlotte	R	8,865	423,679,600	Jefferson	E	12	297,800
Collier	R	13,800	785,170,200	Levy	E	231	7,211,600
Dade	R	95,424	5,130,950,800	Pasco	E	11,576	408,839,800
Duval	R	4,373	319,556,800	Taylor	E	111	3,010,300
Escambia	R	4,495	309,675,500	Subtotal		14,089	$ 491,726,700
Flagler	E	655	23,842,600				
Franklin	E	1,000	36,737,400	*Noncoastal counties*			
Gulf	E	389	11,117,000				
Hillsborough	R	13,447	788,578,800	Subtotal		23,171	$ 1,288,404,000
Indian River	R	4,801	43,623,400				
Lee	R/E	33,608	1,346,771,400	Florida total		531,091	$ 30,563,259,400
Manatee	R	10,549	577,315,000				
Martin	R	5,916	285,064,200	18 Atlantic and Gulf states			
Monroe	R	17,034	789,522,200	coastal counties total		1,164,798	$ 64,668,610,400
Nassau	R/E	753	37,482,800				
Okaloosa	R/E	2,823	228,510,500	All other states total		745,620	$ 33,303,788,600
Palm Beach	R	47,334	3,527,099,000				
Pinellas	R	57,019	3,132,368,200	United States total		1,918,318	$ 97,972,399,000
Santa Rosa	R	1,611	117,517,200				
Sarasota	R	16,467	889,767,600				
St. Johns	R	3,306	220,283,500	Compiled by Dinesh C. Sharma.			
St. Lucie	R/E	6,134	233,698,600	*Source*: Federal Emergency Management Agency, Flood Insurance Administration, Washington, D.C. Personal Communication, October 10, 1981.			
Volusia	R	8,867	622,244,000				
Wakulla	R	352	11,446,400				
Walton	R	1,156	73,556,400				
Subtotal		493,831	$ 28,683,128,700				

lar program. To determine if your community is in the NFIP and for additional information on the insurance, contact your local property agent or call the NFIP's servicing contractor (phone: (800) 638-6620), or the NFIP State Assistance Office at (904) 488-9210. For more information, request a copy of "Questions and Answers on the National Flood Insurance Program" from FEMA (see appendix B under Insurance).

Before buying or building a structure on a barrier beach, an individual should ask certain basic questions:

1. Is the community I'm locating in covered by the emergency or regular phase of the National Flood Insurance Program?
2. Is my building site located in the designated areas of the Coastal Barrier Resources Act, where no federal flood insurance for new structures will be available after October 1, 1983 (see table 5.1)?
3. Is my building site above the 100-year flood level? Is the site located in a V-zone? V-zones are high-hazard areas and pose serious problems.
4. What are the minimum elevation and structural requirements for my building?
5. What are the limits of coverage?

Make sure your community is enforcing the ordinance requiring minimum construction standards and elevations. After Hurricane Frederic (1979) a number of homeowners from Santa Rosa County, whose houses were flooded, put in claims for federal flood insurance. It developed that on direct order from the county com-

missioners the elevation requirements for insurance were not being enforced by the county. One woman who had paid $158 per year for her insurance discovered she should have been paying over $13,000 a year because her house was 5 feet below the 100-year flood level. Prior to construction, her house plans had been approved by the county and no mention was made of the elevation problem. Before payment of her $17,000 claim, the National Flood Insurance Program subtracted her correct $13,000 premium. Later all parties agreed on a lower, but still substantial figure for flood insurance premiums. More than 20 people in the National Flood Insurance Program in the local community were forced to continue paying exorbitant insurance premiums for buildings built below the required elevation because the banks that held their mortgages insisted on it. All of this cost and confusion because county officials said nothing about flood elevations when issuing permits. The then-incumbent county commissioners fared very poorly in the next election!

Most lending institutions and community planning, zoning, and building departments will be aware of the flood insurance regulations and can provide assistance. It would be wise to confirm such information with appropriate insurance representatives. Any authorized insurance agent can write and submit a National Flood Insurance Program policy application. All insurance companies charge the same rates for national flood insurance policies.

The National Flood Insurance Program states its goal as "to . . . encourage state and local governments to make appropriate land use adjustments and to constrict the development of land which is exposed to flood damage and minimize damage caused by flood losses" and "to . . . guide the development of proposed future construction, where practical, away from locations which are threatened by flood hazard." To date, development in the flood-hazard areas continues at a rapid rate.

Revision of minimum flood elevations in the V-zones of coastal counties takes into account the additional hazard of storm waves atop still-water flood levels. Existing FEMA regulations stipulate protection of "dunes and vegetation" in the V-zones, but implementation of this requirement by the local communities has not always been strong. The existing requirements of the NFIP do not address other hazards of "migrating" shorelines, for example, shoreline erosion or shifting of inlets. Thus, buildings may meet the minimum FEMA elevation requirements but at the same time can be located near highly exposed and eroding shorelines. In addition to recognizing the flood hazard, the need exists to incorporate location and structural codes that reflect migrating shorelines, hurricane winds, wave uplift, horizontal pressures, and scouring to minimize the loss of structures as well as the dollars that have supported the insurance program. This is not to say that state and local codes and ordinances have overlooked the latter.

In the past the National Flood Insurance Program has been subsidized and has grown to become a large federal liability. As of August 31, 1981, more than 1.918 *million* flood insurance policies valued at $97.972 *billion* had been sold nationwide. Coastal counties had 1.165 million of these policies valued at $64.667 billion. Florida had more policies and coverage than any other state—531,091 policies valued at $30.563 billion along the coastal coun-

ties with beaches (table 5.2). During 1978–79 the average premium for federal flood insurance policies located in velocity zones was $131 a year. Because of Hurricane Frederic, the average expense and loss per policy was $422, making it a costly subsidy for the nation's taxpayers. Such losses have encouraged the addition of requirements on wave heights to flood elevations and a major revision of the insurance rating system. As a result, insurance rates have been raised significantly.

Recognition of natural hazards and tax subsidy problems provided part of the rationale for Congress to pass the Coastal Barrier Resources Act in 1982. There is an urgent national need to address the problems of developed or developing barrier beaches that were not covered in the act in order to minimize hazards to human lives and loss of property in these areas. Incentive programs to encourage sound land-use planning, limit density of development, improve hurricane evacuation, and allow relocation of damaged structures after hurricanes need to be developed before a disaster hits the coast.

Tarpon Springs on the West Florida coast holds the distinction of having been the first community removed from the NFIP for not abiding by its agreements. Fortunately, the removal was only temporary and the community was reinstated to the program after improving its ordinance language and application forms, stiffening variance procedures, and adding to the staff responsible for administering the program.

Clearly, FEMA is serious about enforcement. If a community is removed from the program, the result is that property owners cannot renew their flood insurance when it expires or buy new policies. Several other communities in Florida are probably in violation of flood insurance requirements and will face loss of insurability if they do not begin to enforce the program's requirements. One of the most common violations that local officials have ignored is the enclosing of ground-level portions of cottages and using them as parts of residences.

There are 2 ways the property owner is likely to get caught if he or she is in violation of the construction requirements. First, FEMA sends out inspectors periodically to see if communities are in compliance. Second, if you file a claim after storm flooding and damage, your property will be inspected. If your structure was in violation of construction requirements, you will be required to pay additional back premiums that could equal and even exceed the amount of the insurance claim. This has happened in Galveston Island, Texas.

Two points are clear. First, the property owner cannot rely solely on the developer, building inspector, or county commissioners to enforce the community ordinances required to qualify for and stay in the NFIP. Second, given the likelihood that developers will be long gone when the question of compliance arises, town and county officials are likely to be held responsible for the inaction in local enforcement and become the defendants in legal actions; that is, elected officials may lose more than the next election for not doing their mandated jobs. In California a group of homeowners who lost their houses in a landslide are suing local officials, claiming they were not warned of the hazard. A homeowner who loses his flood insurance coverage because the developer or community official was irresponsible is likely to take similar action.

Hurricane evacuation

The Disaster Relief Act of 1974 authorized FEMA to establish disaster preparedness plans in cooperation with local communities and states. Hurricane evacuation is a critical problem on barrier islands and coastal floodplains. Due to heavy concentrations of population in areas of low topography, narrow roads, and vulnerable bridges and causeways, plus limited hurricane warning capability (possibly 12 hours or less), it would be impossible to evacuate all of the people prior to hurricanes in many parts of Florida.

Several coastal communities in Florida have formulated detailed hurricane evacuation plans. You should check for hurricane evacuation plans with the county Civil Defense or Disaster Preparedness officer and find out if any potential evacuation problems will exist during a hurricane. They can provide information on the location of hurricane evacuation shelters. These same agencies are responsible for providing emergency and relocation assistance after hurricanes. The Civil Defense office also can provide information on expected losses from hurricanes.

The Florida Coastal Management Program (FCMP)

The Federal Coastal Zone Management Act of 1972 (CZMA) set in motion an effort by most coastal states to manage their shorelines and thereby conserve a vital national resource. Key requirements of the CZMA are coastal land-use planning based on land classification and identification and protection of critical areas. The intentions are to ensure good land use and resource development, conserve resources, and protect the quality of life for citizens of the coastal zone.

While some states passed specific acts to set up state offices of coastal zone management, Florida established a program based on existing state laws. More than 20 statutes serve as the authorities for the Florida Coastal Management Program under the Florida Coastal Management Act of 1978 (Chapter 380, Florida Statutes), which was approved by the federal office of Coastal Zone Management (now the Office of Ocean and Coastal Resource Management) on September 24, 1981. The Department of Environmental Regulation is the designated coastal zone management agency, but it works closely with the Departments of Natural Resources and Community Affairs in implementing the program. The Interagency Management Committee (IMC), consisting of heads of state agencies involved in resource management, was established to solve complex coastal problems through joint efforts between agencies. In addition, the governor's Environment Land Management Study Committee (ELMS) and a legislative Growth Management Committee are reviewing Florida's environmental laws and may suggest legislative or administrative changes that could affect the Florida Coastal Management Program. For specific information, contact the Office of Coastal Zone Management (see appendix B: Coastal Zone Management).

Various aspects of the program are included under the following state programs and acts.

Hazard mitigation

Under the authority of the federal Disaster Relief Act of 1974 (P.L. 93–288) and Florida's Disaster Preparedness Act (Chapter 252, Florida Statutes), as well as other codes, the Bureau of Emergency Management is charged with responsibility for peacetime emergency planning. The purpose of emergency management is to improve public safety by protecting life and property in the event of natural or man-caused hazards. In the coastal zone these hazards include storms, hurricanes, flooding, overwash, shoreline erosion, erosion by shifting streams or channels (avulsion), including inlet migration, dune migration, pollution hazards, and so on (that is, the same hazards on which this book focuses). Hazard mitigation simply means reducing the likelihood of damage from such hazards through actions taken *before* the hazardous process occurs.

According to the state's Comprehensive Emergency Management Plan these are the long-term goals of the state's hazard mitigation effort:

Protection of life and property through the reduction and avoidance of unnecessary and uneconomical uses of hazardous areas.

Preservation and enhancement of beneficial uses of hazard-prone areas.

Protection of natural systems that serve a hazard moderating or mitigation function.

Attention is focused in particular on predictable, recurring hazards, like those noted above, and on seeking nonstructural solutions to hazard mitigation.

The Division of Public Safety Planning and Assistance, Department of Community Affairs, acts as a coordinating agency for developing policy, disseminating information on hazard mitigation, and making recommendations to other units of government. The agency also is responsible for site-specific hazard mitigation studies.

Community officials, planners, and individual property owners in the coastal zone should make use of the services of the Bureau of Emergency Management within the Division of Public Safety and Planning Assistance when evaluating site safety, seeking ways to reduce hazard impact, or planning strategies to meet hazard crises (for example, hurricane warning, evacuation, poststorm recovery).

Florida's Save Our Coast Program

The Coastal Barrier Resources Act of 1982 did not provide any funds for the acquisition of undeveloped barrier islands and beaches for public recreation, habitat protection, or hazard mitigation purposes. In 1981 Florida's governor and cabinet recognized the serious problems associated with the development of barrier islands and beaches such as loss of public access to beaches for recreation, economic losses due to severe erosion and flood dam-

age, logistics for hurricane evacuation, disaster relief assistance costs, and subsidies for infrastructures. As a result, they started programs intended to protect and manage the barrier beaches. Under the $200 million Save Our Coast Program for acquiring undeveloped barrier island and beach properties, the state has a systematic process for the nomination and selection of parcels for purchase. Many of these land parcels are the same as those listed in table 5.1. This new program is in addition to the Conservation and Recreational Land (CARL) Program under which Florida acquires land for public use and recreation.

The governor of Florida signed an executive order to limit the expenditures of state funds for the construction of public infrastructures such as water and sewer systems, roads, bridges, and similar structures in certain hazardous coastal areas. If you plan to acquire or sell properties on a barrier island, it is advisable that you contact the governor's Office of Planning and Budgeting to determine if your property is located in one of the units where the executive order is applicable, or whether the state is interested in acquiring the land under the Save Our Coast Program or the CARL program.

Development of regional impacts

In 1972 the Florida Legislature enacted the Florida Environmental Land and Water Management Act of 1972 (Chapter 380, Florida Statutes) to address the problems of large-scale developments in the state. Under this law "any development because of its character, magnitude or location that would have substantial effect on the health, safety and welfare of citizens of more than one county" is considered a Development of Regional Impact (DRI). Types of projects include, but are not limited to, residential projects, tourist attraction and recreational facilities, shopping centers, office buildings, parks, industrial parks, airports, port facilities, schools, and similar developments.

The procedures and rules pertaining to the determination and review of DRIs are contained in Florida Administrative Code, Rule 9B–16 and Rule 27F–1 Part II. Florida Administrative Code 27F–2 identifies those developments that are specifically presumed to be DRIs. The review and permit process is regulated by the Bureau of Land and Water Management of the Florida Department of Community Affairs (DCA). There are 11 Regional Planning Councils (RPCs) that actually conduct the DRI assessment and review (see appendix B for addresses). We recommend that you contact primarily the Bureau of Land and Water Management and also the appropriate regional planning council to determine if your project is a Development of Regional Impact. Projects located on barrier islands and beaches, around state aquatic preserves, or in environmentally designated areas are given closer scrutiny by the DCA and the RPCs.

Water pollution control and water supply

The Florida Air and Water Pollution Control Act of 1967 and subsequent amendments (Chapter 403, Florida Statutes) govern the discharge and regulation of domestic, municipal, and industrial water pollution. The state law incorporates the requirements of the Federal Water Pollution Control Act Amendments of 1972 and 1977. The Florida Department of Environmental Regulation (DER) has enforcement power over all natural or artificial bodies of water. The state has adopted a comprehensive set of water-quality standards. All waters in the state have been classified into 1 of the 7 classifications for the beneficial use of humans as well as propagation of fish, shellfish, and wildlife.

Water resources are being threatened with pollution, causing economic losses to both local communities and the state. In Florida one-third of all commercial shellfish harvesting areas have been permanently closed due to pollution! Protection of water quality is vital for human as well as other uses. State laws provide additional standards and protection of water quality if the waste disposal affects potable water supply (Class I), shellfish propagation and harvesting waters (Class II), aquatic preserves, or "Outstanding Florida Waters." You need to contact the Department of Environmental Regulation to find out if your property borders on environmentally sensitive waters.

If you plan to locate on a barrier island, check with the local county or city planning and building departments to see if adequate public drinking water supply and sewer hookups are available. In case you plan to build your own sewage disposal facility with a capacity of less than 2,000 gallons per day, your county health department must be contacted for a permit. Minimum standards for septic systems must be met. The first important standard is that the depth to the seasonally high groundwater table must be at least 3.0 feet below the bottom of the drainfield or about 5.0 feet below the ground surface in the wet season. The second important standard is that the drainfield must be set back a minimum of 50 feet from any surface water body. These minimum standards are intended to protect the public health and water quality. For any on-site sewage system or package treatment with a capacity greater than 2,000 gallons per day, contact the Florida DER for rules, regulations and guidelines.

The withdrawal or diversion of drinking water is governed by the Florida Water Resources Act of 1972 (Chapter 373, Florida Statutes). The responsibility for the enforcement of this law rests with the Florida Department of Environmental Regulation, but it is implemented through five water management districts (appendix B). If you obtain your water supply from a public facility or plan to put in a small domestic well, you need no permit from any water management district. However, if you plan to drain the land, divert the water, or put in a large water supply system, contact the appropriate water management district for rules, regulations, and guidelines.

On-site individual sewage disposal facilities

In many instances, development on barrier islands requires individual, on-site sewage disposal and treatment systems when a public sewer system is not available. The installation of on-site septic systems in Florida is regulated by the Department of Health and Rehabilitative Services (DHRS) pursuant to Section 381.272 of Florida Statutes. The local county health departments are responsible for the direct regulation and permitting of these facilities under Rule 10D–6 of Florida Administrative Codes. Rule 10D–6 has specific standards for the capacity of septic tanks, soil types, depth to seasonally high water table, minimum distance from drinking water wells or public water supply, and minimum distance from surface water bodies.

If you plan to install an individual, on-site sewage facility with an estimated daily flow of less than 2,000 gallons for any 1 establishment or structure, you must contact and obtain a permit from your county health department. Subdivisions of 50 or fewer lots, each having a minimum of at least 0.5 acre and a minimum dimension of 100 feet, may be developed with private wells and individual sewage disposal systems, provided satisfactory groundwater can be obtained, and all distance, setback, soil condition, water table elevations, and other requirements of Rule 10D–6 can be met. Residential subdivisions using public water supply systems may be developed with individual sewage disposal facilities for a maximum of 4 lots per acre, provided all other conditions are met.

The installation of septic systems on the highly permeable sandy soils of Florida barrier islands causes pollution of groundwaters as well as surface and estuarine waters. High groundwater tables during wet seasons make the septic systems a health hazard and vulnerable to failures. It is imperative that proliferation of on-site septic systems in highly permeable soils, close to the surface water bodies, and under seasonally high groundwater table conditions, be discouraged to protect public health and water quality.

Dredging and filling

Saltwater and freshwater wetlands are considered extremely valuable natural resources in Florida. Florida legislative goals and policies reflect this concern under Chapter 253 and Chapter 403, Florida Statutes. These policies state in part,

> to prohibit the authorization of the dredging and filling of submerged lands, if such authorization would result in the destruction of resources or interfere with public uses to such an extent as to be contrary to the public interest [and] to prevent and abate pollution and to conserve the waters of the state for the propagation of wildlife, fish and other aquatic life, and for domestic, agricultural, industrial, recreational and other beneficial uses.

To minimize permit problems, delays, and frustrations, we suggest that you do not buy properties located in wetlands of barrier islands and coastal areas.

Barrier islands are characterized by the presence of freshwater and saltwater wetlands. If your plan requires any dredging and / or filling of wetlands or navigable waters, you need to obtain permits from the appropriate state and federal agencies. The dredging and / or filling activity may be associated with the construction of a homesite, access road, boat dock, or erosion control structure. Unauthorized dredging and filling is prohibited and punishable under state and federal laws.

The dredging and filling in Florida waters is governed by Florida Air and Water Pollution Control Act (Chapter 403, Florida Statutes), Florida State Land Trust Fund (Chapter 253, Florida Statutes) and Beach and Shore Preservation Act (Chapter 161, Florida Statutes). State agencies regulating the activities are the Florida DER and the Florida Department of Natural Resources (DNR). Federal laws regulating dredge and fill include the River and Harbor Act of 1899, the Clean Water Act of 1977, and the Marine Protection Research and Sanctuaries Act of 1972. The U.S. Army Corps of Engineers is the federal regulatory agency, while the U.S. Fish and Wildlife Service is another concerned agency. Florida DER and DNR and the Army Corps of Engineers have a joint dredge and fill application to facilitate the permit procedure.

Several local communities in Florida have additional regulations against alteration, cutting, pruning, removal, or destruction of mangrove wetlands. In order to obtain the necessary information on application procedures, regulations, and guidelines, contact local county or city planning and building departments, the Florida Department of Environmental Regulation, or the U.S. Army Corps of Engineers (appendix B). These agencies will assist you in identifying the type and scope of information needed to process your application. There are 2 types of permit applications: short form and regular form, depending upon the size and scope of the project. It should be noted that permit review and approval is more closely scrutinized if a project is located adjacent to Class

I and Class II waters, state aquatic preserves, or "Outstanding Florida Waters."

Local government comprehensive plans

In Florida the Local Government Comprehensive Planning Act of 1975 (Chapter 163, Florida Statutes) mandates that all local governments prepare, adopt, and implement a comprehensive plan that addresses present and future community growth and development needs. The act requires that each unit of local government (county, city, municipality, town, or village) establish a planning process and prepare, adopt, and implement a comprehensive plan. The law requires that the planning process be ongoing, based on effective public participation, and include regular plan review, update, and appraisal. Every community's plan must contain the following required elements: future land-use plan; traffic circulation; sanitary sewer, solid waste, drainage, and potable water supply; conservation; coastal zone (along the coast); recreation and open space; housing; utilities; and intergovernmental relations. For communities in excess of 50,000, 2 additional elements are required: mass transit and port, aviation, and related facilities. The law requires that local governments set forth principles and standards to guide future development. Unfortunately, the law itself does not provide for any minimum standards or enforcement procedures, particularly in regard to the coastal zone.

Almost all of the counties and municipalities in Florida have adopted comprehensive plans. Many of these local plans are quite detailed with specific provisions for the use of beaches, dunes, marshes, bays, barrier islands, and coastal wetlands.

If you plan to buy property or build in the coastal areas of barrier islands, we suggest that you contact your local planning, zoning, and building departments. Their offices are generally located in or near the county courthouse or the city hall. You need to obtain the necessary zoning, subdivision, or building permits from the local government. These agencies will assist you in determining which kinds of development activities are permitted and which are not. The early contact with the local planning or building departments will enable you to find out which, if any, state and federal permits will be necessary for your project.

Coastal construction permits

The low-lying barrier beaches and coastlines of Florida render coastal construction a matter of particular concern to the state and to local communities. The Florida legislature addressed this concern by enacting the Beach and Shore Preservation Act (Chapter 161, Florida Statutes). The requirements and constraints of this law are in addition to those dealing with water-quality control and dredging and filling laws explained earlier. In 1971 the legislature established a goal that stated in part, "The Legislature finds and declares that the beaches of the State, by their nature, are subject to frequent and severe fluctuations and represent one of Florida's most valuable natural resources and that it is in the public interest to preserve and protect them from imprudent construction which can jeopardize the stability of beach-dune system. . . ."

The legislature directed the Florida Department of Natural Resources, Division of Beaches and Shores, to establish Coastal Construction Setback Lines (CCSBLs) that were replaced by Coastal Construction Control Lines (CCCLs) in 1978. The CCCLs are established under Legislative mandate "so as to define that portion of the beach-dune system which is subject to severe fluctuations based on a 100-year storm surge or other predictable weather conditions, and so as to define the area within which special structural design consideration is required to insure protection of beach-dune system, any proposed structure and adjacent properties, rather than to define a seaward limit for upland structure."

The intent of the law is to regulate coastal construction, to establish coastal construction control lines along the sandy beaches, seaward of which construction may not occur without an authorized permit from the DNR, and to administer a beach erosion control grants-in-aid program. The Florida DNR has established a coastal construction control line for each coastal county with sandy beaches fronting the Atlantic or Gulf after conducting a comprehensive study of the areas' coastal resources and processes. Coastal construction is undertaken pursuant to a CCCL permit. The 2 separate permit programs are described in the next few paragraphs.

Coastal Construction Permits (Chapter 161.041, Florida Statutes). The DNR coastal construction permits are required for any construction or change of existing structures and construction or physical activity undertaken for shore protection or erosion control

purposes if that activity is located below the mean high-water line of any tidal water of the state.

Specifically included are such structures as dune walkovers, groins, jetties, moles, breakwaters, seawalls, bulkheads, and revetments. Physical activities, such as artificial beach nourishment, inlet sediment bypassing, excavation or maintenance dredging on inlet channels, and deposition or removal of beach material also require a permit.

Coastal Construction Control Line Permit (Chapter 161.053, Florida Statutes). If any structure is located seaward of the CCCL (or CCSBL) on any sandy shoreline fronting the Gulf of Mexico or the Atlantic Ocean, permits are required from the DNR before undertaking any alteration. Among the activities covered are excavation and construction of any dwelling house, hotel, motel, apartment, condominium, seawall, revetment, pool, patio, garage, parking lot, minor structure, and dune restoration. Driving of motorized vehicles or removal of sea oats on the beaches and dunes seaward of the control line also is prohibited except in 3 Atlantic coastal counties. There are certain counties without sandy beaches, and certain types of structures that are exempt from the law. In order to determine if you need any DNR permit, contact the Division of Beaches and Shores, Department of Natural Resources (appendix B).

In 2 cases (Lee and Pinellas counties) the DNR has delegated authority to the coastal counties and municipalities to administer the CCCL requirement. If you plan to buy or build on the oceanfront it is advisable to check with the county or municipality if your property is located seaward of the CCCL because these areas are extremely hazardous, often unsuitable for permanent structures, and create serious environmental and economic problems for property owners as well as taxpayers.

State Land Lease Permit (Chapter 253, Florida Statutes). If your project involves use of sovereign (state-owned) submerged lands in Florida, you need to obtain appropriate permits from the Bureau of State Lands Management of the Florida Department of Natural Resources (appendix B) pursuant to Chapter 253.77 of the Florida Statutes. Sovereignty lands include tidal lands, islands, sand bars, and lands under navigable waters, whether fresh- or saltwater, which Florida gained title to when it became a state. Generally, permits are more closely scrutinized if the project is in a state aquatic preserve, manatee sanctuary, or other environmentally designated sensitive areas. The rules and regulations for the issuance of permits are contained in the Florida Administrative Code Rule 160-21 (Sovereignty Submerged Lands Management Rule), Rule 160-18 (Biscayne Bay Aquatic Preserves Rule), and Rule 160-21 (Florida Aquatic Preserve Rules).

The most common activities included under this permit program are docks for private and commercial use, reclamation of land lost by erosion or avulsion, and dredging of navigation channels. Certain noncommercial activities that are not located within state aquatic preserves or specially designated manatee areas are exempt from any requirements to make application for consent of use. In general, if you suspect that your proposed construction activity might involve use of state-owned lands, we recommend that you contact the Bureau of State Lands Management to determine whether or not you need a permit from the bureau or other state agencies.

Building codes

For residential dwellings other than mobile homes, Florida requires all communities to adopt 1 of 5 acceptable building codes (Chapter 553, Part VI, Florida Statutes), including the One and Two Family Dwelling Code (after the CABO, Council of American Building Officials), the Standard Building Code, the South Florida Building Code, the National Building Code, and the EPCOT Building Code. Of these the National Building Code is used in Duval County, the South Florida Building Code is used in Dade and Broward counties, and the Standard Building Code is widely used in the remaining coastal counties.

As examples, the Standard Building Code (formerly the Southern Standard Building Code; reference 81, appendix C) and the South Florida Building Code were compiled by knowledgeable engineers, architects, and code enforcement officials to regulate the design and construction of buildings and the quality of building materials. These codes do have certain hurricane resistance requirements, such as continuity, stability, and anchorage, all related to calculated reference wind speed as modified by height above ground and building shape factors to determine design load.

It is emphasized that the purpose of these codes is to provide *minimum* standards to safeguard lives, health, and property. Communities have the right to strengthen the adopted code in order to improve it or to make it more stringent. By law, such improvements in a code cannot discriminate against materials, products, or construction techniques of proven capabilities; and there must be some unique physiographic condition (for example, geographic type or location, topographic features or absence thereof) that warrants the more stringent requirements. All barrier islands and beaches facing the open ocean and the threat of hurricanes should meet the latter requirement. As a result, numerous communities do have specifications that go beyond the Standard Building Code. The Florida Department of Natural Resources has made recommendations for a Coastal Construction Building Code (reference 81, appendix C) to supplement existing codes. Check with your local building inspector to determine the specific code for your area.

Individuals can and should insist on designs and materials that go beyond the *minimum* code requirements (see chapter 6 on construction). Sanibel Island has adopted one of the better codes in Florida with respect to coastal construction. You might contact Sanibel's building inspector's office for a copy of their code to see examples of performance-oriented criteria and coastal issues treated in greater depth. The State Division of Beaches and Shores also provides coastal construction guidelines and may be consulted for advice.

Persons concerned with planning and improving existing building codes should contact the Department of Community Affairs (appendix B). Their Bureau of Emergency Management offers the free publication "Hazard Mitigation through Building Codes."

Mobile home regulations

Mobile homes differ in construction and anchorage from "permanent" structures. The design, shape, lightweight construction materials, and other characteristics required for mobility, or for staying within axle-weight limits, create a unique set of potential problems for residents of these dwellings. Because of their thinner walls, for example, mobile homes are more vulnerable to wind and wind-borne projectiles.

Some coastal states have code requirements for mobile homes that are specific for units locating in hurricane-prone areas. Florida does not, although mobile home construction must meet national code requirements. Regulation is through the Department of Highway Safety and Motor Vehicles.

Mobile home anchorage tiedowns are required throughout Florida. Tiedowns make the structure more stable against wind stress (for recommendations, see the section on mobile homes in chapter 6). Older metal tiedowns may be weakened through corrosion, or violations of anchorage or foundation regulations may go undetected unless there are a sufficient number of conscientious inspectors to monitor trailers. One poorly anchored mobile home can wreak havoc with adjacent homes whose owners abided by sound construction practice. Some mobile home park operators or managers are alert to such problems and see that they are corrected; others simply collect the rent.

The spacing of mobile homes should be regulated by local ordinance. Providing residents with open space between homes, this type of ordinance preserves some aesthetic value for a neighborhood. It also helps to maintain a healthier environment. For example, if mobile home septic tanks are closely spaced, there is the potential for groundwater or surface water pollution. Similarly, if mobile homes are built too closely to finger canals, canal water may become polluted.

Prefabricated structure regulation

Modular unit construction is one of the new approaches to construction of multiple-dwelling structures in the coastal zone (see the section on modular unit construction in chapter 6). These prefabricated units are assembled at the shore as multiplexes and condominiums, commonly 2 to 4 stories in height. The Department of Community Affairs sets the building code standards for all prefabricated buildings, including modular unit dwellings. The department follows standard requirements that include wind design speeds of up to 130 mph in some coastal areas.

All such structures must meet the inspection of an independent, third-party testing architect or engineer who signs the structure off if it meets state requirements. The Department of Community Affairs not only approves the plans for such structures but assigns an insignia when the inspection is approved. It is the local building inspector's responsibility, however, to check for the state insignia as well as making sure that service hookups for the buildings meet the local building code.

Historic and archeologic sites

It is the public policy of the state of Florida to protect and preserve historic sites and properties, artifacts, treasure troves, fossil deposits, prehistoric Indian habitations, and objects of antiquity that have historical values or are of interest to the public. The Florida Archives and History Act of 1966 provides the authority to implement these laws through the Division of Archives, History and Records Management in the Florida Department of State (appendix B).

Barrier beaches and coastal areas of Florida have been sites of historic exploration and early native Indian settlements. If you find that there are objects, sites, or structures of some historic archeologic or architectural value on your property, contact the Bureau of Historic Sites for technical assistance to preserve and protect them.

Endangered fish and wildlife species

Florida's environment is blessed with diverse ecosystems that provide habitats for hundreds of common, endangered, and threatened species of fish and wildlife. The protection of wildlife species and habitat is administered by 2 state agencies: the Game and Fresh Water Fish Commission (GFWFC) and the Department of Natural Resources. The state's enabling laws are the Florida Panther Act of 1978, Florida Manatee Sanctuary Act of 1979, and Feeding of Alligator and Crocodile Act. These state laws provide the protection of particular species of wildlife. Additional protection to endangered and threatened fish and wildlife species is provided by the Federal Endangered Species Act of 1973 and Marine Mammal Protection Act of 1972. The U.S. Fish and Wildlife Service of the U.S. Department of the Interior protects the species listed in the law and regulations.

Barrier islands and beaches are habitats for many endangered and threatened fish and wildlife species. The Florida GFWFC and U.S. Fish and Wildlife Service classify endangered and threatened species into three categories:

Endangered. A species, subspecies, or isolated population that is, or soon may be, in immediate danger of extinction unless the species habitat is fully protected and managed for its survival. The American bald eagle, Atlantic green turtle, Florida panther, and West Indian manatee are some examples.

Threatened. A species, subspecies, or isolated population that is very likely to become endangered soon unless the species or its habitat is fully protected and managed for survival. Some examples of this group are loggerhead sea turtle, eastern indigo snake, brown pelican, and mangrove fox squirrel.

Species of special concern. A species, subspecies, or isolated population that warrants special protection because (1) it may,

due to pending environmental degradation or human disturbance, become threatened unless protective management strategies are employed, (2) its status cannot be classified as threatened until more information is available, (3) it occupies such an essential ecological position that its decline might adversely affect associated species, or (4) it has not recovered sufficiently from a past decline or disturbance. Examples in this category include the American alligator, gopher tortoise, roseate spoonbill, limpkin, pine barrens, treefrog, and beach cotton mouse.

The Florida Game and Fresh Water Fish Commission and the U.S. Fish and Wildlife Service (appendix B) provide technical assistance and coordination to identify endangered and threatened species via the development permit review process. Appendix B provides the legal status of endangered and potentially endangered species in Florida as of July 1982.

Other regulations. In addition to the statutes and regulatory requirements outlined above, the attention of state law also has focused on defining ownership of coastal-zone lands (uplands, tidelands, submerged lands). Title to coastal lands is always more complex than for inland property because of the rapid changes due to submergence, erosion, accretion, or shifting of waterways. When purchasing coastal property, make sure you know exactly what you are gaining title to in terms of private ownership.

Florida's coastal future: more regulation

A drive along Florida's East coast will reveal to even the casual observer that federal, state, and local regulations have not stopped development in coastal high-hazard zones. Such statutes have not halted the addition of engineering structures that ultimately destroy natural protective beach dune systems.

Present and future citizens of coastal communities should *not* assume that existing statutes and ordinances will guarantee their safety, that of their property, or protect existing beaches and dunes. Existing regulations address but do not solve the problems of living in the coastal zone.

Most regulations do not prohibit development in high-hazard zones; they only set limits. The national Coastal Barrier Resources Act may deny flood insurance and federal funds for development of certain barrier islands, but it does not necessarily prohibit such development. The National Flood Insurance Program establishes a minimum standard for structural elevation in a flood zone to qualify for flood insurance, but generally it does not prohibit locating in such a flood zone. Similarly, state and local building codes set minimum standards.

Florida's Beach and Shore Preservation Act is an innovative law, establishing the Coastal Construction Control Line (CCCL); but this line is one of the state permitting jurisdiction, not prohibition. Special structural design may be required for proposed structures beyond the line to protect the structure from hazards and to protect adjacent properties as well as the beach dune system. Variances are given, and therein lies the problem. The delicate balance of providing for beach and dune protection while assuring the reasonable use of private property is difficult to achieve. "Reasonable" may be viewed differently between the property owner and the state; but when construction does take place seaward of

the control line the impact is likely to be that of the pre-CCCL past, that is, ultimate loss of beach and dunes.

Most of the 250 miles of beaches in Florida that are experiencing "critical erosion" had structures placed too close to the water. As a result, many coastal communities in the state are seeking state and federally subsidized beach nourishment projects to protect the threatened properties. These "protective" projects are extremely costly to general taxpayers as well as to property owners, and are only *temporary* in nature. An effective CCCL program should limit the growth of such problems in the future, given *strict* interpretation and enforcement. Keep in mind also that there are no setback requirements for any structures located on nonsandy shorelines of the tidal areas. As explained in chapter 2, such areas also are experiencing significant erosion due to the sea-level rise and drowning of the coastline.

Likewise, the Local Government Comprehensive Planning Act may require planning by local governments, but if this planning takes place without minimum standards or within a system void of land-use planning and zoning that is sensitive to fragile coastal environments and high-energy coastal processes, then it provides no security for the coastal citizen. Even the best of plans is meaningless if there are no provisions and resources for enforcement.

In some respects the approach to coastal regulation is like that of traffic control at a dangerous intersection. The general rules of the road (not to develop in a hazardous zone) are ignored by some drivers, creating unsafe conditions for all (loss of beaches and dunes in front of formerly low-hazard zones). Accidents (property losses) result. Automobile insurance (national flood insurance) spreads the cost to all drivers, recovers a portion of the loss to the victims, but does not make a broken leg whole again or take away paralysis. A group of concerned citizens requests a stoplight (prohibition of unsafe development), but another group believes that a stoplight will back up traffic, slow things down, hurt business (cool the hot economic climate of coastal development). A compromise is reached—the speed limit is reduced (first set of ordinances), but accidents continue to occur (growing property/beach loss), so a blinker light is installed (additional statutes and ordinances). The rules of the road are still being violated (and nature is still gnawing at the shore). Finally a fatal accident occurs; perhaps someone whom all of the community knew and loved is killed (a hurricane strikes, wiping out a community with loss of lives as well as property). Everyone cries, "There should have been a stoplight at that intersection five years ago" (additional legislation is still needed). Perhaps 1 or 2 years will go by while surveys are done; and perhaps another fatal accident or accidents will occur. Eventually there will be a stoplight, but the dead will remain dead.

Although Florida has pioneered the enactment of far-reaching coastal legislation, problems remain. The growth in both tourism and coastal development will increase the likelihood of possible conflict between public access rights and private littoral rights. Florida does not have a mechanism for guaranteeing public beach access, although below the high-water line is state land and in the public domain. New laws or changes in existing regulations should be expected. Similarly, building codes, setback lines, and other minimum protective regulations are likely to be more strictly enforced and stiffened as we experience loss of life, property, and shoreline due to imprudent development. In 1983 a barrier island building code was introduced into the Florida legislature. Although the bill was not passed, similar legislation may be forthcoming. Coastal dwellers should expect future changes in laws and regulations, just as they should expect future changes in the beaches and dunes.

6. Building or buying a house near the beach

In reading this book you may conclude that the authors seem to be at cross-purposes. On the one hand, we point out that building on the coast is risky. On the other hand, we provide you with a guide to evaluate the risks, and in this chapter we describe how best to buy or build a house near the beach.

This apparent contradiction is more rational than it might seem at first. For those who will heed the warning, we describe the risks of owning shorefront property. But we realize that coastal development will continue as some individuals will always be willing to gamble with their fortunes to be near the shore. For those who elect to play this game of real estate roulette, we provide some advice on improving the odds, on reducing (not eliminating) the risks. We do not recommend, however, that you play the game!

If you want to learn more about construction near the beach, we recommend the book *Coastal Design: A Guide for Builders, Planners, and Home Owners* (New York: Van Nostrand Reinhold, 1983), which gives more detail on coastal construction and may be used to supplement this volume. In addition, the Federal Emergency Management Agency's *Design and Construction Manual for Residential Buildings in Coastal High Hazard Areas* is an informative manual for coastal construction that contains much reference material. Also the Florida Department of Natural Resources' *Coastal Construction Building Code Guidelines* when combined with the South Florida or Standard (Southern Stan-

dard) Building Code make outstanding guides for the construction of residential and commercial structures. The DNR publication also has a comprehensive bibliography.

Coastal realty versus coastal reality

Coastal property is not the same as inland property. Do not approach it as if you were buying a lot in a developed part of the mainland or a subdivided farm field in the coastal plain. The previous chapters illustrate that the shores of Florida, especially the barrier islands, are composed of variable environments and are subjected to nature's most powerful and persistent forces. The reality of the coast is its dynamic character. Property lines are an artificial grid superimposed on this dynamism. If you choose to place yourself or others in this zone, prudence is in order.

A quick glance at the architecture of the structures on the Florida coast provides convincing evidence that the reality of coastal processes was rarely considered in their construction. Not too many years back, old-timers wisely lived behind the protection of sand dunes; only recently have city-bred, over-civilized people built in front of dunes to better see the storm come in. Except for meeting minimal building code requirements, no further thought seems to have been given to the safety of many of these buildings. The failure to follow a few basic architectural guidelines that recognize this reality will have disastrous results in the next major storm.

Life's important decisions are based on an evaluation of the facts. Few of us buy goods, choose a career, take legal, financial, or medical actions without first evaluating the facts and seeking advice. In the case of coastal property, two general areas should be considered: site safety and the integrity of the structure relative to the forces to which it will be subjected.

A guide to evaluating the site(s) of your interest on the East Florida open ocean shoreline is presented in chapter 4, along with hazard evaluation maps.

The structure: concept of balanced risk

A certain chance of failure for any structure exists within the constraints of economy and environment. The objective of building design is to create a structure that is both economically feasible and functionally reliable. A house must be affordable and have a reasonable life expectancy free of being damaged, destroyed, or wearing out. In order to obtain such a house, a balance must be achieved among financial, structural, environmental, and other special conditions. Most of these conditions are heightened on the coast—property values are higher, there is a greater desire for aesthetics, the environment is more sensitive, the likelihood of storms is greater, and there are more hazards with which to deal.

The individual who builds or buys a home in an exposed area should fully comprehend the risks involved and the chance of harm to home or family. The risks should then be weighed against the benefits to be derived from the residence. Similarly, the developer who is putting up a motel should weigh the possibility of destruction and death during a hurricane versus the money and other advantages to be gained from such a building. Then and only then should construction proceed. For both the homeowner and the developer, proper construction and location reduce the risks involved.

The concept of balanced risk should take into account the following fundamental considerations:

1. A coastal structure, exposed to high winds, waves, or flooding, should be stronger than a structure built inland.
2. A building with high occupancy, such as an apartment building, should be safer than a building with low occupancy, such as a single-family dwelling.
3. A building that houses elderly or sick people should be safer than a building housing able-bodied people.
4. Because construction must be economically feasible, ultimate and total safety is not obtainable for most homeowners on the coast.
5. A building with a planned long life, such as a year-round residence, should be stronger than a building with a planned short life, such as a mobile home.

Structures can be designed and built to resist all but the largest storms and still be within reasonable economic limits.

Structural engineering is the designing and constructing of

buildings to withstand the forces of nature. It is based on a knowledge of the forces to which the structures will be subjected and an understanding of the strength of building materials. The effectiveness of structural engineering design was reflected in the aftermath of Typhoon Tracy that struck Darwin, Australia, in 1974: 70 percent of housing that was not based on structural engineering principles was destroyed and 20 percent was seriously damaged; only 10 percent of the housing weathered the storm. In contrast, more than 70 percent of the structurally engineered large commercial, government, and industrial buildings came through with little or no damage, and less than 5 percent of such structures were destroyed. Because housing accounts for more than half of the capital cost of the buildings in Queensland, the state government established a building code that requires standardized structural engineering for houses in hurricane-prone areas. This improvement has been achieved with little increase in construction and design costs.

Coastal forces: design requirements

Hurricanes, with their associated high winds and storm surge topped by large waves are the most destructive of the forces to be reckoned with on the coast. Figure 6.1 illustrates the effects of hurricane forces on houses and other structures.

Hurricane winds

Estimates of wind velocity to be used in designing structures along the Florida coast vary somewhat with the building codes. The South Florida Building Code specifies a wind velocity of 120 mph at a height of 30 feet above the ground. The Standard Building Code uses a map to indicate the maximum wind velocity for a given location. It shows winds from 110 to 130 mph along the Florida coast. (The city of Sanibel specifies 130 mph in its code.) Florida's *Coastal Construction Building Code Guidelines* states that "for habitable structures within the coastal construction building zone, the design wind velocity for load computations shall be a minimum of 140 m.p.h at a height of 30 feet above the ground."

The velocity of the wind can be evaluated in terms of the pressure exerted. The pressure varies with the square of the velocity, the height above the ground, and the shape of the object against which it is blowing. A 140-mph wind will exert a pressure about twice that of a 100-mph wind (as $[140/100]^2 = 1.96$). The above-mentioned *Guidelines* offers a table that we quote in part.

Height above ground (in feet)	Minimum velocity pressure (in pounds per square foot)
0 to 5	30
25 to 35	50
100 to 150	75
over 1000	135

The above pressures must be multiplied by shape factors to be obtained from either the South Florida Building Code or the Standard Building Code, whichever applies to your locality.

As an example, the Standard Building Code gives a shape factor of 1.4 for a flat vertical surface, such as a sign. This means that a

WIND

Wind direction ⇨

Pressure

Pressure

Suction

Suction

Arrows show direction of forces on house.

DROP IN BAROMETRIC PRESSURE

Low pressure outside

Normal high pressure inside house

The passing eye of the storm creates different pressure inside and out, and high pressure inside attempts to burst house open.

WAVES

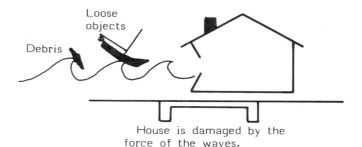

Debris

Loose objects

House is damaged by the force of the waves.

HIGH WATER

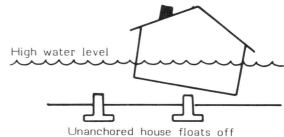

High water level

Unanchored house floats off its foundation.

Fig. 6.1. Forces to be reckoned with at the shoreline.

140-mph wind at 30 feet would exert a pressure of $1.4 \times 50 = 70$ psf against the flat surface instead of the basic 50 psf listed in the table. The effective pressure on a curved surface such as a sphere or a cylinder is less than on a flat surface.

Wind velocity increases with height above ground, so a tall structure is subject to greater velocity and thereby greater pressure than a low structure.

A house or building designed for inland areas is built primarily to resist vertical loads. It is assumed that the foundation and framing must support the load of the walls, floor, roof, and furniture with relatively insignificant wind forces.

A well-built house in a hurricane-prone area, however, must be constructed to withstand a variety of strong wind forces that may come from any direction. Although many people think that wind damage is caused by uniform horizontal pressures (lateral loads), most damage, in fact, is caused by uplift (vertical), suctional (pressure-outward from the house), and twisting (torsional) forces. High horizontal pressure on the windward side is accompanied by suction on the leeward side. The roof is subject to downward pressure and, more importantly, to uplift. Often a roof is sucked up by the uplift drag of the wind. Usually the failure of houses is in the devices that tie the parts of the structure together. All structural members (beams, rafters, columns) should be fastened together on the assumption that about 25 percent of the vertical load on the member may be a force coming from any direction (sideways or upward). Such structural integrity is also important if it is likely that the structure may be moved to avoid destruction by shoreline retreat.

Storm surge

Storm surge is a rise in sea level above the normal water level during a storm. During hurricanes the coastal zone is inundated by storm surge and accompanying storm waves, and these cause most property damage and loss of life.

Often the pressure of the wind backs water into streams or estuaries already swollen from the exceptional rainfall brought on by the hurricane. Water is piled into the bays between islands and the mainland by the offshore storm. In some cases the direction of flooding may be from the bay side of the island. This flooding is particularly dangerous when the wind pressure keeps the tide from running out of inlets, so that the next normal high tide pushes the accumulated waters back and higher still.

Flooding can cause an unanchored house to float off its foundation and come to rest against another house, severely damaging both. Disaster preparedness officials have pointed out that it is a sad fact that even many condominiums built on pilings are not anchored or tied to those pilings, just set on top. Even if the house itself is left structurally intact, flooding may destroy its contents. People who have cleaned the mud and contents of a house subjected to flooding retain vivid memories of its effects.

Proper coastal development takes into account the expected level and frequency of storm surge for the area. In general, building standards require that the first habitable floor of the dwelling be above the 100-year flood level plus an allowance for wave height. At this level a building has a 1 percent probability of being flooded in any given year.

Hurricane waves

Hurricane waves can cause severe damage not only in forcing water onshore to flood buildings but also in throwing boats, barges, piers, houses, and other floating debris inland against standing structures. The force of a wave may be understood when one considers that a cubic yard of water weighs over three-fourths of a ton: hence, a breaking wave moving shoreward at a speed of several tens of miles per hour can be one of the most destructive elements of a hurricane. Waves also can destroy coastal structures by scouring away the underlying sand, causing them to collapse. It is possible to design buildings to survive crashing storm surf as many lighthouses, for example, have survived this. But in the balanced-risk equation, it usually is not economically feasible to build ordinary cottages to resist the more powerful of such forces. On the other hand, cottages can be made considerably more storm-worthy by following the suggestions in the rest of this chapter.

Barometric pressure change

Changes in barometric pressure also may be a minor contributor to structural failure. If a house is sealed at a normal barometric pressure of 30 inches of mercury, and the external pressure suddenly drops to 26.61 inches of mercury (as it did in Hurricane Camille in Mississippi in 1969), the pressure exerted within the house would be 245 pounds per square foot. An ordinary house would explode if it were leakproof. In tornadoes, where there is a severe pressure differential, many houses do burst. In hurricanes the problem is much less severe. Fortunately, most houses leak, but they must leak fast enough to prevent damage. Given the more destructive forces of hurricane wind and waves, pressure differential may be of minor concern. Venting the underside of the roof at the eaves is a common means of equalizing internal and external pressure.

Figure 6.2 illustrates some of the actions that a homeowner can take to deal with the forces just described.

House selection

Some types of houses are better than others at the shore, and an awareness of the differences will help you make a better selection, whether you are building a new house or buying an existing one.

Worst of all are unreinforced masonry houses, whether they are brick, concrete block, hollow clay-tile, or brick veneer, because they cannot withstand the lateral forces of wind and wave and the settling of the foundation. Adequate and extraordinary reinforcing in coastal regions will alleviate the inherent weakness of unit masonry, if done properly. Reinforced concrete and steel frames are excellent but are rarely used in the construction of small, residential structures.

It is hard to beat a wood-frame house that is properly braced and anchored and has well-connected members. The well-built wood house will often hold together as a unit, even if moved off its foundations, when other types disintegrate. Although all of the structural types noted above are found in the coastal zone, newer structures tend to be of the elevated wood-frame type.

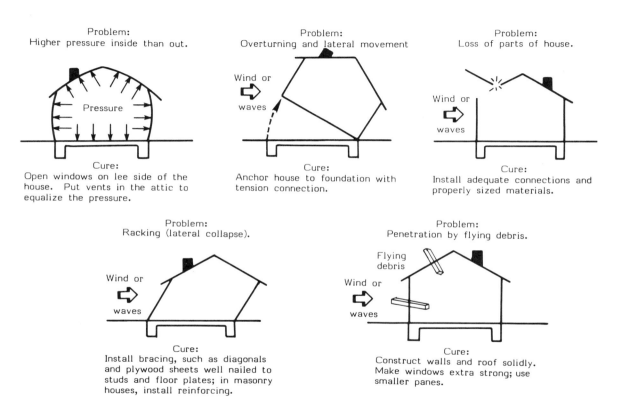

Fig. 6.2. Modes of failure and how to deal with them. Modified from U.S. Civil Defense Preparedness Agency Publication TR-83.

Keeping dry: pole or "stilt" houses

In coastal regions subject to flooding by waves or storm surge, the best and most common method of minimizing damage is to raise the lowest floor of a residence above the expected level. Also, the first habitable floor of a home must be above the 100-year storm-surge level (plus calculated wave height) to qualify for federal flood insurance. As a result, most modern flood-zone structures should be constructed on piling, well anchored in the subsoil. Elevating the structure by building a mound is not suited to the coastal zone because mounded soil is easily eroded.

Current building design criteria for pole-house construction under the flood insurance program are outlined in the book *Elevated Residential Structures*. Regardless of insurance, pole-type construction with deep embedment of the poles is best in areas where waves and storm surge will erode foundation material. Materials used in pole construction include the following:

Piles. These are long, slender columns of wood, steel, or concrete driven into the earth to a sufficient depth to support the vertical load of the house and to withstand horizontal forces of flowing water, wind, and water-borne debris. Pile construction is especially suitable in areas where scouring (soil "washing out" from under the foundation of a house) is a problem.

Posts. Usually posts are made of wood; if of steel, they are called columns. Unlike piles, they are not driven into the ground, but rather are placed in a pre-dug hole at the bottom of which may be a concrete pad (fig. 6.3). Posts may be held in place by backfilling and tamping earth, or by pouring concrete into the

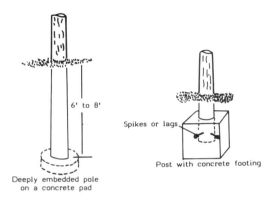

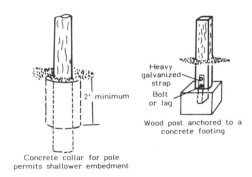

Fig. 6.3. Shallow and deep supports for poles and posts. Source: Southern Pine Association.

hole after the post is in place. Posts are more readily aligned than driven piles and are, therefore, better to use if poles must extend to the roof. In general, treated wood is the cheapest and most common material for both posts and piles.

Piers. These are vertical supports, thicker than piles or posts, usually made of reinforced concrete or reinforced masonry (concrete blocks or bricks). They are set on footings and extend to the underside of the floor frame.

Pole construction can be of two types. The poles can be cut off at the first-floor level to support the platform that serves as the dwelling floor. In this case, piles, posts, or piers can be used. Or they can be extended to the roof and rigidly tied into both the floor and the roof. In this way they become major framing members for the structure and provide better anchorage to the house as a whole (figs. 6.4 and 6.5). A combination of full- and floor-height poles is used in some cases, with the shorter poles restricted to supporting the floor inside the house (fig. 6.6).

Where the foundation material can be eroded by waves or winds, the poles should be deeply embedded and solidly anchored either by driving piles or by drilling deep holes for posts and putting in a concrete pad at the bottom of each hole. Where the embedment is shallow, a concrete collar around the poles improves anchorage (fig. 6.3). The choice depends on the soil conditions. Piles are more difficult than posts to align to match the house frame, as posts can be positioned in the holes before backfilling. Inadequate piling depths, improper piling-to-floor connections, and inadequate pile bracing all contribute to structural failure when storm waves liquify and erode sand support. Just as important as driving the

Fig. 6.4. Pole house, with poles extending to the roof. Extending poles to the roof, as shown in this photograph, instead of the usual method of cutting them off at the first floor, greatly strengthens a beach cottage. Photo by Orrin Pilkey, Jr.

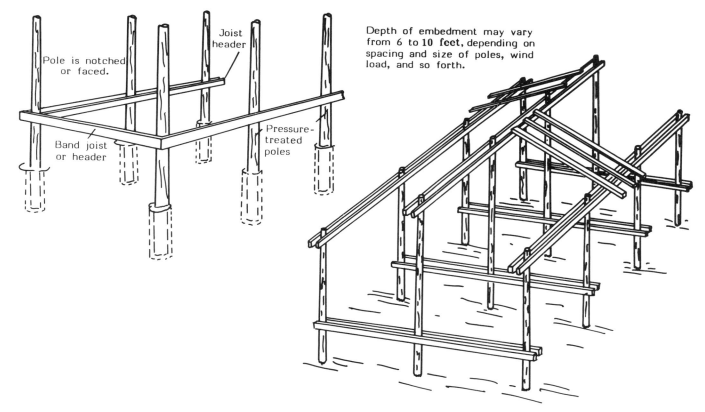

Fig. 6.5. Framing system for an elevated house. Source: Southern Pine Association.

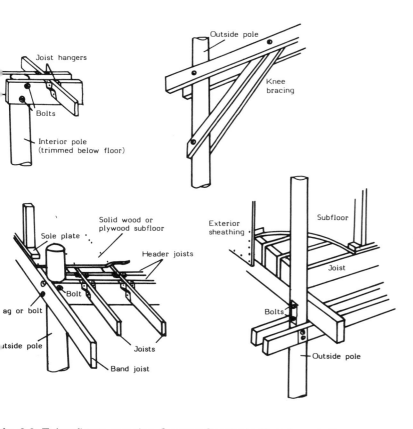

ig. 6.6. Tying floors to poles. Source: Southern Pine Association.

piling deep enough to resist scouring and to support the loads they must carry is the need to fasten them securely to the structure they support above them. Unfortunately, many buildings on Florida's beaches according to local disaster officials are not so anchored. The connections must resist both horizontal loads from wind and wave during a storm and uplift from the same source.

When post holes are dug, rather than pilings driven, the posts should extend 4 to 8 feet into the ground to provide anchorage. The lower end of the post should rest on a concrete pad, spreading the load to the soil over a greater area to prevent settlement. Where the soil is sandy or is the type that the embedment can be less than, say, 6 feet, it is best to tie the post down to the footing with straps or other anchoring devices to prevent uplift. Driven piles should have a minimum penetration of 8 feet. However, most soils require greater embedment, as may code requirements for a specific situation. If the site is near the water, greater embedment is needed.

The floor and the roof should be securely connected to the poles with bolts or other fasteners. When the floor rests on poles that do not extend to the roof, attachment is even more critical. A system of metal straps is often used. Unfortunately, it sometimes happens that builders inadequately attach the girders, beams, and joists to the supporting poles by too few and undersized bolts. Hurricanes have proven this to be insufficient. During the next hurricane on the East Florida coast, many houses and condominiums will be destroyed because of inadequate attachment.

Local building codes may specify the size, quality, and spacing of the piles, ties, and bracing, as well as the methods of fastening the structure to them. Building codes often are minimal requirements, however, and building inspectors are usually amenable to allowing designs that are equally or more effective.

The space under an elevated house, whether pole-type or otherwise, must be kept free of obstructions in order to minimize the impact of waves and floating debris. If the space is enclosed, the enclosing walls should be designed so that they can break away or fall under flood loads, but also remain attached to the house or be heavy enough to sink. Thus, the walls cannot float away and add to the water-borne debris problem. Alternative ways of avoiding this problem are designing walls that can be swung up out of the path of the floodwaters, or building them with louvers that allow the water to pass through. The louvered wall is subject to damage from floating debris. The convenience of closing in the ground floor for a garage, storage area, or recreation room may be costly because it may violate insurance requirements and actually contribute to the loss of the house in a hurricane. The design of the enclosing breakaway walls should be checked against insurance requirements. See *Elevated Residential Structures* by the Federal Insurance Administration, Department of Housing and Urban Development, 451 Seventh Street, S.W., Washington, DC 20410, for more information.

An existing house: what to look for, what to improve

If instead of building a new house, you are selecting a house already built in an area subject to flooding and high winds, consider the following factors: (1) where the house is located; (2) how well the house is built; and (3) how the house can be improved.

Geographic location

Evaluate the site of an existing house using the same principles given earlier for the evaluation of a possible site to build a new house. House elevation, frequency of high water, escape route, and how well the lot drains should be emphasized.

You can modify the house after you have purchased it, but you cannot prevent hurricanes or other storms. The first step is to stop and consider; do the pleasure and benefits of this location balance the risk and disadvantage? If not, look elsewhere for a home; if so, then evaluate the house itself.

How well built is the house?

In general, the principles used to evaluate an existing house are the same as those used in building a new one. It should be remembered that many of the houses were built prior to the enactment of Flood Disaster Protection Insurance and may not meet the standards required of structures or improvements built since then.

Before you thoroughly inspect the building in which you are interested, look closely at the adjacent structures. If poorly built, they may float over against your building and damage it in a flood. You may even want to consider the type of people you will have as neighbors: will they "clear the decks" in preparation for a storm or will they leave items in the yard to become wind-borne missiles?

The house or condominium itself should be inspected for the following characteristics. The structure should be well anchored to the ground. If it is simply resting on blocks, rising water may cause it to float off its foundation and come to rest against your neighbor's house or out in the middle of the street. If well built and well braced internally, it may be possible to move the house back to its proper location, but chances are great that the house will be too damaged to be habitable.

If the building is on piles, posts, or poles, check to see if the floor beams are adequately bolted to them. If it rests on piers, crawl under the house if space permits to see if the floor beams are securely connected to the foundation. If the floor system rests unanchored on piers, do not buy the house.

It is difficult to discern whether a building built on a concrete slab is properly bolted to the slab because the inside and outside walls hide the bolts. If you can locate the builder, ask if such bolting was done. Better yet, if you can get assurance that construction of the house complied with the provisions of a building code serving the needs of that particular region, you can be reasonably sure that all parts of the house are well anchored: the foundation to the ground; the floor to the foundation; the walls to the floor; and the roof to the walls (figs. 6.7, 6.8, and 6.9). Be aware that many builders, carpenters, and building inspectors who are accustomed to traditional construction are apt to regard metal connectors, collar beams, and other such devices as newfangled and unnecessary. If consulted, they may assure you that a house is as solid as a rock, when in fact, it is far from it. Nevertheless, it

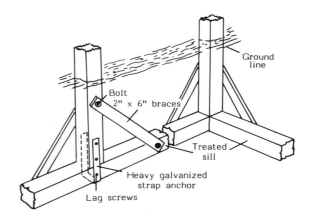

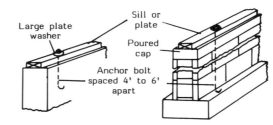

Fig. 6.7. Foundation anchorage. Top: anchored sill for shallow embedment. Bottom: anchoring sill or plate to foundation. Source of bottom drawing: *Houses Can Resist Hurricanes*, U.S. Forest Service Research Paper FPL 33.

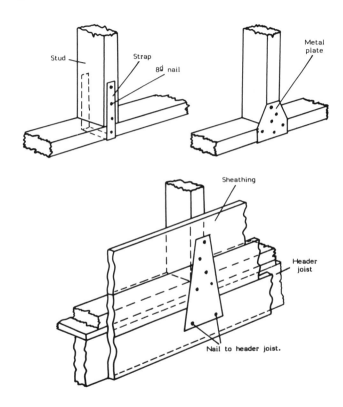

Fig. 6.8. Stud-to floor, plate-to-floor framing methods. Source: *Houses Can Resist Hurricanes*, U.S. Forest Service Research Paper FPL 33.

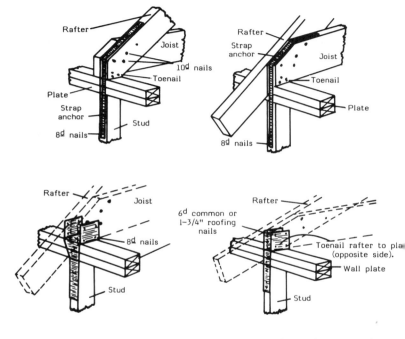

Fig. 6.9. Roof-to-wall connectors. The top drawings show metal strap connectors. Left, rafter to stud; right, joist to stud. The bottom left drawing shows a double-member metal plate connector—in this case with the joist to the right of the rafter. The bottom right drawing shows a single-member metal plate connector. Source: *Houses Can Resist Hurricanes*, U.S. Forest Service Research Paper FPL 33.

is wise to consult the builder or knowledgeable neighbors when possible.

The roof should be well anchored to the walls. This will prevent uplifting and separation from the walls. Visit the attic to see if such anchoring exists. Simple toe-nailing (nailing at an angle) is not adequate; metal fasteners are needed. Depending on the type of construction and the amount of insulation laid on the floor of the attic, these may or may not be easy to see. If roof trusses or braced rafters were used, it should be easy to see whether the various members, such as the diagonals, are well fastened together. Again, simple toe-nailing will not suffice. Some builders, unfortunately, nail parts of a roof truss just enough to hold it together to get it in place. A collar beam or gusset at the peak of the roof (fig. 6.10) provides some assurance of good construction. The Standard Building Code states that wood truss rafters shall be securely fastened to the exterior walls with approved hurricane anchors or clips.

Quality roofing material should be well anchored to the sheathing. A poor roof covering will be destroyed by hurricane-force winds, allowing rain to enter the house and damage ceilings, walls, and the contents of the house. Galvanized nails (2 per shingle) should be used to connect wood shingles and shakes to wood sheathing and should be long enough to penetrate through the sheathing (fig. 6.10). Threaded nails should be used for plywood sheathing. Sheathing is the covering (usually woodboards, plywood, or wallboards) placed over rafters, or exterior studding of a building, to provide a base for the application of roof or wall cladding. For roof slopes that rise 1 foot for every 3 feet or more of horizontal distance, exposure of the shingle should be about one-fourth of its length (4 inches for a 16-inch shingle). If shakes (thicker and longer than shingles) are used, less than one-third of their length should be exposed.

In hurricane areas, asphalt shingles should be exposed somewhat less than usual. A mastic or seal-tab type, or an interlocking shingle of heavy grade, should be used along with a roof underlay of asphalt-saturated felt and galvanized roofing nails or approved staples (6 for each 3-tab strip).

The fundamental rule to remember in framing is that all structural elements should be fastened together and anchored to the ground in such a manner as to resist all forces, regardless of which direction these forces may come from. This prevents overturning, floating off, racking, or disintegration.

The shape of the house is important. A hip roof, which slopes in 4 directions, is better able to resist high winds than a gable roof, which slopes in 2 directions. This was found to be true in Hurricane Camille in 1969 in Mississippi and, later, in Typhoon Tracy, which devastated Darwin, Australia, in December 1974. The reason is two-fold: the hip roof offers a smaller shape for the wind to blow against, and its structure is such that it is better braced in all directions.

Note also the horizontal cross section of the house (the shape of the house as viewed from above). The pressure exerted by a wind on a round or elliptical shape is about 60 percent of that exerted on the common square or rectangular shape; the pressure exerted

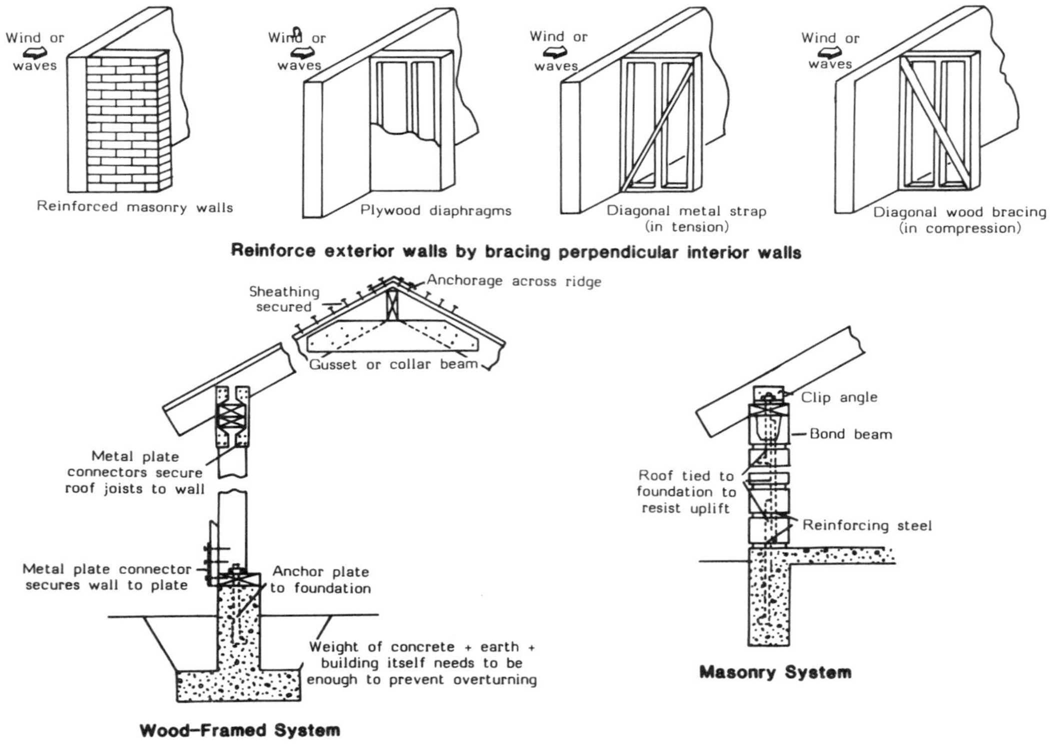

Fig. 6.10. Where to strengthen a house. Modified from U.S. Civil Defense Preparedness Agency Publication TR-83.

on a hexagonal or octagonal cross section is about 80 percent of that exerted on a square or rectangular cross section (fig. 6.11).

The design of a house or building in a coastal area should minimize structural discontinuities and irregularities. It should be plain and simple and have a minimum of nooks and crannies and offsets on the exterior, because damage to a structure tends to concentrate at these points. Some of the newer beach cottages along the Florida shore are of a highly angular design with such nooks and crannies. Award-winning architecture will be a storm loser if the design has not incorporated the technology for maximizing structural integrity with respect to storm forces. When irregularities are absent, the house reacts to storm winds as a complete unit (fig. 6.11).

Brick, concrete-block, and masonry-wall houses should be adequately reinforced. This reinforcement is hidden from view. Building codes applicable to high-wind areas often specify the type of mortar, reinforcing, and anchoring to be used in construction. If you can get assurance that the house was built in compliance with a building code designed for such an area, consider buying it. At all costs, avoid unreinforced masonry houses.

A poured-concrete bond beam at the top of the wall just under the roof is one indication that the house is well built (fig. 6.11). Most bond beams are formed by putting in reinforcing and pouring concrete in U-shaped concrete blocks. From the outside, however, you cannot distinguish these U-shaped blocks from ordinary ones and therefore cannot be certain that a bond beam exists. The vertical reinforcing should penetrate the bond beam.

Some architects and builders use a stacked bond (1 block directly above another) rather than overlapped or staggered blocks because they believe it looks better. The stacked bond is definitely weaker than the latter. Unless you have proof that the walls are adequately reinforced to overcome this lack of strength, you should avoid this type of construction.

In past hurricanes the brick veneer of many houses has separated from the wood frame, even when the houses remained standing. Asbestos-type outer wall panels used on many houses in Darwin, Australia, were found to be brittle and broke up under the impact of wind-borne debris in Typhoon Tracy. Both types of construction should be avoided along the coast.

Ocean-facing glazing. Windows, glass doors, and glass panels should be minimal. Although large open glass areas facing the ocean provide an excellent sea view, such glazing may present several problems. The obvious hazard is disintegrating and inward-blowing glass during a storm. Glass projectiles are lethal. Less frequently recognized problems include the fact that glass may not provide as much structural strength as wood, metal, or other building materials; and ocean-facing glass is commonly damaged through sediment sand blasting, transported by normal coastal winds. The solution to this latter problem may be in reducing the amount of glass in the original design, or installing storm shutters which come in a variety of materials from steel to wood.

Consult a good architect or structural engineer for advice if you are in doubt about any aspects of a house. A few dollars spent for wise counsel may save you from later financial grief.

To summarize, a beach house should have: (1) roof tied to walls,

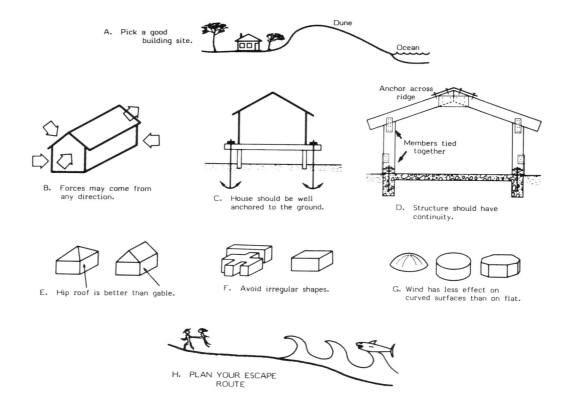

A. Pick a good building site.

Dune

Ocean

B. Forces may come from any direction.

C. House should be well anchored to the ground.

Anchor across ridge

Members tied together

D. Structure should have continuity.

E. Hip roof is better than gable.

F. Avoid irregular shapes.

G. Wind has less effect on curved surfaces than on flat.

H. PLAN YOUR ESCAPE ROUTE

Fig. 6.11. Some rules in selecting or designing a house.

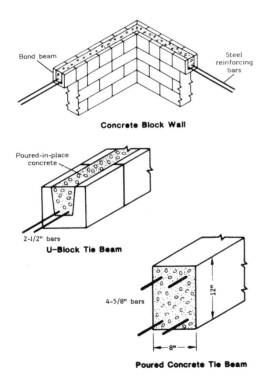

Bond beam

Steel reinforcing bars

Concrete Block Wall

Poured-in-place concrete

2-1/2" bars

U-Block Tie Beam

4-5/8" bars

12"

8"

Poured Concrete Tie Beam

Fig. 6.12. Reinforced tie beam (bond beam) for concrete block walls—to be used at each floor level and at roof level around the perimeter of the exterior walls.

walls tied to foundation, and foundation anchored to the earth (the connections are potentially the weakest link in the structural system); (2) a shape that resists storm forces; (3) floors high enough (sufficient elevation) to be above most storm waters (usually the 100-year flood level plus 3 to 8 feet); (4) piles or posts that are of sufficient depth or embedded in concrete to anchor the structure and to withstand erosion; and (5) piling that is well braced.

What can be done to improve an existing house?

If you presently own a house or are contemplating buying one in a hurricane-prone area, you will want to know how to improve occupant protection in the house. If so, you should obtain the excellent publication, *TR83 Wind Resistant Design Concepts for Residences*, by Delbart B. Ward, reference 69 (appendix C). Of particular interest are the sections on building a refuge shelter module within a residence. Also noteworthy are 2 supplements to this publication, *TR83A* and *TR83B*, which deal with buildings larger than single-family residences in urban areas. These provide a means of checking whether the responsible authorities are doing their jobs to protect schools, office buildings, and apartments. Several other pertinent references are listed in the bibliography (appendix C).

Suppose your house is resting on blocks but not fastened to them and, thus, is not adequately anchored to the ground. Can anything be done? One solution is to treat the house like a mobile home by screwing ground anchors into the ground to a depth of 4 feet or more and fastening them to the underside of the floor systems. See figures 6.13 and 6.14 for illustrations of how ground anchors can be used.

Calculations to determine the needed number of ground anchors will differ between a house and a mobile home, because each is affected differently by the forces of wind and water. Note that recent practice is to put these commercial steel-rod anchors in at an angle in order to better align them with the direction of the pull. If a vertical anchor is used, the top 18 inches or so should be encased in a concrete cylinder about 12 inches in diameter. This prevents the top of the anchor rod from bending or slicing through the wet soil from the horizontal component of the pull.

Diagonal struts, either timber or pipe, also may be used to anchor a house that rests on blocks. This is done by fastening the upper ends of the struts to the floor system, and the lower ends to individual concrete footings substantially below the surface of the ground. These struts must be able to take both uplift (tension) and compression and should be tied into the concrete footing with anchoring devices such as straps or spikes.

If the house has a porch with exposed columns or posts, it should be possible to install tiedown anchors on their tops and bottoms. Steel straps should suffice in most cases.

When accessible, roof rafters and trusses should be anchored to the wall system. Usually the roof trusses or braced rafters are sufficiently exposed to make it possible to strengthen joints (where 2 or more members meet) with collar beams or gussets, particularly at the peak of the roof (fig. 6.10).

A competent carpenter, architect, or structural engineer can review the house with you and help you decide what modifications are most practical and effective. Do not be misled by someone who is resistant to new ideas. One builder told a homeowner, "You don't want all those newfangled straps and anchoring devices. If you use them, the whole house will blow away, but if you build in the usual manner [with members lightly connected], you may lose only part of it."

In fact, the very purpose of the straps is to prevent any or all of the house from blowing away. The Standard Building Code says, "Lateral support securely anchored to all walls provides the best and only sound structural stability against horizontal thrusts, such as winds of exceptional velocity." And the cost of connecting all elements securely adds very little to the cost of the frame of the dwelling, usually under 10 percent, and a very much smaller percentage of the total cost of the house.

If the house has an overhanging eave and there are no openings on its underside, it may be feasible to cut openings and screen them. These openings keep the attic cooler (a plus in the summer) and help to equalize the pressure inside and outside the house during a storm with a low-pressure center.

Another way a house can be improved is to modify 1 room so that it can be used as an emergency refuge in case you are trapped in a major storm. (This is *not* an alternative to evacuation prior to a hurricane.) Examine the house and select the best room to stay in during a storm. A small, windowless room such as a bathroom, utility room, den, or storage space is usually stronger than a room with windows. A sturdy inner room, with more than one wall

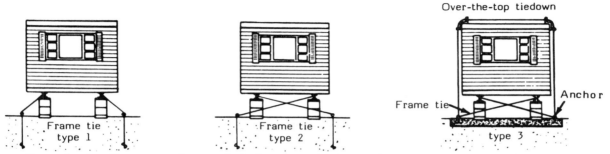

These sketches illustrate various methods for connecting frame ties to the mobile home frame. Type 2 system can resist greater horizontal forces than type 1. Type 3 system involves placement of mobile home on concrete slab. Anchors embedded in concrete slab are connected to ties.

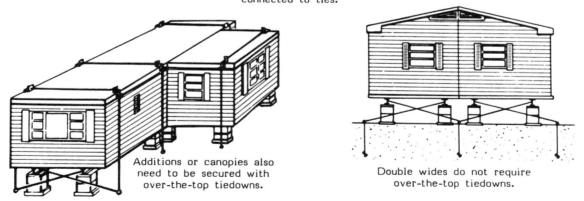

Additions or canopies also need to be secured with over-the-top tiedowns.

Double wides do not require over-the-top tiedowns.

Fig. 6.13. Tiedowns for mobile homes. Source: U.S. Civil Defense Preparedness Agency Publication TR-75.

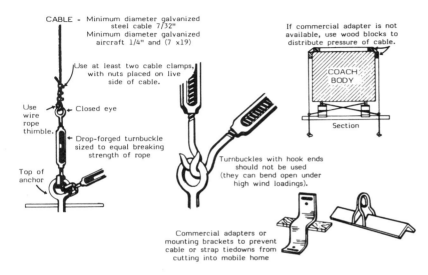

CABLE - Minimum diameter galvanized steel cable 7/32"
Minimum diameter galvanized aircraft 1/4" and (7 x19)

Use at least two cable clamps, with nuts placed on live side of cable.

Use wire rope thimble.

Closed eye

Drop-forged turnbuckle sized to equal breaking strength of rope

Top of anchor

Turnbuckles with hook ends should not be used (they can bend open under high wind loadings).

Commercial adapters or mounting brackets to prevent cable or strap tiedowns from cutting into mobile home

If commercial adapter is not available, use wood blocks to distribute pressure of cable.

COACH BODY

Section

Fig. 6.14. Hardware for mobile home tiedowns. Modified from U.S. Civil Defense Preparedness Agency Publication TR-75.

between it and the outside, is safest. The fewer doors, the better; an adjoining wall or baffle wall shielding the door adds to the protection.

Consider bracing or strengthening the interior walls. Such reinforcement may require removing the surface covering and installing plywood sheathing or strap bracing. Where wall studs are exposed, bracing straps offer a simple way to achieve needed reinforcement against the wind. These straps are commercially produced and are made of 16-gauge galvanized metal with prepunched holes for nailing. These should be secured to studs and wall plates as nail holes permit (fig. 6.10). Bear in mind that they are good only for tension.

If, after reading this, you agree that something should be done to your house, do it now. Do not put it off until the next hurricane hits you!

Mobile homes: limiting their mobility

Because of their light weight and flat sides, mobile homes are vulnerable to the high winds of hurricanes, tornadoes, and severe storms. Such winds can overturn unanchored mobile homes or smash them into neighboring homes and property. Nearly 6 million Americans live in mobile homes today, and the number is growing. Twenty to 30 percent of single-family housing production in the United States consists of mobile homes. High winds damage or destroy nearly 5,000 of these homes every year, and the number will surely rise unless protective measures are taken. As one man whose mobile home was overturned in Hurricane Frederic (1979) so aptly put it, "People who live in flimsy houses shouldn't have hurricanes."

Several lessons can be learned from past experiences in storms. First, mobile homes should be located properly. After Hurricane Camille (1969), it was observed that where mobile home parks were surrounded by woods and where the units were close together,

Table 6.1. Tiedown anchorage requirements

| Wind velocity (mph) | 10- and 12-ft.-wide mobile homes | | | | 12- and 14-ft.-wide mobile homes, 60 to 70 ft. long | |
| | 30 to 50 ft. long | | 50 to 60 ft. long | | | |
	No. of frame ties	No. of over-the-top ties	No. of frame ties	No. of over-the-top ties	No. of frame ties	No. of over-the-top ties
70	3	2	4	2	4	2
80	4	3	5	3	5	3
90	5	4	6	4	7	4
100	6	5	7	5	8	6
110	7	6	9	6	10	7

damage was minimized, caused mainly by falling trees. In unprotected areas, however, many mobile homes were overturned and often destroyed from the force of the wind. The protection afforded by trees is greater than the possible damage from falling limbs. Two or more rows of trees are better than a single row, and trees 30 feet or more in height give better protection than shorter ones. If possible, position the mobile home so that the narrow side faces the prevailing winds. (Australian pines, which blow over too easily, are an exception).

Locating a mobile home in a hilltop park will greatly increase its vulnerability to the wind. A lower site screened by trees is safer from the wind, but it should be above storm-surge flood levels. A location that is too low obviously increases the likelihood of flooding. There are fewer safe locations for mobile homes than for stilt houses.

A second lesson taught by past experience is that the mobile home must be tied down or anchored to the ground so that it will not overturn in high winds (figs. 6.13 and 6.14 and table 6.1). Simple prudence dictates the use of tiedowns, and in Florida tiedowns are required. Many insurance companies, moreover, will not insure mobile homes unless they are adequately anchored with tiedowns. A mobile home may be tied down with cable or rope, or rigidly attached to the ground by connecting it to a simple wood-post foundation system. An alert mobile home park owner can provide permanent concrete anchors or piers to which hold-down ties may be fastened. In general, an entire tiedown system costs only a nominal amount.

A mobile home should be properly anchored with both ties to the frame and over-the-top straps; otherwise it may be damaged by sliding, overturning, or tossing. The most common cause of major damage is the tearing away of most or all of the roof. When this happens the walls are no longer adequately supported at the top and are more prone to collapse. Total destruction of a mobile home is more likely if the roof blows off, especially if the roof blows off first and then the home overturns. The necessity for anchoring cannot be overemphasized: there should be over-the-top tiedowns to resist overturning and frame ties to resist sliding off the piers. This applies to single mobile homes up to 14 feet in width. "Double-wides" do not require over-the-top ties but they do require frame ties. Although newer mobile homes are equipped with built-in straps to aid in tying down, the occupant may wish to add more if in a particularly vulnerable location. Many of the older mobile homes are not equipped with these built-in straps. *Protecting Mobile Homes from High Winds* treats the subject in more detail (see reference 76, appendix C). The booklet lists specific steps that one should take on receiving a hurricane warning and suggests a type of community shelter for a mobile home park. It also includes a map of the United States with lines that indicate areas subject to the strongest sustained winds. In a great hurricane, mobile homes will be destroyed no matter what you do to protect them.

High-rise buildings: the urban shore

A high-rise building on the beach is generally designed by an architect and a structural engineer who are presumably well qualified and aware of the requirements for building on the shoreline. Tenants of such a building, however, should not assume that it is therefore invulnerable. Many people living in apartment buildings of 2 or 3 stories were killed when the buildings were destroyed by Hurricane Camille in Mississippi in 1969. Storms have smashed 5-story buildings in Delaware. Larger high-rises have yet to be thoroughly tested by a major hurricane.

The first aspect of high-rise construction that a prospective apartment dweller or condo owner must consider is the type of piling used. High-rises near the beach should be built so that even if the foundation is severely undercut during a storm the building will remain standing. It is well known in construction circles that shortcuts are sometime taken by less scrupulous builders, and piling is not driven deeply enough. Just as important as driving the piling deep enough to resist scouring and to support the loads they must carry is the need to fasten piles securely to the structure they support above them. The connections must resist horizontal loads from wind and wave during a storm as well as uplift from the same sources. It is a joint responsibility of builders and building inspectors to make sure the job is done right. Hurricane Eloise (1975) exposed the foundation of a just-under-construction high-rise in Panama City Beach, revealing that 30 of the pilings had no concrete around them and were not attached to the building. Such problems probably exist everywhere that high-rises crowd the beach.

Despite the assurances that come with an engineered structure, life in a high-rise building holds definite drawbacks that prospective tenants should take into consideration. The negative conditions that must be evaluated stem from high wind, high water, and poor foundations.

Pressure from the wind is greater near the shore than it is inland, and it increases with height. If you are living inland in a 2-story house and move to the eleventh floor of a high-rise on the shore, you should expect 5 times more wind pressure than you are accustomed to. This can be a great and possibly devastating surprise.

The high wind pressure actually can cause unpleasant motion of the building. It is worthwhile to check with current residents of a high-rise to find out if it has undesirable motion characteristics; some have claimed that the swaying is great enough to cause motion sickness. More seriously, high winds can break windows and damage property, and of course they can hurt people. Tenants of severely damaged buildings will have to relocate until repairs are made.

Those who are interested in researching the subject further—even the knowledgeable engineer or architect who is engaged to design a structure near the shore—should obtain a copy of *Structural Failures: Modes, Causes, Responsibilities* (reference 67, appendix C). Of particular importance is the chapter entitled "Failure of Structures Due to Extreme Winds." This chapter analyzes wind damage to engineered high-rise buildings from the storm at Lubbock and Corpus Christi, Texas, in 1970.

Another occurrence that affects a multi-family, high-rise building more seriously than a low-occupancy structure is a power failure or blackout. Such an occurrence is more likely along the coast than inland because of the more severe weather conditions associated with coastal storms. A power failure can cause great distress. People can be caught between floors in an elevator. New York City had that experience once on a large scale. Think of the mental and physical distress after several hours of confinement, and compound this with the roaring winds of a hurricane whipping around the building, sounding like a freight train. In this age of electricity, it is easy to imagine many of the inconveniences that can be caused by a power failure in a multi-story building.

Fire is an extra hazard in a high-rise building. Even recently constructed buildings seem to have difficulties. The television pictures of a woman leaping from the window of a burning building in New Orleans rather than be incinerated in the blaze are a horrible reminder from recent history. The number of hotel fires of the last few years demonstrate the problems. Fire department equipment reaches only so high. And many areas along the coast are too sparsely populated to afford high-reaching equipment.

Fire and smoke travel along ventilation ducts, elevator shafts, corridors, and similar passages. The situation *can be* corrected and the building made safer, especially if it is new. Sprinkler systems should be operated by gravity water systems rather than by powered pumps (because of possible power failure). Gravity systems use water from tanks higher up in the building. Battery-operated emergency lights that come on only when the other lights fail, better fire walls and automatic sealing doors, pressurized stairwells, and emergency-operated elevators in pressurized shafts will all contribute to greater safety. Unfortunately, all of these improvements cost money, and that is why they are often omitted unless required by the building code.

There are 2 interesting reports on damage caused by Hurricane Eloise, which struck the Florida Panhandle the morning of September 23, 1975. One is by Herbert S. Saffir, a Florida consulting engineer; the other is by Bryon Spangler of the University of Florida. The forward movement of the hurricane was unusually fast, causing its duration in a specific area to be lessened, thus minimizing damage from both wind and tidal surge. The still-water height at Panama City was 16 feet above mean sea level, plus about a 3-foot topping wave. Wind gusts of 154 mph for a period of one-half hour were measured.

At least one-third of the older structures in the Panama City area collapsed. These were beach-front motels, restaurants, apartments, condominium complexes, and some permanent residences. The structures built on piling survived with minimal damage. In one case, part of a motel was on spread footings and part on piles. Just the part on spread footings was severely damaged. (A spread footing is a wide concrete slab resting directly on the ground rather than on piles.)

The anchorage systems, connection between concrete piles or concrete piers and the grade beams, under several high-rise buildings were inadequate to resist uplift loads, illustrating that code enforcement and proper inspection by a qualified professional are essential.

Many of the residences and some of the buildings were built on spread footings that failed because the sand they were resting on washed away with scour. Failure of the footings resulted in failure of the superstructure.

Some of the high-rise buildings suffered glass damage in both windows and sliding glass doors.

Apparently few, if any, of the residences and buildings were built to conform to either the South Florida or the Standard Building Code requirements. (The code was not legally applicable at the time.) If the requirements had been met, much of the damage could have been prevented at a minimum of cost.

Some surprising things were noticed. In almost every case where there was a swimming pool, considerable erosion occurred. Loss of sand beneath the walkways prior to the storm created a channel for the water to flow through and wash out more sand during the storm, which in turn increased both the velocity and quantity of the flow of water in the channel. This ate away the sand supporting adjacent structures, accelerating their failure.

Slabs on grade (on the ground) performed poorly. Often wave action washed out the sand underneath the slab. When this occurred there was no longer support for the structure above it, and failure resulted.

The storms revealed some shoddy construction. Some builders had placed wire mesh for a slab directly on the sand. Then the concrete was poured on top of it, leaving the mesh below and in the sand, where it served no structural purpose. To be effective, it should have been set on blocks or chairs, or pulled up into the slab during the pouring of the concrete.

In some cases cantilevered slabs or overhangs were reinforced for the usual downward gravity loads. Unfortunately, when waves dashed against the buildings they splashed upward, imposing an upward force against the slab for which it was not reinforced, causing it to crack and fail.

Modular unit construction: prefabricating the urban shore

The method of building a house, duplex, or large condominium structure by fabricating modular units in a shop and assembling them at the site is gaining in popularity for development on shoreline property. The larger of these structures are commonly 2 to 3 stories in height and may contain a large number of living units.

Modular construction makes good economic sense, and there is nothing inherently wrong in this approach to coastal construction. These methods have been used in the manufacturing of mobile homes for years, although final assembly on mobile homes is done in the shop rather than on the site. Doing as much of the work as possible in a shop can save considerable labor and cost. The workers are not affected by outside weather conditions. They often can be paid by piecework, enhancing their productivity. Shop work lends itself to labor-saving equipment such as pneumatic nailing guns and overhead cranes.

If the manufacturer desires it, shop fabrication can permit higher quality. Inspection and control of the whole process are much easier. For instance, there is less hesitation about rejecting a poor piece of lumber when you have a nearby supply of it than if you are building a single dwelling and have just so much lumber on the site.

On the other hand, because so much of the work is done out of sight of the buyer, there is the opportunity for the manufacturer to take shortcuts if he is so inclined. It is possible that some modular dwelling units have their wiring, plumbing, ventilation, and heating and air conditioning installed at the factory by unqualified personnel, and it is possible the resulting inferior work is either not inspected or inspected by an unconscientious or inept individual.

Therefore, it is important to consider the following: Were wiring, plumbing, heating and air conditioning, and ventilation installed at the factory or at the building site? Were the installers licensed and certified? Was the work inspected at both the factory and on the construction site? Most important, is the modular dwelling unit built to provide safety in the event of fire? For example, just a few of the many safety features that should be included are 2 or more exits, stairs remote from each other, masonry fire walls between units, noncombustible wall sheeting, and compartmentalized units so that if fire does occur it will be confined to that 1 unit.

It is vital that if 1 unit is placed on top of another, they be adequately fastened together to resist high winds and that they not depend solely on the weight of the upper unit to hold them in place.

In general, it is very desirable to check the reputation and integrity of the manufacturer just as you would when hiring a contractor to build your individual house on site. The acquisition of a modular unit should be approached with the same caution as for other structures.

If you are contemplating purchasing one of these modularized dwelling units, you may be well advised to take the following steps:

1. Check the reputation and integrity of the developer and manufacturer.
2. Check to see if the developer has a state contractor's license.
3. Check the state law on who is required to approve and certify the building.

4. Check what building codes are enforced.
5. Check to see if the state fire marshal's office has indicated that the dwelling units comply with all applicable codes. Also check to see if this office makes periodic inspections.
6. Check to see that smoke alarms have been installed, if windows are the type that can be opened, if the bathroom has an exhaust fan, and if the kitchen has a vent through the roof.

As with all other types of structures, also consider site safety and escape routes(s) for the location of modular units.

An unending game: only the players change

Hurricane or calm, receding shore or growing shore, storm-surge flood or sunny sky, migrating dune or maritime forest, win or lose, the gamble of coastal development will continue. If you choose your site with natural safety in view, follow structural engineering design in construction, and take a generally prudent approach to living at the shore (fig 6.11), then you become the gambler who knows when to hold them, when to fold them, and when to walk away.

Our goal is to provide guidance to today's and tomorrow's players. This book is not the last nor by any means the complete guide to coastal living, but it should provide a beginning. In the appendixes that follow are additional resources that we hope every reader will pursue.

Appendix A. Hurricane checklist

Keep this checklist handy for protection of family and property.

When a hurricane threatens

___ Listen for official weather reports.

___ Read your newspaper and listen to radio and television for official announcements.

___ Note the address of the nearest emergency shelter.

___ Know the official evacuation route in advance.

___ Pregnant women, the ill, and the infirm should call a physician for advice.

___ Be prepared to turn off gas, water, and electricity where it enters your home.

___ Fill tubs and containers with water (one quart per person per day).

___ Make sure your car's gas tank is full.

___ Secure your boat. Use long lines to allow for rising water.

___ Secure movable objects on your property:

    ___ doors and gates   ___ garbage cans

    ___ outdoor furniture   ___ bicycles or large

    ___ shutters   sports equipment

    ___ garden tools   ___ barbecues or grills

    ___ hoses   ___ other

___ Board up or tape windows and glassed areas. Draw drapes and window blinds across windows and glass doors. Remove furniture in their vicinity.

___ Stock adequate supplies:

    ___ transistor radio   ___ flashlights

    ___ fresh batteries   ___ candles

    ___ canned heat   ___ matches

    ___ hammer   ___ nails

    ___ boards   ___ screwdriver

    ___ pliers   ___ ax*

    ___ hunting knife   ___ rope*

    ___ tape   ___ plastic drop cloths,

    ___ first-aid kit   waterproof bags, ties

    ___ prescribed medicines   ___ containers for water

    ___ water purification   ___ disinfectant

        tablets   ___ canned food, juices,

    ___ insect repellent   soft drinks (see

    ___ gum, candy   below)

    ___ life jackets   ___ hard-top head gear

    ___ charcoal bucket and   ___ fire extinguisher

        charcoal   ___ can opener and

    ___ buckets of sand   utensils

___ Check mobile-home tiedowns.

*Take an ax (to cut an emergency escape opening) if you go to the upper floors or attic of your home. Take rope for escape to ground when water subsides.

Suggested storm food stock for family of four

— two 13-oz. cans evaporated milk
— four 7-oz. cans fruit juice
— 2 cans tuna, sardines, Spam, chicken
— three 10-oz. cans vegetable soup
— 1 small can cocoa or Ovaltine
— one 15-oz. box raisins or prunes
— salt
— pet food?
— one 14-oz. can cream of wheat or oatmeal
— one 8-oz. jar peanut butter or cheese spread
— two 16-oz. cans pork and beans
— one 2-oz. jar instant coffee or tea bags
— 2 packages of crackers
— 2 pounds of sugar
— 2 quarts of water per person

Special precautions for apartments/condominiums

— Make one person the building captain to supervise storm preparation.
— Know your exits.
— Count stairs on exits; you'll be evacuating in darkness.
— Locate safest areas for occupants to congregate.
— Close, lock, and tape windows.
— Remove loose items from terraces (and from your absent neighbors' terraces).
— Remove or tie down loose objects from balconies or porches.

— Assume other trapped people may wish to use the building for shelter.

Special precautions for mobile homes

— Pack breakables in padded cartons and place on floor.
— Remove bulbs, lamps, mirrors—put them in the bathtub.
— Tape windows.
— Turn off water, propane gas, electricity.
— Disconnect sewer and water lines.
— Remove awnings.
— **Leave**.

Special precautions for businesses

— Take photos of building and merchandise.
— Assemble insurance policies.
— Move merchandise away from plate glass.
— Move merchandise to as high a location as possible.
— Cover merchandise with tarps or plastic.
— Remove outside display racks and loose signs.
— Take out lower file drawers, wrap in trash bags, and store high.
— Sandbag spaces that may leak.
— Take special precautions with reactive or toxic chemicals.

If you remain at home

— Never remain in a mobile home; seek official shelter.
— Stay indoors. Remember, the first calm may be the hurricane's

eye. Remain indoors until an official all-clear is given.
__ Stay on the "downwind" side of the house. Change your position as the wind changes.
__ If your house has an "inside" room, it may be the most secure part of the structure.
__ Keep continuous communications watch for *official* information on radio and television.
__ Keep calm. Your ability to meet emergencies will help others.

If evacuation is advised

__ Leave as soon as you can. Follow official instructions only.
__ Follow official evacuation routes unless those in authority direct you to do otherwise.
__ Take these supplies:
    __ change of warm, protective clothes
    __ first-aid kit
    __ baby formula
    __ identification tags: include name, address, and next of kin (wear them)
    __ flashlight
    __ food, water, gum, candy
    __ rope, hunting knife
    __ waterproof bags and ties
    __ can opener and utensils
    __ disposable diapers
    __ special medicine

    __ blankets and pillows in waterproof casings
    __ radio
    __ fresh batteries
    __ bottled water
    __ purse, wallet, valuables
    __ life jackets
    __ games and amusements for children
__ Disconnect all electric appliances except refrigerator and freezer. Their controls should be turned to the coldest setting and the doors kept closed.
__ Leave food and water for pets. Seeing-eye dogs are the only animals allowed in the shelters.
__ Shut off water at the main valve (where it enters your home).
__ Lock windows and doors.
__ Keep important papers with you:
    __ driver's license and other identification
    __ insurance policies
    __ property inventory
    __ Medic Alert or other device to convey special medical information

During the hurricane

__ Stay indoors and away from windows and glassed areas.
__ If you are advised to evacuate, **do so at once**.
__ Listen for continuing weather bulletins and official reports.
__ Use your telephone only in an emergency.

— Follow official instructions only. Ignore rumors.

— Keep **open** a window or door on the side of the house opposite the storm winds.

— Beware of the **"eye of the hurricane."** A lull in the winds does not necessarily mean that the storm has passed. Remain indoors unless emergency repairs are necessary. Exercise caution. Winds may resume suddenly, in the opposite direction and with greater force than before. Remember, if wind direction does change, the open window or door must be changed accordingly.

— Be alert for rising water.

— If electric service is interrupted, note the time.

    — Turn off major appliances, especially air conditioners.

    — Do not disconnect refrigerators or freezers. Their controls should be turned to the coldest setting and doors closed to preserve food as long as possible.

    — Keep away from fallen wires. Report location of such wires to the utility company.

— If you detect **gas**:

    — Do not light matches or turn on electrical equipment.

    — Extinguish all flames.

    — Shut off gas supply at the meter.*

    — Report gas service interruptions to the gas company.

— **Water**:

    — The only **safe** water is the water you stored before it had a chance to come in contact with flood waters.

*Gas should be turned back on only by a gas serviceman or licensed plumber.

— Should you require an additional supply, be sure to boil water for 30 minutes before use.

— If you are unable to boil water, treat water you will need with water purification tablets.

Note: An official announcement will proclaim tap water "safe." Treat all water except stored water until you hear the announcement.

After the hurricane has passed

— Listen for official word of danger having passed.

— Watch out for loose or hanging power lines as well as gas leaks. People have survived storms only to be electrocuted or burned. Fire protection may be nil because of broken power lines.

— Walk or drive carefully through the storm-damaged area. Streets will be dangerous because of debris, undermining by washout, and weakened bridges. Watch out for poisonous snakes and insects driven out by flood waters.

— Eat nothing and drink nothing that has been touched by flood waters.

— Place spoiled food in plastic bags and tie securely.

— Dispose of all mattresses, pillows, and cushions that have been in flood waters.

— Contact relatives as soon as possible.

Note: If you are stranded, signal for help by waving a flashlight at night or white cloth during the day.

Appendix B. A guide to local, state, and federal agencies involved in coastal development

Numerous agencies at all levels of government are engaged in planning, regulating, permitting, or studying coastal development and resources in Florida. These agencies provide information on development to the homeowner, developer, or planner and issue permits for various phases of construction and information on particular topics.

Aerial photography, coastal construction control line maps, ortho-photo maps, and remote-sensing imagery

State Topographic–Aerial Survey Engineer
Florida Department of Transportation
Haydon Burns Building
605 Suwannee Street
Tallahassee, FL 32301
(904) 488-2250

Division of Beaches and Shores
Florida Department of Natural Resources
3900 Commonwealth Boulevard
Tallahassee, FL 32303
(904) 488-3180

Coastal Zone Studies
Department of Political Science
University of West Florida
Pensacola, FL 32504
(904) 476-9500

U.S. Geological Survey
325 John Knox Road
Tallahassee, FL 32301
(904) 385-7145

Local county or municipal governments
Attn: planning, zoning, or building departments.

Beach erosion

Information on barrier beach erosion, inlet migration, and erosion control alternatives is available from the following agencies:

Division of Beaches and Shores
Florida Department of Natural Resources
3900 Commonwealth Boulevard
Tallahassee, FL 32303
(904) 488-3180

Coastal Archives Library
Department of Coastal and Oceanographic Engineering
Weil Hall
University of Florida
Gainesville, FL 32611
(904) 392-2710

Coastal Zone Studies
Department of Political Science
University of West Florida
Pensacola, FL 32504
(904) 476-9500

U.S. Army Corps of Engineers
Jacksonville District Office
P.O. Box 4970
400 East Bay Street
Jacksonville, FL 32232

Coastal Engineering Specialist
Florida Sea Grant–Marine Advisory Program
G022 McCarty Hall
University of Florida
Gainesville, FL 32611
(904) 392-2460

Local county or municipal governments
Attn: planning or engineering departments.

Bridges and causeways

The U.S. Coast Guard has jurisdiction over issuing permits to build bridges or causeways that will affect navigable waters. Information for peninsular Florida from Fernandina Beach to Panama City:

Commander, 7th Coast Guard District
1018 Federal Building
51 First Avenue, S.W.
Miami, FL 33130
(305) 350-4108

For areas west of Panama City, contact:

Commander, 8th Coast Guard District
500 Camp Street
New Orleans, LA 70130
(504) 589-6298

Building codes, planning, and zoning

Most communities have adopted comprehensive plans and building codes under the Standard Building Code and in some cases under the improved South Florida Building Code. Check with your county or city building department for permitted uses and building codes. The existing building codes in Florida do not protect the structures from hurricane, flood, wind, and erosion damage. If you intend to build on barrier islands, we advise you to obtain an excellent guide from Texas as well as the Florida codes.

Model Minimum Hurricane Resistant
Building Codes for the Texas Gulf Coast
Texas Coastal and Marine Council
P.O. Box 13407
Austin, TX 78711
(512) 475-5849

Coastal Construction Building Code Guidelines
Division of Beaches and Shores
Florida Department of Natural Resources
3900 Commonwealth Boulevard
Tallahassee, FL 32303
(904) 488-3180

Coastal zone planning and management program

Florida adopted the Coastal Management Program (CMP) pursuant to the Florida Coastal Zone Management Act of 1978 (Chapter 380, Florida Statutes) and the Federal Coastal Zone Management Act of 1972. Florida's CMP did not create any new agency but provides for coordination and consistency in the implementation of various federal and state programs affecting coastal areas and barrier islands. For information on the CMP and designated barrier islands, contact:

Office of Coastal Management
Department of Environmental Regulation
2600 Blair Stone Road
Tallahassee, FL 32301
(904) 488-4805

Dredging, filling, and construction in coastal waters

Florida laws require that all those who wish to dredge, fill, or otherwise alter wetlands, marshes, estuarine bottoms, or tidelands apply for a permit from the appropriate state, federal, and local governments. For information, write or call the following agencies.

For the standard state permit on dredging and filling, contact:

Florida Department of Environmental Regulation
Twin Towers Building
2600 Blair Stone Road
Tallahassee, FL 32301
(904) 488-0130

For short-form dredge and fill application permits, contact appropriate district offices of the Department of Environmental Regulation.

For erosion control structures and coastal construction control line permits, write or call:

Division of Beaches and Shores
Florida Department of Natural Resources
3900 Commonwealth Boulevard
Tallahassee, FL 32303
(904) 488-3180

Easements and submerged land leases for docks, piers, etc., must be obtained from:

Bureau of State Lands Management
Florida Department of Natural Resources
3900 Commonwealth Boulevard
Tallahassee, FL 32303
(904) 488-9120

Federal law requires that any person who wishes to dredge, fill, or place any structure in navigable water (almost any body of water) apply for a permit from the U.S. Army Corps of Engineers.

Permit Branch
U.S. Army Corps of Engineers
P.O. Box 4970
400 East Bay Street
Jacksonville, FL 32232
(904) 791-2887

The Army Corps of Engineers has 10 additional field offices in Florida. Consult your area telephone directory for the U.S. Government listing in the white pages.

Dune alteration and vegetation removal

Florida laws prohibit the destruction, damaging, or removal of sea grasses, sea oats, or sand dunes and berms. Individual counties or cities might have ordinances pertaining to dune alteration and vegetation removal. Permits for certain work and alteration may be obtained from local county or city planning and building departments. For permits to clear or alter dunes or beaches seaward of the coastal construction control lines, write or call:

Division of Beaches and Shores
Department of Natural Resources
3900 Commonwealth Boulevard
Tallahassee, FL 32303
(904) 488-3180

Health, sanitation, and water quality

County health departments are in charge of issuing on-site septic system permits for sewage treatment plants with a capacity of less than 2,000 gallons per day. For the necessary information and permit process, contact your local health department or:

Division of Environmental Services
Department of Health and Rehabilitative Services
1317 Winewood Boulevard
Tallahassee, FL 32301
(904) 488-4070

For sewage systems with a capacity larger than 2,000 gallons per day, the Florida Department of Environmental Regulation issues the permits. (For address, see Dredging and filling listing.)

History and archeology

If you suspect that your property may have an archeologic or historic site, write or call:

Bureau of Historic Sites and Properties
Division of Archives, History and Records Management
Florida Department of State
R.A. Gray Building
Tallahassee, FL 32301
(904) 488-1480, 488-2333

Hurricane information and weather

The National Oceanic and Atmospheric Administration is the best agency from which to request information on hurricanes. NOAA stormflood evacuation maps are prepared for vulnerable coastal areas and cost $2.00 each. For details, call or write:

Distribution Division (C-44)
National Ocean Survey
NOAA
Riverdale, MD 20840
(301) 463-6990

For hurricane probability charts for your area as well as weather and hurricane warning information, contact:

National Hurricane Center
1320 South Dixie Highway
Coral Gables, FL 33146
(305) 666-0413

Hurricane evacuation and disaster assistance

Contact your local county or city Civil Defense or Disaster Preparedness office for hurricane evacuation and hurricane shelter information. Local radio and TV stations provide hurricane warning and evacuation bulletins when storms threaten an area. For information on hurricane disaster response, recovery, and assistance, contact:

Disaster Response and Recovery Assistance
Bureau of Disaster Preparedness
Florida Department of Community Affairs
2571 Executive Center Circle, East
Tallahassee, FL 32301
(904) 488-1900
(904) 488-1320 (in case of emergency)

Federal Disaster Assistance Administration
Region 4 Office
Suite 750
1375 Peachtree Street, N.E.
Atlanta, GA 30309

Insurance

In coastal areas special building requirements must often be met to obtain flood or wind storm insurance. To find out the requirements in your area, check with your local building department and insurance agent. Further information is available from:

Federal Insurance Administration
National Flood Insurance Program
Federal Emergency Management Agency
Washington, DC 20472
(202) 755-5290

Division of Insurance–Consumer Services
Florida Department of Insurance and Treasurer
The Capitol
Tallahassee, FL 32301
(904) 488-2660

Land planning and land use

Local county and municipal governments have adopted comprehensive land-use plans and zoning and building codes under the state law. It is advisable to contact these agencies, preferably before you buy land on a barrier island or coastal area. For additional information, contact:

Division of Local Resources Management
Florida Department of Community Affairs
2571 Executive Center Circle, East
Tallahassee, FL 32301
(904) 488-2356

Large-scale development projects requiring Development of Regional Impact (DRI) studies must meet approvals by the following state agency:

Bureau of Land and Water Management
Florida Department of Community Affairs
2571 Executive Center Circle, East
Tallahassee, FL 32301
(904) 488-4925

Area Regional Planning Council approvals also are necessary for DRIs before state agency approvals are granted.

Land purchase and sales

When acquiring property or a condominium—whether in a subdivision or not—consider the following: (1) Owners of property next to dredged canals should make sure that the canals are designed for adequate flushing to keep waters from becoming stagnant. Requests for federal permits to connect extensive canal systems to navigable waters are frequently denied. (2) Descriptions and surveys of land in coastal areas are very complicated. Old titles granting fee-simple rights to property below the high-tide line may not be upheld in court; titles should be reviewed by a competent attorney before they are transferred. A boundary described as the high-water mark may be impossible to determine. (3) Ask about the provision of sewage disposal and utilities including water, electricity, gas, and telephone. (4) Be sure any promises of future improvements, access, utilities, additions, common property rights, etc., are in writing. (5) Be sure to visit the property and inspect it carefully before buying it.

Land preservation

Several barrier beaches are being considered by the state for public acquisition under 3 state programs: the Environmentally Endangered Lands Program, the Save Our Coast Program, and the Conservation and Recreational Lands Program. If you own large parcels of environmentally sensitive land on barrier islands or coastal areas and prefer to have it preserved for future generations to enjoy, contact the state's Bureau of Land Acquisition (address given below).

On the other hand, if you plan to buy barrier island property, it would be advisable to contact the local government agency as well as the following state agencies to determine if there could be development and permitting problems.

Bureau of Land Acquisition
Division of State Lands
Department of Natural Resources
3900 Commonwealth Boulevard
Tallahassee, FL 32301
(904) 488-2725

Inter-Agency Management Committee
Save Our Coast Program
Office of Planning and Budgeting
Executive Office of the Governor
The Capitol
Tallahassee, FL 32301
(904) 488-5551

Land sales—subdivisions

Subdivisions containing more than 50 lots and offered in interstate commerce must be registered with the Office of Interstate Land Sales Registration (as specified by the Interstate Land Sales Full Disclosure Act). Prospective buyers must be provided with a property report. This office also produces a booklet entitled *Get the Facts . . . Before Buying Land* for people who wish to invest in property. Information on subdivision property and land investment is available from:

Office of Interstate Land Sales Registration
U.S. Department of Housing and Urban Development
Washington, DC 20410

Office of Interstate Land Sales Registration
Atlanta Regional Office
U.S. Department of Housing and Urban Development
230 Peachtree Street, N.W.
Atlanta, GA 30303
(404) 526-4364

Soils and septic systems

Soil type is important in terms of (1) the type of vegetation it can support, (2) the type of construction technique it can withstand, (3) its drainage characteristics, and (4) its ability to accommodate septic systems. For detailed information on soil characteristics and limitations and permitting rules for septic systems, contact:

Local county Soil Conservation Service office, U.S. Department of Agriculture (listing in the telephone book)

Soil Conservation Service
U.S. Department of Agriculture
University of Florida
Gainesville, FL 32611

Local county health department

Environmental Services
Department of Health and Rehabilitative Services
1323 Winewood Boulevard
Tallahassee, FL 32301
(904) 488-4070

U.S. Fish and Wildlife Service
Department of the Interior
P.O. Box 2676
Vero Beach, FL 32960
(904) 562-3909

Water supply and pollution control

If your plan involves draining of land or a large water supply system, contact the appropriate area water management district for rules and permit process. Construction of any sewage or solid waste disposal facilities requires permits from the Florida Department of Environmental Regulation. Contact appropriate district office of the DER. (See Dredging and Filling listing for addresses.)

Wildlife species and habitat protection

For the conservation and protection of fish and wildlife species and their habitat, contact the office of the Game and Fresh Water Fish Commission in your area. Also contact:

Appendix C. Useful references

The following list of references, most of which are annotated, will suffice to get any interested individual into the literature. A major source of publications, information, dates, and advice for all Floridians interested in the marine environment is the Sea Grant Program in Gainesville, Florida. Write or call the Marine Advisory Program, Florida Cooperative Extension Service, G022 McCarty Hall, University of Florida, Gainesville, FL 32611 (904–392–1837), and ask for catalogues and brochures. The extension service may even be able to furnish an expert to advise your community on your particular shoreline problem.

Florida also is blessed with the nation's foremost library of coastal engineering and related subjects in the Department of Coastal Engineering, University of Florida, Gainesville, Florida. For other sources of publications and information see appendix B.

Books by the same authors

1. Living with the Shore series, Orrin H. Pilkey, Jr., and William J. Neal, eds. The series addresses problems and concerns of coastal living and management for all Atlantic Coast, Gulf Coast, and Pacific Coast states, as well as the Great Lakes. Books for North Carolina, Texas, South Carolina, New York, and Louisiana are now available to the public. This text (East Florida) is the sixth book of the series. The series is being published by Duke University Press, 6697 College Station, Durham, NC 27708, and may be ordered from the Press. Cost $9.75 paper; $22.75 cloth.

2. *The Beaches Are Moving: The Drowning of America's Shoreline*, by Wallace Kaufman and Orrin H. Pilkey, Jr., 1979, 1983. This highly readable account of the state of America's coastline explains natural processes at work at the beach, provides a historical perspective of man's relation to the shore, and offers practical advice on how to live in harmony with coastal environments. Originally published by Anchor Press/Doubleday, it is now available in paperback from Duke University Press, 6697 College Station, Durham, NC 27708 ($9.75).

3. *Coastal Design: A Guide for Builders, Planners, and Home Owners*, by Orrin H. Pilkey, Sr., Walter D. Pilkey, Orrin H. Pilkey, Jr., and William J. Neal, 1983. The "umbrella" book for the Living with the Shore series, this volume emphasizes principles of shoreline construction and is intended to be a companion for the individual state books of this series. Van Nostrand Reinhold, New York, 224 pp., $25.50.

General references for the nonspecialist

4. *Waves and Beaches*, by Willard Bascom, 1980. A highly readable primer on beach processes. Available in paperback from most local coastal-zone bookstores. Doubleday/Anchor Press, Garden City, New York.

5. *At the Sea's Edge*, by William T. Fox, 1983. This text is billed as an introduction to coastal oceanography for the amateur naturalist, but it is not easy reading for the nonscientist. Nonetheless, this is the best, most complete, most up-to-date volume available for those who want to learn about the shoreline and are starting from scratch. Prentice-Hall, Englewood Cliffs, NJ 07632, 317 pp.

6. *Barrier Island Handbook*, by Steve Leatherman, 1982. A nontechnical, easy-to-read paperback about barrier island dynamics and coastal hazards. Many of the examples are from the Maryland and New England coasts but are applicable to East Florida as well. Available from Coastal Publications, 5201 Burke Drive, Charlotte, NC 28208 ($5.75).

7. *Sea Islands of the South*, by Diana and Bill Gleasner, 1980. An excellent visitor's guide to the southeastern coast of the United States, including both naturalist information and descriptions of developed barrier islands. You will find descriptions, explanations, and identifications of everything from dunes to tides to birds to shells, guides to visitor information centers, accommodations, activities, and sightseeing points of interest. This guide is especially handy to the first-time traveler through North Carolina to Florida, but may be of interest to natives, too. Available in most coastal bookstores. Published by the East Woods Press.

8. *Barrier Island Ecology of Cape Lookout National Seashore*, by Paul Godfrey. An excellent summary of how islands in North Carolina have evolved. It includes emphasis on the role of overwash and the role of vegetation in island evolution. This book is pertinent to an understanding of Florida's islands. National Park Service, Department of the Interior, Washington, DC, Scientific Monograph #9.

9. *Florida Sea Grant Publications Catalog*. An annual publication listing a wide variety of useful publications for the coastal dweller. Many of these publications are free and can be obtained from the Sea Grant Marine Advisory Program, G022 McCarty Hall, University of Florida, Gainesville, FL 32611.

10. *Florida Coastal and Environmental Information*, by Lucille Lehmann and Todd L. Walton, Jr., 1979. A useful pamphlet of addresses and sources for all kinds of information for the coastal dweller. Available from the Marine Advisory Program, Florida Cooperative Extension Service, University of Florida, Gainesville, FL 32611.

11. *Environmental Quality by Design: South Florida*, by A. R. Veri, W. W. Jenna, and P. E. Bergamaschi, 1975. A nicely illustrated book discussing how to live with South Florida's numerous natural environments. University of Miami Press, Coral Gables, Florida, 192 pp.

12. *Appraisal Report on Beach Conditions in Florida*, by the U.S. Army Corps of Engineers, Jacksonville District, 1965. A summary of beach/island characteristics, which is out of date

but still useful. Available from the U.S. Government Printing Office, Washington, DC 20402, and from U.S. Army Corps of Engineers' offices, 42 pp., plus appendix.

13. *Cat Five*, by Robert P. Davis, 1977. Although not in a class with John D. MacDonald's *Condominium*, this novel graphically dramatizes the effect of a Saffir-Simpson Scale 5 hurricane on Palm Beach. William Morrow and Co., New York.

Books for the specialist or hardworking nonspecialist

14. *The Encyclopedia of Beaches and Coastal Environments*, edited by M. L. Schwartz, 1982. A very informative and complete volume that discusses everything you wanted to know on the subject. It is written for the geologist rather than the lay person, however. Hutchinson-Ross Publishing Co., Stroudsburg, Pennsylvania.

15. *Our Changing Coastlines*, by F. P. Shepard and H. R. Wanless, 1971. A state-by-state rundown of the recent geologic history of all the U.S. shorelines. Illustrations are mainly aerial photographs. Book is now a bit out of date, but it still furnishes dramatic proof of the highly dynamic nature of our shorelines. McGraw-Hill, New York, 579 pp.

16. *Coastal Mapping Handbook*, by M. Y. Ellis, ed., 1978. A primer on coastal mapping that outlines the various types of maps, charts, and photography available; sources for such products; data and uses; state coastal mapping programs; information appendixes; and examples. A valuable starting reference for anyone interested in maps or mapping. For sale by the Superintendent of Documents, U.S. Government Printing Office, Washington, DC 20402 (stock no. 024-001-03046-2), 200 pp.

17. *Coastal Ecosystem Management*, by John Clark, 1977. This 928-page text covers most aspects of the coastal zone from descriptions of processes and environments to legal controls and outlines for management programs. Essential reading for planners and beach community managers. John Wiley and Sons, New York. Available in most university libraries.

18. *Terrigenous Clastic Depositional Environments*, by Miles Hayes and Tim Kana, 1976. Although compiled for a professional field course, this text provides an excellent, detailed treatment on various coastal sedimentary environments that makes good reading for the interested nonscientist. The numerous photographs and diagrams support the text description of depositional systems in rivers, dunes, deltas, tidal flats and inlets, salt marshes, barrier islands, and beaches. Most of the examples are from South Carolina. Technical Report No. 11-CRD (184 pp.) of the Coastal Research Division, Department of Geology, University of South Carolina, Columbia, SC 29208. Probably easiest to obtain through a college or university library.

19. *Barrier Islands from the Gulf of St. Lawrence to the Gulf of*

Mexico, edited by Steve Leatherman, 1979. This collection of technical papers presents some of the current geological research on barrier islands. Of particular interest to students of East Florida barrier islands is the lead paper by Miles Hayes entitled "Barrier Island Morphology as a Function of Tidal and Wave Regime." Published by Academic Press and available through most college and university libraries.

20. *Beach Processes and Sedimentation*, by Paul Komar, 1976. The most widely used textbook on beaches and beach processes. Recommended only to serious students of the beach. Published by Prentice-Hall, Englewood Cliffs, NJ 07632. Available in university libraries.

21. *Coastal Geomorphology*, edited by D. R. Coates, 1973. A collection of technical papers including R. Dolan's "Barrier Islands: Natural and Controlled." Interesting reading for anyone willing to overlook or wade through the jargon of coastal scientists. Published by the State University of New York, Binghamton, NY 13901. Available in university libraries.

22. *Geological Highway Map of the Southeastern Region*, compiled by A. P. Bennison and others. Although this map is not aimed specifically at the coast, it provides the layman with a semitechnical treatment of the regional geology of Florida and adjacent states. In addition to the map, there is a discussion of the geological development of the region and its rock and mineral resources, a description of the Everglades, a photographic map, subsurface cross sections, descriptions of gemstones and fossils, and a list of points of geologic interest.

Available from the American Association of Petroleum Geologists, P.O. Box 979, Tulsa, OK 74101.

23. *Florida, Satellite Image Mosaic* (scale 1:500,000), by the U.S. Geological Survey, 1973. This large composite was compiled from NASA ERTS-1 satellite images and shows the entire state of Florida. Because the image is produced in false-color infrared, vegetation appears red, giving the illustration an overall dominant color of pink to red. Coastal features such as barrier islands, keys, bays, marshes, and swamps stand out clearly, and distinct inland ridges mark old shoreline positions from former high stands of sea level. Published by the U.S. Geological Survey, Reston, VA 22092.

24. *The Florida Coastal Management Program, Draft Environmental Impact Statement*, prepared by the Office of Coastal Zone Management, National Oceanic and Atmospheric Administration, and the Florida Office of Coastal Management, Department of Environmental Regulation, 1981. This massive document provides the background to the Florida Coastal Management Program (FCMP) and includes discussions of Florida coastal management legislation, programs, goals, and initiatives. A wealth of information is incorporated into the report, including descriptions of important natural environments such as barrier islands, why they are hazardous for development and difficult to maintain artificially. Students of coastal land-use regulation will find this report to be a good example of the wide spectrum of land-use demands, often conflicting, that are placed on the coastal zone. One can sym-

pathize with the "regulators" who must walk a thin line to meet the wide range of objectives from preservation of the environment to encouragement of economic growth as set forth in the document. Although the volume was not published for sale, it was widely distributed to public and private agencies concerned with coastal issues. You may find a copy in your community's planning office or through various state departments that deal with coastal issues.

Films

25. *It's Your Coast*, NOAA. A 28-minute film on coastal zone management problems and selection. Available from the Marine Advisory Program, University of Florida, Gainesville, FL 32611.

26. *Portrait of a Coast*. A spectacular 29-minute film showing among other things a major storm on the Massachusetts coast. It addresses the interrelated problems of rising sea level, coastal erosion, and shoreline stabilization. This film is very pertinent to the Florida situation. Available from Circle Oak Productions, 73 Girdle Ridge Drive, Katonah, NJ 10536.

27. *Tornadoes*, NOAA. This 15-minute film shows how the tornado warning system works, plus scenes of tornado damage. Available from the Marine Advisory Program, University of Florida, Gainesville, FL 32611.

28. *Hurricane before the Storm*. This 29-minute film is centered on Hurricane Eloise, which hit northeast Florida. The film discusses how to save life and property. Available from the Marine Advisory Program, University of Florida, Gainesville, FL 32611.

Shoreline engineering

29. *Shore Protection Manual*, by the U.S. Army Corps of Engineers, 1973. The "bible" of shoreline engineering. Published in 3 volumes. Request publication 08-0022-00077 from the Superintendent of Documents, U.S. Government Printing Office, Washington, DC 20402. Price $14.25.

30. *Help Yourself*, by the U.S. Army Corps of Engineers. Brochure addressing the erosion problems in the Great Lakes region. May be of interest to barrier island residents; it outlines shoreline processes and illustrates a variety of shoreline engineering devices used to combat erosion. Free from the U.S. Army Corps of Engineers, North Central Division, 219 South Dearborn St., Chicago, Il 60604.

31. *Publications List, Coastal Engineering Research Center (CERC) and Beach Erosion Board (BEB)*, by the U.S. Army Corps of Engineers. A list of published research by the Corps. Free from the U.S. Army Corps of Engineers, Coastal Engineering Research Center, Kingman Building, Fort Belvoir, VA 22060.

32. *Low-Cost Shore Protection*, by the U.S. Army Corps of Engineers, 1982. A set of 4 reports written for the layman under this title includes the introductory report, a property owner's

guide, a guide for local government officials, and a guide for engineers and contractors. The reports are a summary of the Shoreline Erosion Control Demonstration Program and suggest a wide range of engineering devices and techniques to stabilize shorelines, including beach nourishment and vegetation. In adopting these approaches, one should keep in mind that they are short-term measures and may have unwanted side effects. The reports are available from John G. Housley, Section 54 Program, U.S. Army Corps of Engineers, USACE (DAEN–CWP–F), Washington, DC 20314.

33. *Shore Management Guidelines* and *Shore Protection Guidelines*, by the U.S. Army Corps of Engineers, 1972. These publications are designed to instruct the public on the use of the shore and the use of structural solutions in solving erosion problems. Both are available from the Department of the Army, Corps of Engineers, Washington, DC 20314.

34. *Shoreline Stabilization with Salt Marsh Vegetation*, by Paul L. Knutson and W. W. Woodhouse, Jr., 1983. Use of salt marsh as an erosion buffer on the lagoon sides of islands is discussed. This is a much preferable alternative to bulkheading. Coastal Engineering Research Center Special Report #9, Kingman Building, Fort Belvoir, VA 22060.

35. *Beach Nourishment in Florida and on the Lower Atlantic and Gulf Coasts*, by Todd L. Walton, Jr., 1977, *Shore and Beach*, pp. 10–18. A technical report discussing the successes and failures of a number of beach replenishment projects.

36. *Beach Dune Walkover Structures*, by Todd L. Walton, Jr., and Thomas C. Skinner, 1976. A primer on walkover structures with plans detailed enough to hand to your contractor (or to do it yourself). Available from the Marine Advisory Program, University of Florida, Gainesville, FL 32611.

Hurricanes

37. *Early American Hurricanes, 1492–1870*, by D. M. Ludlum, 1963. An excellent summary of the storm history of the Atlantic and Gulf coasts that provides a lesson on the frequency, intensity, and destructive potential of hurricanes. Published by the American Meteorological Society, Boston, Massachusetts. Available in public and university libraries.

38. *Hurricanes and Coastal Storms*, edited by Earl Baker, 1980. Technical papers dealing with hurricane and storm awareness, evacuation, and mitigation presented at a 1979 national conference in Orlando, Florida. Good reading for planners, developers, and coastal community officials. Available from the Marine Advisory Program, University of Florida, Gainesville, FL 32611.

39. *Bibliography on Hurricanes and Severe Storms of the Coastal Plains Region and Supplement*, by the Coastal Plains Center for Marine Development Services, 1970 and 1972. A reference list that provides a good starting point for persons seeking detailed information on hurricanes and hurricane research. Available through college and university libraries.

40. *Hurricane Information and Gulf Tracking Chart*, by NOAA, 1974. An important brochure that describes hurricane characteristics and lists safety precautions. Available from the Superintendent of Documents, U.S. Government Printing Office, Washington, DC 20402.

41. *Post-Disaster Reports*. Available from both the Jacksonville and Mobile district offices of the U.S. Army Corps of Engineers. These posthurricane reports provide valuable documentation of storm damage and are particularly useful for those who wish to prevent disaster recurrences.

42. *Lower Southeast Florida Hurricane Evacuation Study Technical Data Report*, 1983. This is a report prepared for Monroe, Dade, Broward, and Palm Beach counties by a private contractor and the Corps of Engineers. This report gives a lot of numbers, such as evacuation time estimates, tables of numbers of endangered people, etc.; a somewhat distressing report. Available from county governmental offices and the Corps of Engineers.

43. *Hurricane Evacuation Plan: A Model for Florida's Coastal Counties*, by the Florida Division of Disaster Preparedness, 1978. A summary of the procedures and organization needed to evacuate endangered communities, 42 pp.

44. *Florida Hazard Analysis*, by the Florida Division of Disaster Preparedness, 1977. A summary of the natural hazards of Florida, available in local libraries, 93 pp.

45. *Florida Hurricane Survey Report*, 1965. A post-Hurricane Betsy report of damage and storm characteristics. Available in the University of Florida Coastal Engineering Library, Gainesville, Florida, 81 pp.

Site selection

46. *Ecological Determinants of Coastal Area Management* (two volumes), by Francis Parker, David Brower, and others, 1976. Volume 1 defines the barrier island and related lagoon-estuary systems and the natural processes that operate within them. Outlines man's disturbing influences on island environments and suggests management tools and techniques. Volume 2 is a set of appendixes that include information on coastal ecological systems, man's impact on barrier islands, and tools and techniques for coastal area management. Also contains a good barrier island bibliography. Available from the Center for Urban and Regional Studies, University of North Carolina at Chapel Hill, 108 Battle Lane, Chapel Hill, NC 27514.

47. *Coastal Ecosystems: Ecological Considerations for Management of the Coastal Zone*, by John Clark, 1974. A clearly written, well-illustrated book on the applications of ecological principles to the major coastal-zone environments. Available from the Publications Department, Conservation Foundation, 1717 Massachusetts Avenue, NW, Washington, DC 20036.

48. *Coastal Environment Management*, prepared by the Conservation Foundation, 1980. Guidelines for conservation of resources and protection against storm hazards, including ecological descriptions and management suggestions for coastal

uplands, floodplains, wetlands, banks and bluffs, dunelands, and beaches. Part 2 presents a complete list of federal agencies and their authority under the law to regulate coastal-zone activities. A good reference for planners and persons interested in good land management. Available from the Superintendent of Documents, U.S. Government Printing Office, Washington, DC 20402.

49. *Natural Hazard Management in Coastal Areas*, by G. F. White and others, 1976. The most recent summary of coastal hazards along the entire U.S. coast. Discusses adjustments to such hazards and hazard-related federal policy and programs. Summarizes hazard management and coastal land-planning programs in each state. Appendixes include a directory of agencies, an annotated bibliography, and information on hurricanes. An invaluable reference, recommended to developers, planners, and managers. Available from the Office of Coastal Zone Management, National Oceanic and Atmospheric Administration, 3300 Whitehaven Street, NW, Washington DC 20235.

50. *Guidelines for Identifying Coastal High Hazard Zones*, by the U.S. Army Corps of Engineers, 1975. Report outlining such zones with emphasis on "coastal special flood-hazard areas" (coastal floodplains subject to inundation by hurricane surge with a 1 percent chance of occurring in any given year). Provides technical guidelines for conducting uniform flood insurance studies and outlines methods of obtaining 100-year storm-surge elevations. Recommended to island planners. Available from the Galveston District, U.S. Army Corps of Engineers, Galveston, TX 77553.

51. *Report of Investigation of the Environmental Effects of Private Water-front Lands,* by W. Barada and W. M. Partington, 1972. An enlightening reference treats the effects of finger canals on water quality. Available from the Environmental Information Center, the Florida Conservation Foundation, Inc., 935 Orange Avenue, Winter Park, FL 32789.

52. *Know Your Mud, Sand, and Water: A Practical Guide to Coastal Development*, by K. M. Jurgensen, 1976. A pamphlet describing the various island environments relative to development. Clearly and simply written. Recommended to island dwellers. Available from UNC Sea Grant, North Carolina State University, Box 8065, Raleigh, NC 27695.

Water

53. *Your Home Septic System, Success or Failure.* Brochure providing answers to commonly asked questions on home septic systems. Lists agencies that supply information on septic tank installation and operation. Available from UNC Sea Grant, North Carolina State University, Box 8065, Raleigh, NC 27695.

54. *Water Resources Development.* Water projects of the U.S. Army Corps of Engineers in Florida. Available from U.S. Army Corps of Engineers, Jacksonville, Florida, 191 pp.

Vegetation

55. *Mangroves: A Guide for Planting and Maintenance*, by John Stevely and Larry Rabinowitz, 1982. How to identify, plant, and maintain mangroves, and why they are important. Available from Sea Grant Marine Advisory Program, University of Florida, Gainesville, FL 32611.

56. *Dune Restoration and Revegetation Manual*, by Jack Salmon and others, 1982. A manual of use to both homeowners and community officials anywhere in the southeastern United States. Available from the Sea Grant Marine Advisory Program, University of Florida, Gainesville, FL 32611.

57. *Stabilization of Beaches and Dunes by Vegetation in Florida*, by John Davis. Guidelines for the use of vegetation in Florida nearshore areas. Available from Sea Grant Marine Advisory Program, University of Florida, Gainesville, FL 32611.

58. *How to Build and Save Beaches and Dunes*, by John A. Jagschitz and Robert C. Wakefield, 1971. Outlines how to build dunes using brush, snow fencing, or American beach grass. Most of the discussion pertains to the planting and care of beach grass. Available from Rhode Island Agricultural Experiment Station, Woodward Hall, University of Rhode Island, Kingston, RI 02881, *University of Rhode Island Marine Leaflet Series No. 4*, 12 pp.

59. *Building and Stabilizing Coastal Dunes with Vegetation* (UNC–SG–82–05) and *Planting Marsh Grasses for Erosion Control* (UNC–SG–81–09), by S. W. Broome, W. W. Woodhouse, Jr., and E. D. Seneca, 1982. These publications on using vegetation as stabilizers are available from UNC Sea Grant, North Carolina State University, Box 8650, Raleigh, NC 27695. State publication number with your request.

60. *The Dune Book: How to Plant Grasses for Dune Stabilization*, by Johanna Seltz, 1976. Brochure outlining the importance of sand dunes and means of stabilizing them through grass plantings. Available from UNC Sea Grant, North Carolina State University, Box 8605, Raleigh NC 27695.

Flood Insurance

61. *Questions and Answers/National Flood Insurance Program*, by the Federal Emergency Management Agency (FEMA), 1983. This pamphlet explains the basics of flood insurance and provides addresses of FEMA offices. Free from Federal Emergency Management Agency, Washington, DC 20472.

62. *Coastal Flood Hazards and the National Flood Insurance Program*, by H. Crane Miller, 1977. This publication describes in detail the nature of flood hazards in the coastal zone and the basic features of the flood insurance program. The third and most interesting portion of this article is the attempt to assess the impact that this program has had on those interested in building in the coastal zone. Available from National Flood Insurance Program, Federal Emergency Management Agency, Washington, DC 20472, 50 pp.

63. *Entering the Regular Program, No. 3.* Intended for use by community officials during the period when a community enters the regular Federal Insurance Administration program. Explains the responsibilities of FEMA and the local community that must be met to enter the regular program. It includes a timetable that should be followed. Available from Federal Emergency Management Agency, Washington, DC 20472.

64. *Guide for Ordinance Development, No. 1e.* A guidebook designed for use by community officials in preparing floodplain management measures that satisfy the minimum standards of the national flood insurance program. It organizes the program's standards into a simple ordinance and provides an explanatory narrative. Available from Federal Emergency Management Agency, Washington, DC 20472.

Building, home improvement, and repair

65. *Elevated Residential Structures, Reducing Flood Damage Through Building Design: A Guide Manual*, prepared by the Federal Insurance Administration, 1976. An excellent outline of the flood threat, essential for proper planning and construction. Illustrates construction techniques and includes a glossary, references, and worksheets for estimating building costs. Order publication 0-222-193 from the Superintendent of Documents, U.S. Government Printing Office, Washington, DC 20402, or contact an office of the Federal Emergency Management Agency.

66. *Design and Construction Manual for Residential Buildings in Coastal High Hazard Areas*, prepared by Dames and Moore for the Department of Housing and Urban Development on behalf of the Federal Emergency Management Agency, Federal Insurance Administration, 1981. A guide to the coastal environment with recommendations on site and structure design relative to the National Flood Insurance Program. The report includes design considerations, examples, construction costs, and appendixes on design tables, bracing, design worksheets, wood preservatives, and a listing of useful references. The manual is available from the Superintendent of Documents, U.S. Government Printing Office, Washington, DC 20402 (publication number 722-978/545), or contact an office of the Federal Emergency Management Agency.

67. *Structural Failures: Modes, Causes, Responsibilities*, 1973. See especially the chapter entitled "Failure of Structures Due to Extreme Winds," pp. 49-77. Available from the Research Council on Performance of Structures, American Society of Civil Engineers, 345 East 47th Street, New York, NY 10017. Price $4.00.

68. *Flood Emergency and Residential Repair Handbook*, prepared by the National Association of Homebuilders Research Advisory Board of the National Academy of Science, 1980. Guide to floodproofing as well as step-by-step cleanup procedures and repairs, including household goods and appliances. Available from the Superintendent of Documents, U.S.

Government Printing Office, Washington, DC 20402. Order stock No. 023-000-00552-2 for $3.50.

69. *Wind-Resistant Design Concepts for Residences*, by Delbart B. Ward. Displays with vivid sketches and illustrations construction problems and methods tying structures down to the ground. Considerable text and excellent illustrations devoted to methods of strengthening residences. Offers recommendations for relatively inexpensive modifications that will increase the safety of residences subject to severe winds. Chapter 8, "How to Calculate Wind Forces and Design Wind-Resistant Structures," should be of particular interest to the designer. Available as TR83 from the Civil Defense Preparedness Agency, Department of Defense, the Pentagon, Washington DC 20301; or from the Civil Defense Preparedness Agency, 2800 Eastern Boulevard, Baltimore, MD 21220.

70. *Hurricane-Resistant Construction for Homes*, by T. L. Walton, Jr., 1976. An excellent booklet produced for residents of Florida. A good summary of hurricanes, storm surge, damage assessment, and guidelines for hurricane-resistant construction. Technical concepts on probability and its implications on home design in hazard areas. A brief summary of federal and local guidelines. Available from Florida Sea Grant Publications, Florida Cooperative Extension Service, Marine Advisory Program, Coastal Engineering Laboratory, University of Florida, Gainesville, FL 32611.

71. *Hurricane-Resistant Construction for Homes*, by Todd L. Walton, Jr., 1983. A quick summary of construction principles in hurricane-prone areas, with an excellent bibliography. This Florida Cooperative Extension Marine Advisory Bulletin is available from Sea Grant Marine Advisory Program, G022 McCarty Hall, University of Florida, Gainesville, FL 32611, 31 pp.

72. *Houses Can Resist Hurricanes*, by the U.S. Forest Service, 1965. An excellent paper with numerous details on construction in general. Pole-house construction is treated in particular detail (pp. 28-45). Available as Research Paper FPL 33 from Forest Products Laboratory, Forest Service, U.S. Department of Agriculture, P.O. Box 5130, Madison, WI 53705.

73. *Pole House Construction* and *Pole Building Design*. Available from the American Wood Preservers Institute, 1651 Old Meadows Road, McLean, VA 22101.

74. *Standard Details for One-Story Concrete Block Residences*, by the Masonry Institute of America. Contains 9 foldout drawings that illustrate the details of constructing a concrete block house. Principles of reinforcement and good connections aimed at design for seismic zones but apply to design in hurricane zones as well. Written for both the layman and designer. Available as Publication 701 from Masonry Institute of America, 2550 Beverly Boulevard, Los Angeles, CA 90057. Price $3.00.

75. *Masonry Design Manual*, by the Masonry Institute of America. A 384-page manual that covers all types of masonry including brick, concrete block, glazed structural units, stone, and veneer. Very comprehensive and well presented. Probably of more interest to the designer than to the layman. Available as publication 601 from the Masonry Institute of America, 2550 Beverly Boulevard, Los Angeles, CA 90057.

76. *Protecting Mobile Homes from High Winds* (TR-75), prepared by the Civil Defense Preparedness Agency, 1974. An excellent booklet that outlines methods of tying down mobile homes and offers means of protection such as positioning and wind breaks. Publication 1974-0-537-785, available free from the Superintendent of Documents, U.S. Government Printing Office, Washington, DC 20402; or from the U.S. Army, AG Publications Center, Civil Defense Branch, 2800 Eastern Boulevard (Middle River), Baltimore, MD 21220.

77. *Coastal Design: A Guide for Builders, Planners, and Homeowners.* See entry 3 in this appendix.

78. *Coastal Construction Practices*, by Christopher P. Jones and Leigh T. Johnson. Includes an address list of state and local agencies involved in regulation of coastal construction. Marine Advisory Publication available from Marine Advisory Program, University of Florida, Gainesville, FL 32611.

79. *Guidelines for Beachfront Construction with Special Reference to the Coastal Construction Setback Line*, by Courtland Collier and others, 1977. The Sea Grant catalog says this publication illustrates criteria for evaluating variances that will uphold the purpose and philosophy of the Coastal Construction Setback Law wherever construction seaward of this line is justified. We find this approach distressing because a setback line can have *no* exceptions if it is to succeed. At any rate, this publication can be obtained from the Marine Advisory Program, University of Florida, Gainesville, FL 32611.

80. *Building Construction on Shoreline Property.* A fact sheet on shoreline construction, available from the Marine Advisory Program, University of Florida, Gainesville, FL 32611.

Building codes

81. *Coastal Construction Building Code Guidelines*, edited by R. R. Clark, 1980. This excellent volume is designed to serve as a supplement to the 2 building codes listed below. The guidelines from Clark's volume are intended to strengthen the 2 codes to meet structural design considerations required by Section 161.053, Florida Statutes: *Standard Building Code*, 1979 edition, available from the Southern Building Code Congress, 1116 Brown Marx Building, Birmingham, AL 35203; and *South Florida Building Code (Broward County Edition)*, 1979, available from Broward County governmental offices. The guidelines are available as Technical Report No. 80-1, Division of Beaches and Shores, Florida Department of Natural Resources, 3900 Commonwealth Blvd., Tallahassee, FL 32303. A must for the conscientious builder.

82. *Model Minimum Hurricane Resistant Building Standards for the Texas Gulf Coast*, by the Texas Coastal and Marine Council, P.O. Box 13407, Austin, TX 78711. The problems encountered on the coast of east Florida are similar to those on the Gulf Coast of Texas, making this splendid book appropriate.

Appendix D. Field guide to the beaches of Dade County

The islands of Miami Beach, Virginia Key, and Key Biscayne are the most southerly of the sand barrier islands along the east coast of the United States (fig. D–1). The material making up these islands is a mixture of quartz sand, which has traveled south by longshore drift from northern Florida and Georgia, and more locally derived calcium carbonate grains from the breakdown of mollusk shells and other marine skeletal remains. In addition, recent beach nourishment projects have added sands from various sources that were not naturally part of the beach system.

As this guide was going to press, a number of changes were taking place in Dade County. The drawbridge on Rickenbacker Causeway was being replaced by a new high bridge (designed to make storm evacuation safer). The city of Miami was in the beginning stages of developing northern Virginia Key as a recreational park facility. A large amount of new sand was scheduled to be pumped up on the beaches of central and southern Key Biscayne in 1984. And, as noted earlier, Miami Beach recently has been the site of the largest and most costly beach replenishment project in American shoreline history.

The guide begins at the entrance to Rickenbacker Causeway (reached by Interstate 95, exit 1 to Key Biscayne). The tour leads you out the causeway across Virginia Key to Key Biscayne to visit natural and developed beaches on this southernmost barrier island. This portion of the trip could best be enjoyed by bicycle, whether you pedal in from the causeway entrance or rent bicycles at some of the stops. The park areas have bicycle paths and numerous beach accesses. Once the new bridge is completed, bicycle access from the mainland will be much safer.

The tour next examines the sediment-starved shoreline of Virginia Key, after which you will then return to the mainland, drive north through Miami, and head out to the south tip of Miami Beach via the MacArthur Causeway. The massive new renourishment beach of Miami Beach is accessible at numerous points. Three stops are recommended, including one at Government Cut jetty at the south end.

The final stop on the tour is at Bakers Haulover Beach, an area that has received renourishment several times but which still has sand generally similar to that originally found on Miami Beach.

0.0 Toll booth at the entrance to the Rickenbacker Causeway (toll $0.75).

Drive out on the Rickenbacker Causeway (which becomes Crandon Boulevard on Key Biscayne) to Cape Florida State Park at the south end of Key Biscayne.

Rickenbacker Causeway was built during and just after World War II. The fill areas, including much of the roadway on Virginia Key, have restricted water circulation in Biscayne Bay. This causeway and five others to the north have divided northern Biscayne Bay into a number of sepa-

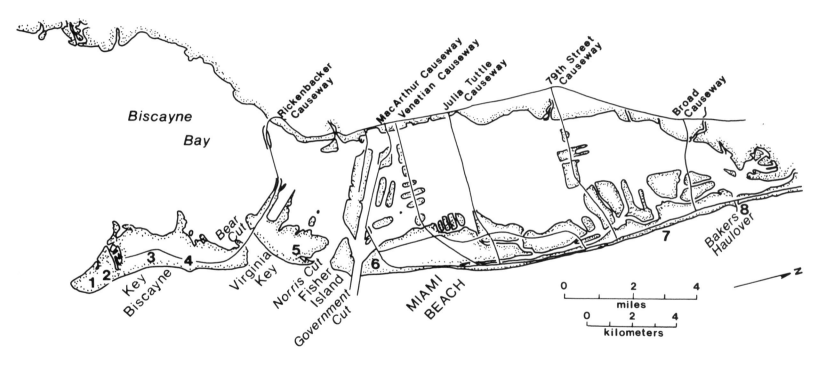

Fig. D-1. Map of the Miami area and coastal barrier islands showing locations of stops for this field trip.

rate bays. Each of these causeways serves as an evacuation route for island residents. However, all of them become impassible during the early stages of a hurricane's approach.

2.5 On the left, Planet Ocean, created by the International Oceanographic Foundation, is an outstanding and enjoyable place to visit to learn about our oceans and also our shorelines. It is well worth your time.

2.8 The Seaquarium on the right has an exhilarating display of marine life.

2.9 On the right is the University of Miami's Rosenstiel School of Marine and Atmospheric Science. It has tours for the public on Mondays at 1 p.m. (There also is a nice cafeteria on the water.)

On the left are the laboratories of the National Oceanic and Atmospheric Administration and the Tropical Marine Fisheries Center.

3.0 **Take the bridge** across Bear Cut, which separates Virginia Key and Key Biscayne. Bear Cut is a natural tidal inlet that is noted on maps from the earliest exploration of Florida waters. The tidal currents through Bear Cut have shifted much of Virginia Key's southward-drifting beach sand seaward, forming a broad, shallow, underwater sand platform seaward of northern Key Biscayne.

3.5 Come on to Key Biscayne. The Australian pines (*Casurina*) that dominate this northern tip of Key Biscayne are exotic trees that rapidly grow on disturbed or filled land—in this case fill associated with causeway construction. These beautiful trees are a great hazard to the inhabitants of Key Biscayne. They are shallow-rooted and as a consequence are readily blown over during hurricanes. They will block passage on and off the island.

5.6 Enter the central one-third of Key Biscayne, which is residential and commercial.

7.0 Enter Bill Baggs Cape Florida State Park, which occupies the southern one-third of Key Biscayne. It is open from 8 A.M. to sundown; the entrance fee is $.50 per person. Write to the superintendent for a waiver of fees for educational groups (Key Biscayne, FL 33149).

7.8 Turn left into the parking lot and park as soon as possible. Walk out to the beach.

Stop 1. Natural shoreline with sea oat stabilization, beach ridges, and controlled access walkways.

In 1950 the bulk of Cape Florida was filled by a developer to its present elevation by dredging material from the bay side (fig. D-2). Only the section of beach ridges at this stop and at an area near the lighthouse remain in their original natural state (fig. D-3). Hence, the dominance of Australian pines throughout the park. Prior to filling, this southern third of Key Biscayne was a series of southward-arching, sandy beach ridges that in some cases were separated by mangroves or small ponds (fig. D-2). Each ridge of sand was once at the tip of the island, clearly showing that Cape Florida grew southward.

On the walk out to the beach, you will cross several beach ridges. These are quite young, having only sea oats and shrub vegetation. This is one of the few sections of beach in Dade County that has been building out during the last 50 years. By coring into these ridges we have learned that each one was formed during a major storm, and that sea oats subsequently grew on the ridges and caused some further growth as they trapped finer sand blown or washed onto the ridges during lesser storms.

Here as elsewhere sea oats and other coastal vegetation are important to assure stabilization and preservation of the beach ridges and dunes. The beach ridges in the park were severely damaged in areas where foot traffic destroyed the vegetation. In 1982 Cape Florida park began a program of restricting access to the beaches by putting up fences to define walkways. Notice the difference in the beach ridge elevations at and away from the walkways.

The shrubs of the round-leafed seagrape, the low, crawling vines of the beach peanut and the beach star, and the other grasses also are important to stabilization of the ridges.

To encourage recovery of the previously damaged beach ridges, the park planted 20,000 sea oat plants in 1982 and 1983. As you will see at the next stop, the park also is beginning to construct board walkways across beach ridges, a program they plan to expand.

Seaward of the beach is a very broad, shallow, littoral sand platform on which the seagrass *Thalassia* flourishes. Though important to the stabilization of the offshore sands, the blades wash ashore in great abundance after winter storms, detracting from the aesthetic quality of the beach to many beachgoers. The various parks have various ways of handling this problem. Wisely, park managers of Cape Florida either do not disturb this seagrass wrack or they rake it to the edge of the beach ridges as a protection to the ridge and as shore mulch. This, at the same time, deters foot traffic in from the beach. Only litter is removed from the beach. To simply gather the seagrass from the beach and carry it away also would remove precious beach sand.

The beaches of southeast Florida differ from those farther north (from Palm Beach north) in that the Bahamas to the east protect the shores from large waves coming in from the open Atlantic. In addition, certain stretches are protected by seaward reef ridges near the edge of the continental shelf. These break up larger waves generated in the Straits of Florida. Seaward of Key Biscayne, for example, is a shelf edge ridge rising from the deeper seafloor to a depth of 9 to 12 feet. In addition, north and south Key Biscayne have broad, shallow, littoral sand platforms extending about 1 mile seaward of the shore. These further dampen incoming wave energy. As a result of the relatively small waves, the beaches of Key Biscayne are composed of somewhat finer-grained sand than is present on the more

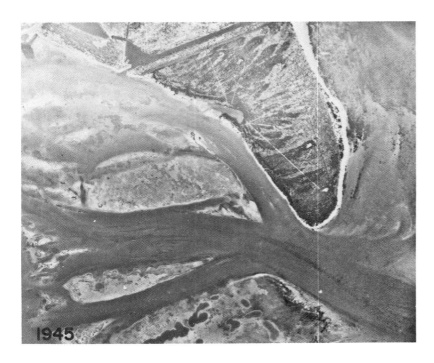

Fig. D-2. Aerial photographs from 1945, 1951, and 1972 of Cape Florida, southern Key Biscayne. Cape Florida Channel, just left of Key Biscayne, was severely modified in 1950 when dredged to provide fill for nearly t entire cape area. This fill covered the curving beach ridges that record

1972

he natural southward growth history of Key Biscayne (in 1945 photo).

exposed beaches farther north.

From the beach here you can look north to the developed part of Key Biscayne, Crandon Park, Fisher Island, and Miami Beach (the buildings in the distance).

To the south you can see Cape Florida Lighthouse (fig. D-3), and if you look due south you may be able to see Soldier Key, the northernmost of the Florida Keys. Soldier Key is composed of coral limestone—a reef formed some 120,000 years ago during a previous interglacial stage when sea level was about 22 feet higher than it is at present.

Beach sand that is transported south past Key Biscayne is mostly carried southeastward across an elongated, shallowly submerged sand ridge that extends south about as far as the level of Soldier Key. Directly south of Key Biscayne is a carbonate mud bank cut by numerous tidal channels. Tidal ebb flow through these channels is responsible for shifting the southward-drifting beach sand seaward.

It is from this southeastward extending sandbank that sand was obtained for the Key Biscayne beach nourishment in 1984. The sand will be spread on the beach from just north of this stop northward through the park and in front of the commercial sector.

Return to your car and drive on south through the parking lot. Continue on the drive around Cape Florida unless you want to stop at the lighthouse.

As you drive through the Australian pine forest here you can see that almost nothing lives on the forest floor except

Fig. D-3. Cape Florida Lighthouse (1978) with the eroded beach to the northeast.

the Australian pines. The needles fall off these trees in such profusion that other growth is stifled. This, combined with the aforementioned shallow root systems and ease of blow-over, make this pine a less-than-desirable barrier island inhabitant.

The Cape Florida Lighthouse, constructed in 1825, was active until 1878 when it was replaced by Fowey Rock light at the shelf edge reef (visible to the southeast about 3 miles distant). The old lighthouse has now been restored, and together with a replica of the lightkeeper's home is open for tours.

When constructed, the lighthouse was apparently about 200 feet from the shoreline. Gradual erosion has left the lighthouse at the water's edge, with only concrete seawalls protecting it from erosion. The 1984 beach nourishment program added sand and an erosion control structure near the lighthouse.

When Cape Florida was filled in 1950 (fig. D-2), the sediment was dredged from the Cape Florida channel and from the carbonate mud bars along the southwest side of Cape Florida, and a seawall was added along the entire southwest shore. The deep, broad channel produced by this dredging is a trap for beach sands carried south past the lighthouse and is a major cause of shore erosion at the south tip of Key Biscayne.

On the drive beyond the lighthouse you can see "Stilts-ville" to the south. These are weekend homes built on pilings along the edge of tidal channels in the mud bar belt. This area is presently being incorporated into Biscayne National Park, and by the turn of the century these houses will be removed.

8.9 No Name Harbor. This small harbor has been a refuge

from hurricanes since early explorers first traversed these waters. In 1982, scout groups began planting red mangrove seedlings in the riprap shore margin.

9.2 Cross the main park road and park in the parking lot. (The lot is sometimes closed on weekdays; if so, park along the roadway and walk 100 yards to the beach.) Walk across the clearing to the beach.

Stop 2. Natural beach with boardwalks. This is a somewhat less used portion of the Cape Florida beach. In 1983, to reduce stress to the vegetation on the beach ridges, 3 boardwalks were constructed across to the beach. At least 3 more are planned. Very shortly visitors should be able to compare the influence of vegetation here with the areas to the south where boardwalks are absent.

From here north, beach fill was added in 1984. From here south, the shoreline has been stable or building out during the past 100 years, but there has been less build-up recently than at Stop 1.

Leave the parking lot and turn right (north) on the main park road toward the exit.

9.8 On the left, just beyond the park exit, is Pines Canal. This is an artificial canal constructed about 1920. It briefly separated Cape Florida from the rest of Key Biscayne, but since there were no significant jetties constructed, it quickly filled in on the beach side with sand carried in by longshore drift.

On the right, the Towers of Key Biscayne Condominium was built on a "compacted sand foundation" on the filled portion of the canal. The beach has a small bulge here (probably caused by the filling of Pines Canal) giving a false sense of beach protection. The seawall (also the front of the more seaward building) lines up with the beach shoreline to the north and south.

10.2 **Turn right** on Seaview Drive.

10.4 **Stop at the corner** of Seaview Drive and Ocean Drive. The large building in front of you, the 26-story Casa del Mar, in contrast to the Towers of Key Biscayne, is built on deep pilings and has a massive, sloping seawall whose foundation is supposed to extend 30 feet below sea level (limestone bedrock begins at about 20 feet). The purpose of deep pilings is to help the building survive a big storm if the beach erodes right out from under the foundation.

There is theoretically a public access just to the left (north) of the Casa del Mar entrance. The gate is usually locked.

10.4 **Turn left** on Ocean Drive.

10.5 Key Biscayne Hotel and Villas was constructed in 1952. When first built, it had more than 100 feet of beach in front of the present seawall. This beach lost more than 25 feet of shoreline in Hurricane Donna (1960), another 25 feet during Hurricane Betsy (1965), and has had minor erosion since. There has been little to no beach since 1965 (fig. D–4).

Fig. D-4. View along the seawall of the Key Biscayne Hotel during a winter storm in January, 1982. Note how the seawalls completely reflect incoming waves. This tends to move what sand is near the shore back seaward off the beach. Hence seawalls, while protecting basic structures built close to the beach, tend to destroy the beach. Of course the beach was the reason the buildings were built there to begin with.

(*Note*: Public beach access on the commercial section of Key Biscayne is presently poor but may improve somewhat after the 1984 nourishment project. Good public access is required because tax money will pay part of the replenishment bill. The various hotels offer good access to the shore and are, of course, open to the public for drinks and meals. This guide does not suggest that hotels offer public beach access for individuals or large groups.)

10.6 Key Biscayne Beach Club. There is another theoretical public beach access to the left of the entry drive.

By October 1983 the seawalled properties to the north and south of the Key Biscayne Beach Club had no beach even at low water. The beach at the club had eroded back to a naturally cemented layer containing mangrove roots.

10.7 **Turn left** on Galen Drive.

11.0 **Turn right** (north) on Crandon Boulevard.

11.3 **Turn right** on East Drive. The older homes in the development on the right are mostly low and were severely inundated during Hurricane Betsy (1965). Federal flood insurance regulations now require first-floor elevations to be 10 feet above mean sea level on the east side of Crandon Boulevard and 9 feet on the west side.

11.7 **Turn right** on Ocean Drive.

Stop 3. Developed shoreline of Key Biscayne. You have 2 choices here: (a) Turn left into Silver Sands and Sand Bar Restaurant. Park and walk up the stairs to the bar overlooking the beach where there is a nice view of the beach system; (b) or park at Sonesta Beach Hotel and walk through the main entrance to the beach at the back.

The Silver Sands, built prior to Hurricane Betsy, was damaged and the seaward part of the structure undermined by both that storm and Hurricane Inez a year later (1966). Figure D–5 shows conditions along this shore during a winter storm.

The Sonesta Beach Hotel was built following these storms. The hotel is set back from the beach (as it is prior to renourishment) about the same distance that the now beachless villas of the Key Biscayne Hotel were when first constructed more than 30 years ago.

The effective beach was more than 100 feet wide at the Sonesta (prior to the 1984 renourishment). However, the beach is severely eroding at present—not laterally but vertically. The beach ridges that used to be here were stripped of vegetation as recreational use increased, and the beach ridges and back-beach area have had over 2 feet of lowering, or vertical erosion. This can be seen by the exposed roots of the palms extending about 2 feet above the sand surface. The heavily used portions of Crandon Park to the north display similar vertical erosion.

This vertical erosion means that there is less volume of sand present to act as a buffer to storm erosion. Storm waves also will more easily overtop the now lower beach. This shoreline may thus severely erode laterally during the next significant hurricane.

Fig. D–5. Seagrass wrack along the beach at the Sonesta Beach Hotel during a winter storm.

Looking north, you can see Crandon Park beyond the condominiums. Sand pushed by the tides through Bear Cut at the north end of Key Biscayne has formed a permanent offshore bar. This bar is about 1 mile offshore at the north end of Key Biscayne, and southward it angles toward the shore.

You can see this bar just offshore by the Silver Sands and Sonesta. It joins the shore just north of the Key Biscayne Beach Club. If there is an onshore wind, the waves will be breaking on it. This essentially is a permanent feature that protects the adjacent beaches from some of the offshore wave energy.

Disturbance of this bar by dredging off northern Key Biscayne in 1969 caused large volumes of sand to drift south. This drifting sand may eventually provide a "natural" pulse of beach nourishment on the commercial sector of Key Biscayne.

Return to Crandon Boulevard.

12.1 **Turn right** (north) on Crandon Boulevard.

13.1 **Turn right** into Crandon Park just beyond the police station and park in the lot (entrance fee $1.00). Walk out to the beach at the north end of parking lot #1.

Stop 4. Crandon Park Beach. To the south of the loop walk with the curved seawall, the beach is very broad. This is partly because the seawall is set well back from the shore and partly because the offshore sandbar in about 1975

moved onshore here. Prior to that time the offshore bar was separated from the beach by a trough 50 to 200 feet wide and 10 to 12 feet deep.

The heavy recreational use, uncontrolled flow of pedestrian traffic, and use of heavy equipment on the shore prevent effective vegetation from stabilizing the back-beach area. Again, the exposed roots of palm trees are an indication of the vertical erosion, or beach lowering, that has taken place in portions of the beach and the grassed picnic areas behind (seen to the north of the loop).

In 1969 a small amount of sand was pumped onto the beach from the north end of Key Biscayne south to the north end of the parking lot. The source for this sand was a "borrow" area 1,500 feet offshore (inside of an offshore sand ridge) on a seagrass-stabilized portion of the nearshore platform. Both the sand put on the beach and the sand exposed offshore by the dredging were quite fine-grained (having been trapped and stabilized there by the seagrasses). Most of this nourishment is now gone, and the offshore borrow pit became quite dynamic for about 10 years. Breaking waves actually eroded the inner margin of the borrow pit, and the sand released spread both shoreward (smothering other extensive areas of seagrass) and southward parallel to the offshore ridge. The area is gradually restabilizing as the seagrass comes back.

One of the reasons that the portion of Crandon Park north of the loop has been eroding is that, in conjunction with development of the park in the early 1950s, an elongated trench was dredged just offshore from the beach. Extending from just north of the loop to just north of the northernmost parking lot, this trench has an uncertain purpose. Perhaps it was to provide fill for the parking areas. Whatever, it has not only been the site of numerous unfortunate drownings over the years but also a sink for sand shifting southward along the coast. The trench is now largely filled.

The absence of vegetation-stabilized beach ridges in the developed part of Crandon Park leads to the landward loss of a great amount of sand by wind. If appropriate dune vegetation was present, this sand would be trapped and would build up the dunes.

As this park is a major beach recreation area for the county, the park managers attempt to keep it free of seagrass wrack. A large scraper-loader moves up the beach scraping the wrack (and some sand). In the past they have dug a trench along the base of the seaward-most dune (north of the parking lots) to deposit the material so it can decay. The sand was then returned to the beach. This served two purposes. It cleaned the beach without removing sand from the system, and the trench minimized the landward loss of sand from the beach zone. Unfortunately, on my last trip to the dump (which is on the west side of Crandon Boulevard) I noticed large mounds of seagrass wrack and sand there—a quite permanent loss of sand from the system.

If you feel adventurous, the walk to the north tip of the island is pleasant and normally much less peopled than near the parking lots. At the north end of the island is a rocky intertidal platform. It is actually an exposure of the 2 oldest beach ridges on Key Biscayne (formed about 3,000 years ago) that were subsequently partly inundated by later sea-level rise. As black mangroves colonized the area (about 2,000 years ago), their roots penetrated the former beach ridges. With time, the roots were fossilized and became quite hard on exposure. These cemented beach ridges are very important to the stability of northern Key Biscayne. The area appears erosional, but comparison with surveys made in 1770 indicates that there has been very little long-term erosion of this rocky platform.

Return to Crandon Boulevard. (Mileage includes a 0.5-mile circuit in Crandon Park; adjust if necessary.) Continue north.

15.0 Marina and Bear Cut Beach. If you wish to visit Bear Cut Beach, park in the Marina on the left and carefully cross the causeway. The north tip of Key Biscayne also can be reached by walking along the shore from this side. Much of the shore is an eroding forest of red and black mangroves, capped by a thin beach ridge.

Continue driving across Bear Cut Bridge. Bear Cut has been here a long time. It is shown on a 1520 map.

The beaches on both sides of Bear Cut are officially

closed to swimming. Strong tidal currents and sharp drop-offs cause numerous drownings each year.

The city of Miami has acquired much of the shoreline of Virginia Key and is developing it as a waterfront park area. Much of the area is presently closed except on weekends.

15.9   **Turn right** on "Sewer Beach Road." This city of Miami, Virginia Key Park is presently open from 8 A.M. to 8 P.M. This, together with the name of the road, is likely to change.

The area along the left side of the road was a major county dump and landfill until the late 1970s. It is now being colonized by Australian pines.

17.4   **Turn right** (carefully) on the dirt road that leads to the beach. Stop at the shore.

Stop 5. Virginia Key Beach. In 1952 the raw sewage that was seriously damaging Biscayne Bay was abruptly diverted through a new sewage treatment plant on Virginia Key and then released at an outfall about 1 mile seaward. The large green structure just to the north is a pumping station. The outfall pipe has recently been extended to beyond the shelf edge and sewage is now released in the Straits of Florida.

Prior to the hurricane of 1835, the island of Virginia Key was connected to Miami Beach to the north. After formation, the inlet (Norris Cut) remained narrow and shallow through the mid-1960s.

To the north you can see Fisher Island and Miami Beach. Fisher Island was created in 1905 when the narrow southern spit of Miami Beach was severed with the dredging of Government Cut. As jetties were extended seaward of the cut to prevent it from being filled by the longshore drift of beach sand from Miami Beach, the areas to the south became sediment-starved. The granite rubble jetties are visible extending seaward from Fisher Island and Miami Beach. The northern jetty extends about 1 mile seaward of the beach.

Since about 1912 essentially no beach sand has come south past Government Cut. Prior to that time about 100,000 cubic yards of sand per year were probably drifting south. That means the beaches south of Government Cut have been deprived of about 7 million cubic yards of sand over the last 70 years. This sediment starvation has had a severe negative impact on the shorelines of Fisher Island, Virginia Key, and northern Key Biscayne (fig. D-6).

During the development boom in the 1920s Carl Fisher placed extensive fill on the back side of his Fisher Island property with the dream that it would become the deep water port of Miami. That dream died with the hurricane of 1926. The original natural beach on the seaward side is completely eroded away, and the beach is composed of Carl Fisher's rubble fill.

Norris Cut has been almost completely flushed of sand, much of it being swept into deep-dredge channels within the bay or onto the shallow flats behind northern Virginia Key.

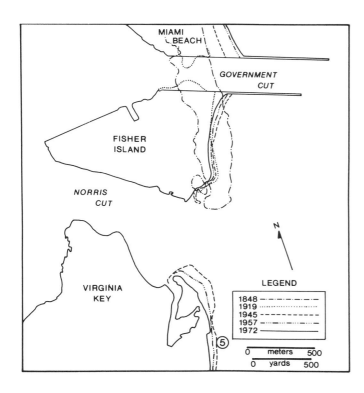

Fig. D-6. Shoreline changes of southern Miami Beach, Fisher Island, and northern Virginia Key between 1848 and 1972. This view was taken before beach fill was added to Virginia Key or Miami Beach.

An area of shallow, littoral sand seaward of the beach at this stop was once extensively carpeted with seagrasses. Sediment starvation caused the loss of most of this seagrass-covered bottom, resulted in rapid deepening of the offshore area, and left the beach exposed to greater wave energy (fig. D-7).

As a result, the beach on northern Virginia Key has eroded by more than 300 feet. The granite groins visible here were installed in 1973 prior to a major renourishment program on 2.1 miles of beach. This innovative project took fossil quartz beach sand being dredged as a part of a Government Cut deepening project and placed it along the northern and central portions of Virginia Key, completely burying the groins. This was innovative because it killed two birds with one stone. The channel was dredged, and the beach was replaced, both in the same operation. At that time the shoreline along this entire portion had cut back essentially to the treeline. As you can see at the northern and southern ends, the sand is again essentially gone. Some sand remains in the central area.

As the offshore sand reservoir and protection has been largely depleted, the future of Virginia Key's beach is not bright. Though not a developed shoreline, this is of special concern because the major sewage treatment facility lies only a few hundred yards inland.

The north end of Virginia Key, in from the shore edge, has received several episodes of fill during Government

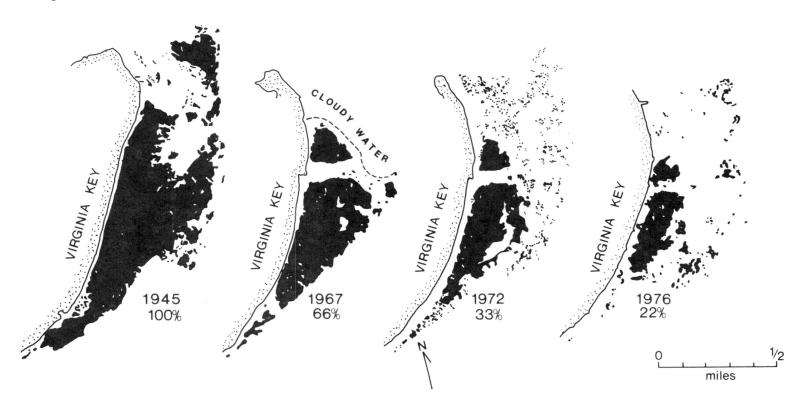

Fig. D-7. Maps showing the loss of seagrass (black in color) on the shallow shelf seaward of the beach on Virginia Key. Percentage of cover with respect to 1945 conditions is noted. This loss is caused by the cutting off of the sand supply by jetties at Government Cut.

Cut deepening programs. Though some of this fill has been trucked to other sites, this area has the highest land elevations in Dade County.

Return to the Rickenbacker Causeway.

19.2 **Turn right** (west) on the Rickenbacker Causeway. Continue off the causeway. Stay in the right lane to follow the exit to I-95 North.

21.8 **Exit to I-95 North.**

24.2 **Take right exit** to I-395 to Miami Beach.

25.5 MacArthur Causeway; continue.

After crossing the drawbridge, you are on Watson Island, a fill island. Chalks International Airline, the world's oldest commercial airline, operates seaplanes to the Bahamas from here.

To the right is Dodge Island, Miami's port and the port for a number of cruise ships.

To the left is Venetian Causeway, the oldest causeway across Biscayne Bay. During the 1926 hurricane the winds suddenly went calm, and many people drove out the causeway to see the damage to Miami Beach. As the calm eye of the storm passed, more than 100 people were trapped and drowned on the causeway by rising water.

All of the causeways and residential and industrial islands in the Bay are artificial. Most were filled in the early 1920s. However, the eastern part of Dodge Island was filled to its present configuration in the early 1980s. The fill on some of the older islands has compacted, and because of the leeward elevations these islands are partially inundated by exceptional spring tides.

Just to the right of the roadway is Government Cut. It was recently dredged to a depth of 42 feet to accommodate the cruise ship SS *Norway.*

As you cross the bridge at the east end of the causeway, you can see Fisher Island to the right. The red-tile roofed buildings are the old U.S. Quarantine Station, now used as a marine geology station by the University of Miami.

28.9 Come on to Miami Beach. Continue east on 5th Street.

29.5 **Turn right** (south on Ocean Drive).

30.0 At the end of the road, park and walk out to the beach south of the pier.

Stop 6. South Miami Beach and Government Cut. Walk south to the jetty at the north side of Government Cut. On the way down you may see the sign:

Beach Erosion Control and
Hurricane Protection Project
Protection Jetty Sand Tightening Project
Beach Erosion Control Project
U.S. Army Corps of Engineers

Though a wide, renourished beach provides protection from total beach erosion during a hurricane, it does not provide protection from flooding. A common misconception is that beach renourishment will provide complete protection from hurricanes. As we will see, the big artificial berm (the ridge on the inner beach) may actually cause increased flooding. The "protection jetty sand tightening project" means that the spaces between the rubble making up the jetty are being filled with sand and rubble so sand cannot wash through into Government Cut.

There is a small dune near the jetty, west of the new fill, where one can see what the old, natural beach material looked like. It is a tannish sand composed of quartz and polished shell fragments, quite coarse.

Government Cut was cut in 1905 and had to be dredged repeatedly to remove sand that was filling it in. This replaced Cape Florida channel as the main access to Biscayne Bay. Government Cut was generally useless until 1912 when jetties were completed on the north and south sides of the cut. Several phases of redredging, deepening, and extending the jetties have brought Government Cut to its final form.

The cut and jetties have formed a nearly complete block to the southern drift of shore sand since 1912. Much of this southward-drifting sand backed up against the north jetty, producing a broad beach that extended north to about 13th Street (figs. D–8 and D–9). Some sand was diverted seaward, shallowing the offshore zone in this area.

From the jetty you can look south to Fisher Island. As noted earlier, the present beach on Fisher Island is rubble

Fig. D–8. Oblique aerial view (1972) looking south across south Miami Beach, Government Cut, Fisher Island, Norris Cut, Virginia Key, Bear Cut, and a part of Key Biscayne (top left). Note the sand buildup against the jetty at Miami Beach.

fill retreating at several feet per year. To the south, you can see Virginia Key and Key Biscayne. Note the erosional offset of Fisher Island and Virginia Key. Remember that Fisher Island once formed a continuous, straight-line beach with Miami Beach (fig. D–6). Beyond you can see the three

Fig. D-9. Oblique aerial view north from the south end of Miami Beach in 1978, prior to the major beach widening project.

sections of Key Biscayne.

This southern end of Miami Beach has received 2 phases of beach fill. The first took place as a part of the Government Cut deepening program. This sand contained an abundance of limestone and coral rubble. The contract for filling stipulated that all grains larger than *12 inches across* were to be screened out!

This minor project has been overshadowed by the massive $68 million project that widened the beach some 300 feet for the entire length of Miami Beach (fig. D-10). Included in this project is an artificial berm about 11 feet in elevation along the inner portion of the beach fill. This project was begun in 1979 and completed in 1981, working from north to south. This project is, thus, only recently finished, and the waves are now "adjusting" the beach profile.

As there was no suitable volume of natural beach sand for this project, an offshore sediment was selected. In from the edge of the platform, the fossil limestone forms a series of submerged linear ridges paralleling the shore. The limestone surface dips down to more than 50 feet below sea level between these ridges, and these elongated depressions are largely filled with a calcareous sand. This sand between the ridges was dredged for the beach fill.

Though approved as a beach sand, this sediment contains very few characteristics of a natural beach sand. More than 30 percent of the sand is sufficiently fine-grained that

Fig. D-10. Oblique aerial view north along Miami Beach in May 1980, just after the major beach fill. Note the murky water just seaward of the new beach.

it tends to readily move in suspension. Many of the coarser grains that were presumed suitable for a beach environment are either very porous and have a very low effective density in water or are thin, platy grains that move much more easily than the robust shell and spherical quartz grains of the preexisting beach. Much of the larger calcareous material is delicate and highly susceptible to fracture breakage when placed in the surf zone.

If there is an onshore wind and waves, the water will probably appear quite murky, a problem rarely observed before nourishment. This fine calcareous mud in suspension was partly in the beach fill and is partly produced by the rapid breakage of the coarser grains in the surf zone.

Near the jetty you may see some large piles of coral rubble. The beach fill contained significant amounts of limestone rubble either as coral heads scattered through the sands or as limestone pieces sucked in when the dredge slipped a bit. Initial reprofiling and erosion of the beach fill by natural processes concentrated these in the swash zone. A rock removal and crushing program costing more than $1 million, thus, had to be added.

The need for beach nourishment in the southern portion of Miami Beach began with the hurricane of 1926. In the early 1920s Miami and Miami Beach were rapidly developing. Resorts were built too near the water's edge. Then the storm struck. The following description is from P. W. Harlem, *Aerial Photographic Interpretation of the*

Historical Changes in Northern Biscayne Bay, Florida: 1925 to 1976 (University of Miami Sea Grant Technical Bulletin 40, 1976).

The 1926 hurricane of September 14–22 advanced on South Florida at a rate of over 18 miles per hour until the 17th when it crossed the coast at Miami and slowed down to 11 miles per hour (Mitchell, 1927). The eye of the storm passed over Miami and Homestead at 6:45 on the morning of the 18th, passing just to the south of Little River. Winds, reported by the local weather bureau, were 8 miles per hour the evening before, 57 miles per hour at 1:50 a.m. on the 18th, and had peaked at about 115 miles per hour (indicated) from the northeast at 5:00 a.m. when the instrument was blown into the street. An hour and one-half later, as the eye passed, the wind was variable at 10 miles per hour. Most of the 242 deaths attributed to this storm occurred after the eye passed as people were caught unprotected on the streets and causeways. At least one hundred million dollars of property damage was incurred in a period of hours. Between Ft. Lauderdale and Miami 4,725 homes were destroyed and another 9,100 damaged. The highest storm tide along Miami and Miami Beach bayshores coincided with the second phase of the storm, after the eye passed, as the 120 miles per hour plus wind changed direction to the east and southeast. Besides inundating the city of Miami Beach, a tidal surge in the Miami River wrecked large numbers of boats put there for safe anchorage. The storm tide in the Miami Canal at Hialeah reached 3 m (10 feet). Storm tides of 2.3 m (7.5 feet) occurred north of MacArthur Causeway, 3.6 m (11.7 feet) at the Miami River mouth and 3.3 m (10.6 feet) at Miami Beach, both south of the causeway.

This marked the end of the first development boom of Miami and Miami Beach. Though there was severe damage, some of the shorefront hotels survived. The beach, however, had eroded, leaving some of the hotels partly in the water and many with waves washing against their walls. Wooden groins were constructed in an attempt to bring some of the sand back to the beach.

Though Miami Beach got off to a poor start because structures were built too near the beach, there has really been very little subsequent erosion. The massive beach nourishment project just completed was, for the southern portion of Miami Beach, an attempt to solve a problem created 55 years earlier. The problem is the same one we see developing in many areas of South Florida today—construction too close to the beach.

As you walk back to your vehicle, note the old South Beach "fishing pier" now (in 1984 at least) mostly extending across the new beach fill.

Drive north on Ocean Drive. As you drive from the south to the north end of Miami Beach, you will progress from the earliest developments to areas built up only in the late 1970s.

30.4 Public park.

At 15th Street there was no beach prior to renourishment, and for several blocks north and south the shore consisted of vertical seawalls (fig. D-11). Incoming waves reflected back offshore, creating a permanent offshore bar inhibiting shoreward movement of sand.

31.3 **Jog left** one block at 15th Street and continue north on Collins Avenue.

Following major hurricanes, Collins Avenue and the first floor of many hotels were commonly filled with sand. This was bulldozed back to the beach. There have been no hurricanes since 1966 (none since beach nourishment), so the response of the new beach fill has not yet been tested.

32.0 Public access and parking at 21st Street.

At 24th Street we join Indian Creek, the remnant of a tidal inlet that opened near 70th street in the mid-1800s. The inlet migrates south because of southward-drifting longshore sand transport. It was sealed off by natural processes in 1820.

32.9 Public access and parking at 34th Street.

33.0 Public access and promenade at 35th Street.

33.5 **Jog left** around the Fontainebleau Hotel. You are again riding along Indian Creek.

Fig. D-11. Oblique aerial photograph of Bakers Haulover Cut following the 1926 hurricane. The cut had been opened only the year before. A portion of the bridge survived; the rest of the cut and the access roadway were destroyed. In the foreground note the flattened mangrove trees at the north end of Miami Beach. Near the top of the photograph the mangrove trees are upright but defoliated. Source: Peter W. Harlem, Aerial Photographic Interpretation of the Historical Changes in Northern Biscayne Bay, Florida: 1925–1976, University of Miami Sea Grant Technical Bulletin No. 40 (1979).

33.8   Public access and parking.

As the road moves away from Indian Creek and into a canyon of condominiums, one can consider some of the alternatives for Miami Beach. This area was only recently developed. There was a significant beach here prior to beach fill.

There is presently a lot of very wide beach. If this beach is washed away in the future, is it worth renourishing for recreational or economic reasons? Who should bear the cost? Should nourishment projects be small but with good-quality sand, or large with mediocre fill (such as this one)? What would happen when an area with this extent of development is not nourished to prevent undermining? As more and more beach areas in Florida lose their beaches, where will all the money come for replenishment at $1 million to $6 million per mile?

35.7   Public access and parking.

36.4   Public access at North Shore Community Center. Parking is across the street.

36.8   Between 79th and 87th streets is a section of shoreline that was converted from private homes to a public park as a part of the recent beach nourishment program.

Stop 7. Park to the left in the lot or along the street at 81st or 82nd streets. Walk across Collins Avenue and over one of the boardwalks to the beach.

Near the foot of the boardwalk you may be able to see the brownish quartz and calcareous sand of the old natural beach. The quartz is medium to fine in grain; the grain of the rounded, calcareous shell fragments is medium to coarse.

Beyond is the new beach. Standing here shortly after the new fill had been added, I heard a proud, elderly gentlemen proclaim to his out-of-town visitors, "Isn't it wonderful—but my God it is hard on the feet!"

In October 1983 there was a total width of 300 feet of new beach fill here, 85 feet of which was the wave-swash zone of the beach. This section of beach is about 3 years older than that seen at the south end of Miami Beach. It has had a bit more time to reprofile and erode.

Laboratory analyses of the fill by the author suggest that only about 30 percent of the fill is suitable for beach sand. The sheer volume of sediment, however, will take time to rework.

As you walk across the new beach to the water, note the "hurricane" berm. As mentioned earlier, aspects of beach nourishment projects are commonly advertised as providing protection against hurricanes. The one protection that is provided is volumes of sand between a structure and most wave action.

The 11-foot-high berm is commonly noted as a hurricane protection element. Yes, so long as it is preserved, it will prevent moderate storms, waves, and surges from over-topping it from the seaward side. No, it will not prevent flooding on the bay side of the berm. In fact, it may even cause worse flooding on the island. Water pushed north in Biscayne Bay by a storm will have nowhere to exit except Bakers Haulover. Water may build up in northern Biscayne Bay, seriously flooding the island. In other words, the berm may act like a dam for the storm waters trying to escape from the bay.

In the Great Labor Day Hurricane of 1935, Elliot Key, a coral limestone island forming the southern seaward boundary to Biscayne Bay, was severely flooded for more than 5 hours by waters piled up in southern Biscayne Bay. The elongated Marathon Key, in the middle Florida Keys, also is commonly flooded by hurricane surges piled up on 1 side of the island. In contrast, small Pigeon Key just to the west is generally not flooded by hurricanes. Water easily flows around it.

This problem may be compounded in hurricanes with strong rainfall which will increase the volume of water that must escape the bay. Along most of the U.S. East Coast, evidence that indicates that inlets are formed and maintained by water rushing back to the sea after a storm has passed. The opening of Norris Cut in 1835, for example, appears to have been from the bay side. Freshwater build-up may be important.

At this location the coarser sand you see at the surface of the fill is what has been concentrated by the action of the wind in removing the finer grains. Quartz grains, the major constituent of the original natural beach, make up only a small portion of the new beach.

This presently broad beach has only existed for a few years. You might wonder what will happen to this broad back-beach area in the future. Will it become covered with vegetation (sea oats, sand spurs)? Will rainwater acting on the surface cause the calcareous material of the broad back beach to dissolve or become cemented?

Note that the lifeguard stands are on skids so they can be moved to adjust for future erosion.

Return to your car; continue north on Collins Avenue.

38.4 96th Street, Bal Harbor Shopping Center; continue north.

39.0 Bakers Haulover Bridge. Bakers Haulover prior to 1925 was a narrow zone of the beach where small fishing boats could be pulled across into and out of northern Biscayne Bay. There were no inlets for a considerable distance to the north or south. Bakers Haulover was cut through in 1925. It is unclear whether it was cut to relieve pollution in northern Biscayne Bay or to provide boat access between the bay and offshore. A bridge across the cut also was put in at this time.

As shown in the photograph (fig. D–11), the hurricane of 1926 had devastating effects on this area, leaving a portion of the bridge but washing out the roadway accesses and severely eroding the shoreline adjacent to the inlet. Much of the sand was swept into the bay.

Following the hurricane, the bridge was rebuilt and a series of groins were installed on the beach north of Bakers Haulover.

This inlet is like most of the other inlets along Florida's east coast, which are artificially created or artificially maintained. Longshore-drifting sand sucked into the inlets by flood tides (fig. D-12) or swept seaward by ebb tides is the major cause for loss of beach sand and hence accentuated beach erosion.

Just bayward of Bakers Haulover is the Intracoastal Waterway. Repeated dredging is necessary to keep the growing flood-tidal delta (the body of sand swept into the bay by flood tide) from blocking the waterway.

39.6 Just north of the bridge, turn right to Haulover Beach and park in the lot (there may be a $1.00 fee). Walk to the beach.

Stop 8. Haulover Beach. This beach has been renourished several times since 1926. In some cases the sand has been derived from the dredging that maintains the Intracoastal Waterway; in others, more costly offshore material was used.

Nonetheless, the size and composition of the sand on the beach is similar to that which naturally occurred on both this beach and Miami Beach.

During the winter season you may see the waves breaking on an offshore bar. This bar is seasonal and forms as

Fig. D-12. Oblique aerial photograph of Bakers Haulover Cut in August 1935 showing the beach sand that has been swept into Biscayne Bay through the inlet to form a fan-shaped tidal delta. Active lobes of sand (light in color) are encroaching into the dredged Intercoastal Waterway. Darker areas (arrows) are areas of stailization by seagrasses and algae. Source: Peter W. Harlem, Aerial Photographic Interpretation of the Historical Changes in Northern Biscayne Bay, Florida: 1925–1976, University of Miami Sea Grant Technical Bulletin No. 40 (1979).

the stronger waves from winter storms transfer some sand from the shore seaward. This sand will move back to the beach during smaller wave conditions of the late spring and summer. This annual beach cycle including an apparent narrowing of the beach during the winter is an important, natural part of beach dynamics. Too often, development activities have ignored the natural dynamics of beaches when building in the shore zone.

If you have a mask and snorkel, the beach north of the fishing pier is usually an excellent spot to enjoy first-hand the dynamic shore zone.

End of trip. We hope it was both enjoyable and enlightening.

In summary, the beaches of Dade County vary from extremely intense development (all of Miami Beach and the central part of Key Biscayne) to undeveloped shorelines that are sites of moderate to intense recreational activity. Historical erosion rates are very minor. Had it not been for man's activities, there would be only minor shore erosion problems today. Unfortunately, man's misguided influences on the shore, such as construction of walls and groins and the dredging of channels, have increased over the years to the point that nearly the entire shore system is being adversely affected. In an attempt to counteract the resulting problems, minor to massive beach renourishment programs have been carried out. The success of the massive Miami Beach program (that is, how long will the beach stay in place, and will it help or hinder the community in a hurricane) remains to be seen. In other areas (Fisher Island, Virginia Key, northern Key Biscayne) the resultant problems along the shoreline have not really been addressed.

The next 20 years will be a time during which the citizens of Dade County will have to make some hard choices, especially if recent predictions of rising sea level are realized.

Index

Date Due

Due	Returned	Due	Returned
JUN 05 1987		JUN 27 1994	
MAY 19 1987	MAY 01 1987		
OCT 26 1987	OCT 04 1987	APR 28 1994	
		APR 06 1995	
DEC 01 1988		JUN 20 1995	MAY 07 1995
		APR 29 1996	
JAN 09 1989			MAR 21 1996
APR 23 1989	APR 16 1989	JUN 05 1996	
NOV 14 1990			MAY 14 1996
		JUN 17 1997	16 1997
JAN 07 1991	MAR 05 1991	JUL 09 1997	JUN 23 1997
MAR 04 1991			
DEC 17 1991	DEC 17 1991		
APR 08 1992	MAR 31 1992		
NOV 30 1992	DEC 14 1992		
MAR 01 1993	MAR 19 1993		
APR 16 1993	APR 28 1993		
JAN 04 1994			
	DEC 13 1993		
MAY 14 1994	12 1994		